Raymond Bradforth was born in Yorkshire, and for the next thirty years lived in various parts of the country before finally settling in Surrey. His management experience covered over twenty-five years as a manager in industry, in business and consultancy, in processing, production, construction, and information systems and technology in the UK. His twenty-five years' teaching experience as a college and university business school lecturer and tutor covered management, business, marketing, management information systems, computing, and six years in research. This was followed by ten years as an EU management adviser during which time he made fifty visits to companies throughout Eastern Europe. He was educated in production at Birmingham University, in management and business studies at Aston College of Advanced Technology, at Edinburgh University as a Diploma in Management student, as a graduate by examination of the British Institute of Management, at Cranfield College of Aeronautics as a research fellow, and at Henley the Management College where he gained a Master's degree, and later became a Doctor of Philosophy.

To Aunty May and Uncle Rex

Raymond Bradforth

My Kaleidoscopic Life

Austin Macauley Publishers™
LONDON • CAMBRIDGE • NEW YORK • SHARJAH

Copyright © Raymond Bradforth 2022

The right of Raymond Bradforth to be identified as author of this work has been asserted by the author in accordance with section 77 and 78 of the Copyright, Designs and Patents Act 1988.

All rights reserved. No part of this publication may be reproduced, stored in a retrieval system, or transmitted in any form or by any means, electronic, mechanical, photocopying, recording, or otherwise, without the prior permission of the publishers.

Any person who commits any unauthorised act in relation to this publication may be liable to criminal prosecution and civil claims for damages.

All of the events in this memoir are true to the best of author's memory. The views expressed in this memoir are solely those of the author.

A CIP catalogue record for this title is available from the British Library.

ISBN 9781398431379 (Paperback)
ISBN 9781398431386 (ePub e-book)

www.austinmacauley.com

First Published 2022
Austin Macauley Publishers Ltd®
1 Canada Square
Canary Wharf
London
E14 5AA

Table of Contents

Foreword	9
The Beginning	11
North Wembley	17
Castle Bromwich	21
A Respite	23
Back to Bradford	25
BelleVue	37
Sussex by the Sea	46
West Kensington	49
The Brewing Industry	55
Birmingham	59
Cape Hill	65
Social Birmingham	70
National Service	74
Hong Kong	89
Swinging Birmingham	104
Birmingham Brewing School	109
Cape Hill Shift Brewer	118
St Helens	131
Edinburgh	144

The Doldrums	152
Mortlake	158
America	162
Northampton	165
Cranfield	178
Computing	185
Executive Life	189
The Wilderness	200
Real Management	203
Nadir	208
Convalescence	215
Management Education	222
Gypsy Hill	228
Henley	236
Marketing	242
Academia	249
Doctorate	255
Resurrection	266
Czech Republic	274
Hungary	280
Slovakia	289
Serbia	296
Afterlife	303
The Chessboard	307

Foreword

Every time a kaleidoscope is shaken, a completely different pattern is revealed. My life has unfolded in a similar manner. My original reason for writing about events that had long since passed was primarily for the benefit and possible amusement of a small select group of friends who, like me, had worked in the brewing industry. I simply wrote about my experiences in the industry. The industry and the once privileged occupation of a brewer had changed out of all recognition from half a century earlier. My own part in it was not typical, and my friends seemed to find my writing somewhat unusual, and even mildly interesting. As a result, I then somehow felt the incentive to write more about the rest of my life. I realised subsequently that I seem to suffer a form of senile dementia, which my late father had once characterised himself as 'being cursed by a photographic long-term memory'. I appear to have inherited from him this unfortunate long-term trait. Furthermore, I seem to continue to be able to record in an absurdly minute detail many of the activities and events which may have been unlikely to have been recalled by more mentally well-balanced geriatric individuals. Unfortunately, in contrast, I cannot always remember what I did yesterday. Nevertheless, I have found that recalling and writing an account of my kaleidoscopic past has proved to be remarkably therapeutic for me, although somewhat addictive. It may prove to be of less benefit to other readers. In an attempt to avoid any intellectual discomfort that might affect readers due to the repeated shaking of the kaleidoscope, the text has been divided into small sections rather than conventional chapters. I hope that this may help to reduce any possible adverse effects of tedium in the narrative.

Raymond Bradforth 2020

The Beginning

I belong to a very small ethnic minority. I am half Yorkshire, and half Welsh. To make this heritage even rarer, my great grandfather was a Devonian, and my great grandmother was Irish.

When I was born, my mother and father were in their mid and late twenties. My father was one of ten children. In contrast, my mother who was only slightly younger had only a sister who was six years older. As a young woman, my mother had been a hairdresser in an upmarket department store. She had lived all of her life in Bradford, where her mother and father lived in a middle-class area on the outskirts of the city. Both parents were Victorians. My grandfather had the unusual forename of 'Taylor'. He had been a cloth buyer who had been made redundant during the Great Depression but had saved enough money to own his own house. He was a keen cricketer as a young man and subsequently had been secretary of the local cricket club. In contrast, my grandmother had begun work at the age of twelve as a 'part timer' – working in the mill during the morning and attending school in the afternoon. I was their only grandchild, and they were both caring and affectionate, particularly my grandmother. Her greatest admonishment to my grandfather when he occasionally attempted to behave sternly was, "Taylor – that's early Victorian."

One of my father's elder brother called Raymond, after whom I was named, died at the age of fifteen. Raymond and his friend had been swimming in a pool on the nearby mountainside. They both drowned when one of the boys was in swimming difficulties and they clutched one another together. The boys were brought down from the mountain on an open farm cart, which was then driven through the street and parked in front of my father's home. Raymond's body was then delivered to his parents. Such practices as these apparently were common at the beginning of the twentieth century.

My father was the youngest but one of a family of ten children. Both of his parents had died in the pneumonia epidemic at the end of the First World War.

He was brought up as an orphan at the age of thirteen by his seventeen-year-old sister who refused to allow him to be sent to an orphanage in the same way as his younger sister. When the First World War ended, my father heard the news from a passenger of a train that arrived at Pontypool Road station where my father was 'train spotting'. The passenger was waving a newspaper out of the carriage window and shouting that an armistice had been signed, and the war was over. My father promptly burst into tears, bitterly disappointed that he would now be unable to fight in the army in the war – unlike his only brother who was still serving in Palestine. This brother, my Uncle Tom, had gone one Sunday from Cardiff with his friend on a day-trip on a steamer-boat to Ilfracombe. When they returned to Cardiff, they both enlisted in the Royal Field Artillery. Apparently, when Uncle Tom returned home, my grandparents were not amused. He left his parents, not on very good terms, but he would never see either of them again.

My father was unhappy at school, particularly due to a sadistic schoolmaster who considered frequent vigorous caning as the most effective form of teaching. As a result, my father left school unilaterally at the age of thirteen and took a job at the local steelworks. His first job was as a 'knocker up'. He had to go around to employees' houses at five o'clock each morning and tap on their windows to wake them for work. In some cases, the houses were remote cottages on the mountainside. As a thirteen-year-old, he found this very frightening in the dark. The other part of his job was collecting pots of beer during the day for the factory steelworkers. On one occasion, he slipped near the steel rolling mill and fell on to the fast-emerging sheet of hot steel. He travelled for some yards before being rescued by one of the workers. Finally, at the age of fifteen, he decided to join the army. He travelled to the military depot at Brecon and enlisted in the Royal Horse Artillery. When his sister discovered this, she also travelled to Brecon to inform the colonel that my father was only fifteen years old. She wished to take him home. She was told that her wishes were irrelevant, since my father had claimed to be eighteen, signed his name and must therefore remain enlisted.

My father became an expert horse rider, and when the regiment was posted to Ireland, he was selected to become a member of the Royal Artillery Mounted Rifles. The role of this small elite unit was to ride over rural areas of Ireland and hunt down armed members of Sin Fein who were engaged in the ongoing civil war. His previous service had been in Dublin where Michael Collins was besieged in the Four Courts beside the River Liffey. He later described that when the artillery guns were fired from the road on the opposite side of the river, they gradually demolished the stonewall behind them. The guns then had to be moved each time to be opposite to the next piece of unbroken wall.

When my father was finally discharged at the age of twenty, after five years' service, he received a very brief training for civilian life. This apparently was advice on how to become a salesman. For some reason, he first started his sales career in Leeds and began carefully creating advertisements and then putting them in the local newspaper for the products he was selling. One day whilst in the office of the Yorkshire Post newspaper, he was approached by an older man, who first looked at the advertisements and then asked him why – at his age – was he daring to wear a Royal Artillery tie? Apparently, the man was a director of the Yorkshire Post and Bradford Telegraph Argus. After receiving my father's explanation, he immediately offered him permanent employment with the newspaper as an advertisement salesman in Bradford. Thus, began my father's career in the newspaper industry, which continued for the rest of his civilian working life.

My grandparents lived in Undercliffe, a rather bleak suburb on the Northern outskirts of Bradford. My mother had lived there all of her unmarried life. After leaving school, she worked as a hairdresser at Brown and Muffs, a large rather up-market department store in Bradford. She was attractive and apparently enjoyed the glamour and entertainment of the 'Flapper' years of the 1920s and beginning of the '30s. She and her colleagues often used to watch from behind the shop window people passing and peering in at the displays. Like most young girls, they took particular note of young men, and speculated, judged them, and imagined their potential as boyfriends. Apparently, my father was observed and received a very high score. The girls then speculated on how to manage to make a 'date' with him. My mother, who apparently was considered to be very attractive, determined that she would win the challenge. Apparently, she alone succeeded, with the result that they were married secretly a few months later.

They went on their honeymoon to Filey, a resort on the Northumbrian coast, from where, during their stay, my father had to return alone briefly to Bradford to attend a meeting. My mother's family discovered her marriage a few weeks later. My grandmother stated that the news was the 'biggest disappointment' of her life. However, everyone eventually became reconciled to the events, particularly when I was born over a year later.

I was born on 8th December 1932 at Apperly Bridge in the valley of the River Aire, just outside the northeast boundary of the city of Bradford, in the West Riding of Yorkshire. My earliest recollections are from the age of about three, when my parents had moved closer to Bradford, to a new bungalow in the quiet fairly rural residential Bradford suburb of Bolton. I remember a number of unconnected events such as playing in the garden, playing with picture blocks with railway engine pictures on them, eating Weetabix, and climbing over the wall to the neighbours' house to be read stories. One of the stories, which I suspect may have been of a 'Sunday School' variety, was 'The House with the Golden Windows', in which a boy had walked up the side of the valley and seen a house with golden windows. Every time he returned and approached the house, the windows ceased to be golden, because the gold was the light of the sun. I suspect that this story was my first introduction to curiosity, revelations and possible subsequent disappointment. On one occasion when I climbed over the wall, I slipped and received a very deep gash on my left knee. The doctor who was called Tordoff had a reputation for being somewhat unsympathetic towards patients. He examined and dressed the wound and declared that it was not worth stitching for such a young child. When I joined the army nearly twenty years later, it was then two inches long and half an inch wide. Its existence was duly recorded in my Pay Book as a distinguishing identification feature, presumably useful in the event of my death.

There were very, very, few cars in the mid-1930s, but the next-door but one neighbours had a car with a so-called 'dickie' seat at the rear in which one or two passengers could sit outside the car above the boot. On one occasion, I was allowed to sit in it. This was the only car in the road of approximately fifty modern houses.

I remember being taken to Leeds to be bought a cowboy suit, with which I was slightly disappointed because it had a straw hat instead of a felt or canvas Stetson one. My father worked for the Bradford newspapers the 'Telegraph and Argus' and the 'Yorkshire Post'. His great friend and colleague Harold Williams was a reporter, and they were also great beer drinking partners. Harold was tall, with a typical Yorkshire Dales accent and intonation, and he had a small dark plump wife Kathleen and three daughters. They lived at Saltaire at the other side of Bradford, where we used to visit them in a large three-storey terrace house high above the main road. I much admired the middle daughter Barbara who was two or three years older than me and was usually given the task of 'looking after' me. On one hot day in the summer when we visited them, an older male cousin was staying with them. He wore an open-necked shirt and clearly had no vest. In contrast, I always had to wear a warm woollen vest all the year around and was very resentful that my mother would not allow me to remove it.

On Saturdays, at lunchtime after work, my father used to meet his friend Harold, and I remember one Saturday when my father came home merrily and very good naturedly drunk. My mother berated him, and unused to my parents arguing, I hid beneath the gate-leg dining table, somewhat alarmed. Many years later, my father recounted how Harold's wife Kathleen's response to his drunkenness on one similar occasion had been to throw a glass of beer on her husband's face when she had an argument with him in a pub. Harold's only reaction was to look mildly surprised and say, "Well, I never," and to dry himself. I remember being able to recognise the names of all of the fishes on a set of cigarette cards, much to the amazement of my father and visitors. I was also able to recognise the contents of gramophone records, presumably because I recognised the labels. I remember a neighbour, Eric Foster, who I think, I must have had heard my father refer to as a 'pest'. When he knocked at the door one day, I called out in a loud voice, "Here is that pest Eric Foster." Apparently much to the embarrassment of my parents. On a number of occasions, I was taken down the hill with my mother to catch the 'Trackless' (as electric trolley buses were then known) into Bradford. These trolley buses were very early single and double deck versions. From a small child's point of view, they had two enormously high steps at the rear side to ascend in order to board them. Once aboard, they were characterised by a sound of constantly repetitive loud clicking as the driver notched the speed up and down with the foot pedal.

The bungalow was about two hundred feet up on the side of a wide shallow valley through which ran a tributary to the River Aire, a branch of the Leeds and Liverpool Canal, and the LMS Railway. From the garden at the back of the bungalow, we could see right across to the other side of the valley about a mile away. One beautiful bright summer evening when we were in the garden, we saw a most unusual unique and elegant sight. A huge airship, the *Graf Zeppelin* flew gently and almost silently up the centre of the valley heading towards Bradford at almost the same height as our garden. Many years later, my father claimed that the Germans had been photographing a number of industrial centres in Britain prior to the Second World War.

On one occasion, my father, who had been an expert horse rider in the army, took me into the field behind the house to look at, stroke and pat the horses whilst talking to the owner, who I assume was the farmer. Subsequently, I ventured into the field on my own, to pat and stroke the horses, and was admonished by the same man, presumably because of the serious potential danger to me. I was very chastened and upset. Finally, I remember being taken to the infants' school; a typical Victorian Bradford blackened stone building. At the school, the children spent the morning playing and later sleeping on camp beds with a blanket on to which had been sewn a picture of some animal or other, so that they could recognise their own blanket. On the way home in the afternoon, my mother would buy me a bar of white 'Five Boys' chocolate. After spending only a few weeks at the school, my father got a job on the Westminster Press, a newspaper group in Fleet Street, and we moved to London.

North Wembley

My life in London, or to be more precise, in North Wembley in Middlesex was idyllic. We moved into a semi-detached house in a brand new Middle-Class 'Garden' estate consisting almost entirely of wide avenues, with cherry blossom trees on grass verges on either side of the roadways. I was sent to a brand-new primary school about half a mile away in South Kenton. Beyond the school was a vast area of parkland leading to Moor Park and was virtually open country. My grandfather who visited us subsequently used to take me to the parkland where I was able to fly a simple small balsa wood kite shaped like an aeroplane, which was catapulted into the air with a rubber band. My school days there were, for almost the only time in my life, very happy. The school was modern and spacious and was surrounded by grassed open spaces. I used to walk to and from the school, which was about a half a mile away lower down the estate through the passageways which connected the other avenues. In summer, there were always ice creams available from a white coated man on a Walls Ice Cream tricycle who waited in the next avenue at the end of one of the alleyways. The 'ice creams' were all coloured and were what would later be called iced lollies. They were about four inches long, triangular in section and came in packs of about eight. The packs of ices were broken into their individual triangular sleeves and sold for a penny each. If children were short of money, they would be cut in half with the seller's penknife and sold for a halfpenny. On Sunday mornings, I would join our United Dairies milkman on his horse and cart to help him deliver milk. I recall in my second year celebrating 'Empire Day' in the school playing fields where we had games and races. I was an enthusiastic reader and read Enid Blyton and Rupert Bear books which were bought for me by my father. I coloured a picture in a competition in a comic and won an Enid Blyton book about a character called Mr Pennyfether.

On the way to our house from North Wembley station was a pathway on the side of the railway cutting from which it was separated by a five-foot diamond-wire fence. The six tracks were not only the main LMS line from Euston to the Midlands and North but also the suburban lines to the Home Counties and the electrified lines of the Bakerloo and LMS. From behind the fence here, I and my school friends used to collect locomotive numbers of the LMS trains. From time to time, my parents would take me on the line for picnics either to Carpenters Park, which was in the heart of the countryside, or to Cassiobury Park and the watercress beds at Watford. We used to travel from South Kenton, and I was always fascinated by the Euston electric trains coming down the gradient from North Wembley and rolling and swaying violently from side to side like ships at sea.

My two school friends were Donald Pride and Colin Blundell. Whilst Colin lived halfway between me and the school, Donald lived about a mile away at North Wembley in a terraced house backing on to the railway line. Whilst Donald's parents appeared to be rather poor, Colin's were clearly well off and extremely generous to him. He had a large Hornby electric train set and expensive model buses to the same scale. I had a rather smaller clockwork train set consisting of a Hornby clockwork red Midland Compound locomotive, a number of wagons, an oval of track, and a foot-bridge with a yellow signal clipped to it. I did not have a brake van for the wagons or a station. The front bogie wheels had an unfortunate tendency to keep coming off the rails, and I found this rather frustrating. My father attempted to make me a wooden platform to serve as a station and a box to form an engine shed. Unfortunately, although my father was always enthusiastically well intentioned, his carpentry and mechanical skills were severely limited. I was therefore rather disappointed by his rather amateurish efforts. As a result of the limitations of my own layout, I took every opportunity to play at Colin Blundell's home with his quite extensive layout with carriages and stations. In contrast, I have no recollection of ever playing at Donald Pride's much smaller home – rather that he used to come and play at mine. We frequently met my father at North Wembley station when he came home from his office in Fleet Street. He always carried a tightly rolled umbrella, which was an obligatory city fashion at the time. After being in the rain, he often used to demonstrate how to roll it and explained that it would have cost him sixpence in the city to have had it rolled professionally. He would invariably bring home two tubes of a new sweet, 'Smarties', that had just been introduced. On one occasion, he failed to do this, and Donald asked, "Where were the Smarties?" My father was somewhat shocked at what he considered to be minor rudeness.

I had also been bought a high-quality James black tricycle. This was something of a disappointment to me, since I had wanted a red one to match my red model locomotive. However, Donald, who did not have a cycle, and I took great pleasure in riding around the estate. On either side of the quiet wide roads on the outer side of the grass verges were concrete pathways. We pretended that these were railway tracks. When I pedalled the cycle, Donald would stand on the frame above the back axle. I would be the train driver and Donald was the guard. We would stop at the small rectangular manhole covers which were located every twenty yards or so beside the path. Donald, as the guard, would jump off and after pausing would wave a small green flag that my mother had made out of a short raspberry cane and a green handkerchief. We would periodically change places. This entire charade was inspired by watching railway guards on the local electric trains. The LMS electric trains shared the route of the Bakerloo line. Station platforms were a compromise between the different sizes and heights of the two types of train. It was necessary to step down nearly a foot to the tube trains and climb up a similar distance to the LMS electrics. However, at Queens Park station, the trains had separate platforms, which were the appropriate height for each type of train. The guards of the Euston Electrics belonged to the 'old school' of railway servants. They would walk forward about forty feet along the train, blow their whistle and then insert the brass sleeve on the end of their green flag between two bare wires which were suspended above the platform. This rang a bell at the front of the train, and the driver would then start the train. Acceleration was rapid, and the guard would then turn and with a rather elegant acrobatic movement grasp the passing brass handrail, leap on to the footboard and re-enter his compartment. Some sixty years later, I read a railway magazine article which described a day excursion of railway employees and their families. At every station at which their train stopped, all of the holidaying guards would get out of the train along the length of the train. They would all then wait for the train to start and leisurely perform their working habit of leaping onto the moving train before closing their compartment doors.

Life began to change rapidly when we were issued at school with gas masks. These were in cardboard boxes with a piece of string with which we wore them around our necks. Shortly afterwards, on a Sunday morning when I was at home, playing with Donald, we heard Neville Chamberlin on the radio announce the start of the Second World War. A few minutes later, Donald announced that he thought he could smell gas but did not have his gas mask with him. My father immediately advised him not to be frightened but to run home as fast as possible. Shortly after war was declared, the 'Phoney War' began, and children in London were evacuated to the country. My Uncle Rex and Aunty May lived in Castle Bromwich just outside the outskirts of Birmingham. They and my parents decided that it was a suitable place to which I could be evacuated 'privately'. My parents agreed to take me to Banbury by taxi from where I could be picked up in my uncle's car. Unfortunately, because of the short notice of the decision, they had little ready cash available for a taxi fare. My father enterprisingly decided to raid my savings moneybox. This was a chromium-plated steel oval bank moneybox specifically designed not be opened other than in a bank branch. My father's efforts to break into the box first with a tin opener, then with a hacksaw were embarrassing but as a result of much persistence were successful.

Castle Bromwich

When I arrived at Castle Bromwich, I was immediately enrolled at the local 'Village School'. The 'BBC' accent of any child from a middle-class London suburb differed significantly from elsewhere in Britain. The broad 'Birmingham' accent was in total contrast to my 'BBC' accent. On my second day at school, the headmaster asked me to stand on the stage in the small assembly hall. He then proudly announced to the whole school that he was delighted to say that 'this boy has perfect English diction and accent'. Perhaps unsurprisingly, my subsequent progress in the school was somewhat limited. The climax came almost immediately, after I had been knocked over in the school playground and called a 'stuck up little cunt'. I had no idea why I was being attacked or what the word meant. It was quite outside any experience that I had encountered or observed in North Wembley. However, I later recounted it to my Uncle Rex. After a visit by him to the headmaster, the miscreants were 'spoken to' and the bullying ceased. Nevertheless, I did not attempt to acquire a 'Birmingham' accent.

The house in Castle Bromwich backed onto a farm owned by Mr Winterton, where, I spent a great deal of my leisure time. I was allowed to join in herding the cows in for milking. I became quite bold at this, but on one unfortunate occasion, I was turned on and knocked over by a white cow called 'Daisy' who had recently produced a calf, to which she had presumed I was a threat. Fortunately, she had no horns, and I was rescued by one of the farm workers, who explained the problem to me. Shortly afterwards, I received my first instruction in how to distinguish cows from bulls. The labourer that I asked was obviously somewhat amused, if not surprised. Realising the delicacy of the situation, he first explained that it was nothing to do with whether they had horns or not. He then simply put his arm around my waist and patted my stomach with his open hand and explained that cows had a bag of milk teats hanging down and bulls didn't.

One of my most important tasks when visiting the farm was to go to the local village shop to obtain for the farm workers open paper packets containing five 'Woodbines' cigarettes for sixpence. I was also allowed to help with the haymaking. Astonishingly, on one occasion, due to the wartime shortage of labourers during haymaking, I was asked to drive the tractor towing the hay cart and keep it in a straight line. Since I could hardly reach the pedals or control the steering wheel, I found this a rather difficult task.

One of my disappointments at leaving home was that I had been unable to bring any toys with me. I particularly missed my model trains. However, my uncle and aunt had a pair of small wooden Dutch clog ornaments hung up with a small brass hook and eye. I was able to link these together, push them around the carpet, and pretend that they were a locomotive and tender. Shortly afterwards, my aunt bought me a four-wheeled Hornby tinplate coach, which I was able to push around the carpet instead. It was all rather infantile and pathetic, but there were no other local children known to my aunt and uncle with whom I could play. However, they did know one family who lived a few miles away that I could reach by bus. I visited them on a couple of occasions and was incredibly impressed by the fact that they owned a 'TrixTwin' train set with two electric locomotives. These were very early small-scale models, and the first that I had seen. They had the unique facility of being able to be operated independently, and at the same time, on the same piece of track.

The farm was the highlight of my stay in Castle Bromwich. However, on one occasion, I was returning on the bus from a visit to the TrixTwin trains. I was eagerly looking forward to getting back to my aunt and uncle's house, changing, and then going to the farm. Their house was directly opposite the bus stop on the other side of the road. When the bus stopped, I went down the steps and rushed around the front of the bus and into the house. My uncle greeted me and gave me a very severe scolding. Despite having warned me previously to be cautious and careful and look before I crossed the road, I had apparently nearly been knocked down by a car that was overtaking the stationary bus. It was probably the most dangerous incident in my entire life.

A historic feature of the location of my aunt and uncle's house was that a few hundred yards behind it the land sloped down to the rest of Birmingham. Opposite, in the land below was located the Dunlop and other factories. In front of them was a runway on which newly manufactured Spitfires were tested and flown off to their service squadron destinations.

A Respite

After a few months, the 'Phoney War' apparently ended, and I was returned to North Wembley. In the meantime, my father had joined the Local Defence Volunteers, more popularly known as the LDV, and later as the home guard. He was issued with an armband and a forage cap. Frequently, he would bring home a Canadian rifle, which he used to take out each night when on guard-duty in the parkland near Moor Park. He recounted later, when the London Blitz took place, that from there they used to watch streams of German bombers heading towards the landmark of Harrow-on-the-Hill, before 'turning left' towards the centre of London.

For a few months, life appeared to return to near normality. During that time, inexplicably a small Italian boy joined our school class. It was during the winter, and for some reason I befriended him. He had apparently never seen snow before, and I was able to walk home with him. In a very superior and rather patronising way, I was able to demonstrate to him how to slide along in the snow on the grass verges alongside the roads in the avenues. I was never able to work out why he had left Italy or what happened to him subsequently.

When the London Blitz began, North Wembley was affected very little. Despite air raid warnings, each night only one bomb ever fell within a mile of our house. That was a direct hit on a small modern single-storey church that had been built as part of the new estate. Fortunately, it was deserted at the time of the demolition. However, anti-aircraft fire occurred every night and shrapnel, which tended to be scattered widely, was eagerly collected by schoolchildren the following day. At the same time, at night, the red glow of light from London's devastating fires could be seen easily from Wembley.

My father was very concerned about the safety of my mother and me whilst he was out on LDV patrol each night. We had no air raid shelter in the garden so as an alternative he tried to provide some safety indoors. He brought his and my mother's double bed downstairs. He put a house brick under each of the bed legs in order to enable my mother and me to sleep underneath instead of on top of the bed. He hoped that the diamond-patterned wire mattress frame on top of the bed would then provide some protection against any falling debris. Finally, the soft-spring padded mattress was placed under the bed, and my mother and I slept on that.

My mother had received letters from my grandparents in Bradford telling her that they were preparing for air raids by creating a shelter under the stone cellar stairs. However, they had so far not received any air raids at all. Compared with sleeping under the bed in North Wembley for the last couple of weeks, this sounded to me to be a significantly better option than our current situation. More importantly, my father had received his call-up papers and was due to join (or rejoin) the army within a few weeks. The decision was therefore made by my parents that my mother and I would return to Bradford and live with my grandparents. At the same time, we would vacate our house, which was rented, in North Wembley and put our furniture into storage. Fortunately, the house next door was occupied by a police inspector and his family. They had a 'spare room' upstairs, in which they would be happy, for a modest fee, to store our furniture for the duration of the war. Fortunately, the inspector, as a member of the police force, would be exempt from call-up to the armed forces.

Shortly afterwards, my mother and I left for Yorkshire with two suitcases, and arrived in Bradford to live with my grandparents. My life was about to change beyond all recognition.

Back to Bradford

My grandparents lived in Undercliffe, on higher northern outskirts of the city. The house, on the edge of a hill, was one of a dozen blackened stone two-storey terraced house with a large attic on the roof, on a steeply sloping cobbled street somewhat misleadingly called Beech Grove. Like most of the other houses, it was separated from the house next door by a passageway closed by a wooden door. The back of the house overlooked allotments, beyond which was a golf course, fields, and about a mile away an unusual very large grass-covered mound. I subsequently discovered that this was 'Myra Shea', a disused coal pit shale tip from the previous century. Beyond this was a sloping built-up cobbled main road along which ran local trams. When ascending the road, despite their distance from Beech Grove, the motors of these trams could be heard emitting a forlorn wailing sound. On the evening when I first arrived at my grandparent's house and heard this distant sound, I was immediately alarmed. I had mistakenly interpreted this as an 'air-raid siren', the sound of which I had so recently become familiar in London.

On my first day living with my grandparents, I was taken to meet Michael Thornton, a boy of almost the same age as myself, who lived half a dozen doors away at the end of the row of houses. He was pleasant and friendly and offered to take me down to the local newsagent's shop just beyond the bottom of the road. The shop was small, with a raised counter behind which stood the friendly middle-aged shopkeeper. With a beaming smile, she welcomed me with the immortal phrase, "*Doosta like spice, lad.*" I was totally uncomprehending, at which she continued, "*Nay, lad – I recon tha' must.*" I was eventually to learn that from broad Yorkshire Bradford dialect that translated to 'Do you like sweets, boy? No, boy – I think you must.' I was soon to learn more of the Yorkshire schoolboy dialect. In particular – "*Ey oop – lad. A ta lakin out t'nite?*" This translated to the invitation 'Hello, lad – are you coming to play outside tonight?' Michael and his slightly older brother lived in the end house of the row. They used to play cricket with a cricket bat and tennis ball in front of a wicket chalked on the wall. They kindly invited me to join them. Within a very short time, I made a lifelong discovery. I was totally incapable of throwing, catching, or hitting any size or type of ball. These severe handicaps remained with me for the rest of my life.

My grandparents had arranged for me to be admitted to the local Hanson Primary School about half a mile away beyond the bottom of the hill. The next day, my mother took me to meet the headmaster. As we waited in the corridor outside his office, the door was opened suddenly by a middle-aged man wearing a brown double-breasted pinstriped suit. On the end of his arm was the ear of a small rather ragged boy to whom he directed what to me seemed an extraordinary utterance. "If thou ever does that again, lad, I shall clatter thee." I later learned that 'clattering' was the colloquial term for slapping. The brown-suited man was my new headmaster.

My introduction to Hanson Primary School as a pupil was a life-changing and somewhat alarming experience. In contrast to the gentle civilised middle-class environment of North Wembley and Middlesex, the vast majority of my fellow schoolchildren came from abysmally poor homes. Many of them wore wooden clogs with brass-studded leather uppers, rather than shoes or sandals, and the clothing of the majority was shabby and even ragged. Fights in the school play-yard were frequent, and as well as punching, the practice of 'clogging' or kicking their opponents with their heavy clogs was common. All of the teachers used to enforce discipline in class by using canes. These 'canes' ranged from long thin bamboo to short inflexible walking sticks. These were sometimes hung in the corner of the classroom or hidden in the teacher's desk. However, the quality of the curriculum, and its teaching was superb. Every effort was made by teachers to prepare pupils for the examination for ten-year-olds, which later became known as the 'Eleven Plus'. Like all primary schools at the time, the classes were all mixed sex, but there was little social contact between boys and girls. Boys and girls used to deliberately ignore one another.

Beside the lower end of Beech Grove, two or three very large public airraid shelters had been built. These were covered with soil and overgrown with grass. Normally, they were locked; presumably, they were to be unlocked by Air Raid Wardens in the event of a raid. To my knowledge, they were never used, since Bradford had only one very brief air raid throughout the war. One day on the way home from school with Michael Thornton, we were ambushed by a gang of older boys, none of who either of us knew. We were taken in to one of the shelters that for some reason was unlocked. Both Michael and I were understandably frightened, and neither of us had any idea why we were there. The boys simply taunted us, poked and pushed us, threatened to leave us and lock us in the shelter. However, the boys released us eventually, and Michael and I ran home. We never saw the boys again and never had any idea of why we had been so treated.

Winters in Bradford were on a different scale to any of those that I had encountered in the South or Midlands. They were colder, had bitter winds, lasted longer and above all else had much more and deeper snow. One of the major disadvantages to this was that boys only wore short trousers – never long ones. The physiological effect of this was dreadful. Quite apart from being extremely cold, my legs and knees used to become 'chapped', a condition that made them raw, cracked and painful. A partial solution to this was the generous application of lanolin, which was purified sheep fat. However, tobogganing or 'sledging', as it was universally known, was a delight. Nevertheless, the combination of sledging and short trousers was especially unpleasant. In practice, I managed to overcome this by using a pair of my mother's very old 'slacks', which she allowed me to use. I looked forward to the time that I would go to high school, where almost all boys wore long trousers.

Because of my age, my mother was exempt from the potential conscription to work in a factory, or on the 'War Effort' that was in force for all young women. Apart from helping my grandmother to cook and clean, she really had little else to do. Although the 'married family' allowance from my father's army pay was considerably less than his civilian pay, my mother and I were never short of money. We also enjoyed the advantage of living rent free with my grandparents. However, my mother still had a circle of female friends from her life before she was married. She used to meet a group of them regularly in a tearoom in the city. One member of the group was Ruth Watkins, a thirty-five-year-old who was not married and had not been one of my mother's pre-war circles of friends. After a short time, she and my mother became very close friends, since Ruth, like my mother, had few real domestic or time-consuming family responsibilities. Later, her new friendship proved to be invaluable to us all.

Kenny Poole was in the same form as me at Hanson Primary School and lived in a rather poorer area near to my grandparents' home. He was a pleasant lad but had his own circle of friends, and he and I were friendly; we were never close. His elder brother was in the army in the Black Watch, and news arrived that he had been killed in North Africa. I could never understand, until thirty years later, why a Bradford lad should be in a Scottish Highland infantry regiment. I discovered the reason was that in the First World War, Bradford, like many other cities, had raised 'Pals' Regiments, which consisted only of local men, many of whom had known one another all of their lives. Often these regiments were suddenly and tragically totally annihilated in the trench fighting in France. The families in whole areas of their home cities were then bereaved at the same time. In the Second World War, the authorities had sensibly avoided this by posting many recruits to County Regiments, which were unconnected with their homes.

The variety of regional dialects was brought home to me when my grandfather took me to his home village of Scholes, five miles outside Bradford in a rural area near Cleckheaton. We used to visit his sister who was married to a local farmer. On one occasion, I was sent out to play with a few of the local Scholes children of my own age. After a short time, although in a very friendly manner, they began to mock me. Apparently, my Bradford accent was completely alien to them and quite unlike their own Cleckheaton Yorkshire accents. We always returned from Scholes with the luxury of half a dozen new-laid eggs. The current wartime ration was one egg per person per week. We used to buy our weekly rations from a small grocer's shop opposite to my grandparent's house. On one occasion, Kenny Poole's mother was explaining to the shopkeeper that when she had tried to cook Kenny's egg for breakfast as a weekly treat she had found it to be rotten. The shopkeeper very ungraciously and rather reluctantly allowed her to buy a replacement egg. In contrast to shopping, milk, which was not rationed, was delivered daily to my grandparents' house from a horse and two-wheeled cart. The cart, otherwise known as a trap, contained two or three milk churns. Eddie the milkman used to transfer the milk to an oval bucket on which was a lid, which was retained by a metal strap. Inside the bucket were two ladles, one of which could hold a pint and the other was a half-pint size. Eddy would come through the passageway to the back door and then ladle the milk into a large jug handed over by my grandmother. The only bottled milk available could be bought at the local grocer's shop. This milk was pasteurised and had a distinctive flavour which I liked, although many people did not. It was only bought by my grandmother when she occasionally ran out of milk.

Possibly because of my mother's social awareness, she became concerned about two of my features that she regarded as serious shortcomings. Firstly, my 'second' upper front teeth were prominent and twisted, and I suppose inevitably somewhat unsightly. My mother therefore took me to a local dentist, who somewhat bizarrely, rejoiced in the name of Mr Pullen, who duly fitted me with a gold-wired brace and springs. My teeth had already earned me the nickname in some quarters of 'Tusker'. The other feature that she considered embarrassing and highly undesirable was my now inevitable broad Bradford accent. To counteract this, she registered me with an elocutionist on the other side of the city. Fortunately, his small first-floor studio room was on my way home from Belle Vue School. Both of these initiatives by my mother were in fact beneficial to me. Although I was never very close to her, whatever her motivation, her help proved to be invaluable to me for the rest of my life, and for which I have been eternally grateful ever since.

The elocutionist was Mr John Dale. He was in his very early thirties and was physically handicapped and had a very severe limp. This was presumably the reason why he was not in the armed forces. It was inevitable that my weekly elocution lessons would be highly successful. Having less than two years previously had a ringing endorsement of my 'perfect English accent', it was quite effortless for me to restore and reproduce it whenever it was required. Mr Dale's syllabus was based on the examinations and certificates of the 'London School of Elocution, Music, and Drama'. This involved learning pieces of poetry and drama and presenting them verbally in a professional manner in front of an audience. Initially, the audience was John Dale, but for examinations, it was before an independent professional panel of examiners from the London School. On a number of occasions later, I was invited to present before audiences of as many as fifty or a hundred people. I also won prizes on a number of competitive occasions. Unsurprisingly, I rapidly passed all of the examinations effortlessly, and eventually, John Dale considered that I should take up acting as a profession. Fortunately, I never had any real inclination to do so.

Perhaps unsurprisingly, no pupils at Hanson Primary School ever scored high enough marks to be selected for Bradford Grammar School. The alternative 'Secondary' schools were Hanson High School, which was next door, or Belle View High School, which was on the opposite side of the city. Failure to obtain high enough marks for either of these left only the option of admission to 'Barking Road Modern'. This was about a mile up the main road to Bradford

Moor and had a fearsome reputation. It was renowned for initiation ceremonies of pushing schoolboys' heads into toilets and for frequent fights and 'beatings up'. I was unenthusiastic about returning to Hanson High School and hoped to opt for Belle Vue. I was literally terrified at the unthinkable prospect of going to Barking Road.

My only real school friend was Peter Newton. He was intelligent, amiable, and most importantly, tall. He was rarely challenged by other boys and in reality was my potential bodyguard. Apart from fist fighting, two of the popular aggressive practices of boys were stone throwing and 'gobbing'. 'Gobbing' was spitting skilfully and accurately at the maximum possible distance, usually towards one's opponents. They also competed to see who could 'pee' out the furthest. I was obliged to learn and practice all of these skills. I never mastered fist fighting and relied hopefully on Peter Newton to discourage any potential threats to me. After eighteen months at Hanson, we both passed the examination to go to secondary school and were the only two boys accepted for Belle Vue High School. There was also a Belle Vue Girls High School next door to that for boys. None of the girls in our class at Hanson Primary School had been accepted there.

The other important life-changing influence was that my grandparents' next-door neighbours, Mr and Mrs Cawthra, were Methodists. They introduced me to the local Methodist Church, at which I began to attend Sunday school. This allowed me to enter a very pleasant world that was completely different from the ghastly environment of Hanson Primary School. Among the new friends that I met there was David Bonney. He was at Woodhouse Grove School, a private school at Apperly Bridge. However, most importantly, he collected gramophone records and introduced me to classical music, of which he was an enthusiast. This was another life-transforming experience. Following his example, I began to collect what would later be described, somewhat derisively, as 'popular' classics. Tchaikovsky's and Grieg's First piano concertos, Handel's Water Music, and Mendelssohn's Fingal's Cave were my first acquisitions. These were old-fashioned twelve-inch wax discs. I used to play these in my grandparents' attic where there was an old 'wind up' acoustic gramophone that had been used when my mother was a young woman. In due course, one of the two main springs broke, and due to wartime shortages, these were almost impossible to replace. However, I did eventually find a supplier in Shipley on the other side of Bradford. In order to replace the spring, I had to dismantle the gramophone, and the spring was duly replaced. A few weeks later, the other spring broke. Once again, I had it repaired and replaced it.

After my efforts at repairing the gramophone, David Bonney explained the differing sound quality between acoustic and electrical gramophones, later to become known as 'record players'. He also made me aware of the deterioration of the record discs that occurred as a result of using steel needles on their wax grooves. I discovered that I could obtain a new arm and head that would produce an electrical output signal to replace the existing acoustic one. The new head not only produced a better sound but was also lighter. The output from the new head was through a telephone jack plug. I discovered, somewhat to the surprise of my grandparents, that at the back of their old Philips radio there was a jack plug socket. I had also learned from my friend David that fibre needles were available that minimised record wear. Apparently, these were made from natural rose thorns and had to be sharpened periodically by using a special small sharpening device. Armed with all of this newly acquired knowledge and technology, I acquired these as Christmas presents. I had prematurely and enthusiastically anticipated and entered the future world of 'hi-fi'.

Entertainment during the war was restricted largely to the radio and the cinema. My mother, grandmother, and I used to visit the local, curiously named, 'Oxford' Cinema in Undercliffe once a week. The cinema was somewhat unusual in that it was simply a single ground floor with no circle or other levels. I also used to visit with Peter Newton the large West End Cinema in Bradford on Saturday afternoons. The big entertainment of the year was the Christmas Pantomime at the Alhambra Theatre. This always starred Norman Evans as the pantomime 'dame'. He always included his then famous music hall act of 'Over the Garden Wall'. This was a brilliant sketch of a bespectacled rotund middle-aged Northern housewife gossiping with her neighbour in her back garden. It was an extremely perceptive observation of North Country domestic life, which I, and apparently the rest of the audience, found both recognisable and very funny. The character was also copied many years later by the splendid television comedian Les Dawson.

Our daily leisure entertainment was the BBC radio. I used to listen to Children's Hour at five o'clock, and my grandfather used to listen to the News at six. On Monday nights, I was allowed to stay up to a variety programme called somewhat unimaginatively as 'Monday Night at Eight'. On Children's Hour, Arthur Ransom's 'Winter Holiday' was currently narrated. I completely fell in love with the book and immediately went to the local Lending Library to obtain a copy. I subsequently read all of Arthur Ransom's Swallows and Amazons books.

Shortly after we had moved to Bradford, my father was conscripted into the Royal Artillery. He was posted to Deepcut on Salisbury Plain and was trained as an artillery surveyor. The function of a surveyor was to identify and plot targets for the guns of the battery or regiment to which they were attached. However, shortly afterwards, he was posted to the Officer Cadet Training Unit at Llandrindod Wells in the middle of Wales. Unfortunately, having served previously for five years as a regular soldier, he apparently took unkindly to being 'ordered about stupidly' by one young officer with whom he disagreed. As a result, he was 'posted out' to another regiment without completing the course. This was the 136 Field Artillery Regiment at Stamford Bridge in East Yorkshire. The regiment was a Liverpool Territorial Army unit and therefore consisted almost entirely of 'Liverpudlians'. Many of these were dockworkers or 'whackers', most of whom proved to be great opportunists. My father had absolutely nothing in common with any of them. However, he tended to be amused by and sometimes subsequently benefited from their well-practiced ability to 'acquire' items of value that happened to pass and come within their reach. This became of particular benefit, especially in the case of food items, when they subsequently travelled on a troopship. One of the skills of the Liverpudlian gunners was in train travel. The origin and destinations of almost all train tickets at that time were pre-printed on small cards. However, the destinations of minor obscure stations distant from the issuing station had to be hand-written by the station booking clerks. The Liverpool homes of most of the gunners involved approximately three hundred miles of rail travel. Clearly, this was unaffordable for weekend leave. Their solution was simple. They bought a return ticket to the nearest small railway station for which there were no printed tickets. They then carefully erased the hand-written destination and replaced it with an equally small unimportant destination close to Liverpool.

After visiting us on a couple of weekend leaves in Bradford, my father left with his regiment, which had now been posted overseas. On each occasion, he brought me two or three very large blocks of Cadbury's Dairy Milk chocolate. Presumably, these were by courtesy of his Liverpool comrades' commercial activities. Having left England, the convoy travelled out into the Atlantic Ocean by a route selected to avoid U-boat attacks. Until they arrived in India, no one on the ship knew of their final destination. Finally, in India, he left the regiment and became a sergeant in the Intelligence Corps. He and his previous regiment were then posted to the Burma campaign. Whilst he was abroad he sent regular airmail letters home, often with money postal orders for my mother and me.

I had a Sunday school friend called Peter Furness. He, like Peter Newton and David Bonney, had no brothers or sisters. Both Peter Furness and David came separately to play with me at my grandparents' house on a number of occasions. On one Christmas Eve when Peter Furness was with me, his parents had gone off to an evening carol service. They returned on a trolley bus from Undercliff and alighted some distance from Beech Grove in order to take Peter home. As they walked around the back of the bus, they were both killed instantly by an oncoming vehicle in the opposite direction. Peter had become an orphan. Perhaps fortunately, the implications and significance of the tragic news did not register fully until later, after he had been taken home by some local neighbours who had received the tragic news.

An important social activity that my Sunday school friends introduced to me was cigarette smoking. Although I was only ten years old, the practice was common amongst Bradford lads of that age. It was commonly known as 'baccering' and usually took place in quiet locations where there were few adults. In the case of my new friends, the location was the local allotments on the way home from Sunday school. The cigarettes were always Wills' Woodbines, the cheapest cigarettes on the market, and these were readily available in paper packets of five. In order to maintain credibility amongst other boys, it was essential to inhale. I continued to smoke, albeit modestly and socially rather than addictively for the next ten years. However, I never smoked when alone and never really enjoyed smoking, nor was there any chance of me ever becoming an addict. I regarded cigarette smoking simply as a necessary social activity.

My other social activity was to join the Wolf Cubs at the local Parish Church. The uniform was simply schoolboy short trousers and a grey jersey with a coloured scarf, which was held at the front by platted leather 'woggle'. A green cap with yellow piping completed the ensemble. On attendance nights, 'cubs' were split into groups of six, somewhat unimaginatively called 'Sixes'. Each six had its own distinctive colour, and this was identified by a triangular strip of cloth sewn on to the upper sleeve. I was recruited into the Red 'Six'. Inevitably, and perhaps prophetically, my father commented that the red triangle was the historic trademark of Bass Brewery and its beer. After attending regularly for a few weeks, I was promoted to become a 'Second'. This entitled me to a yellow band, sewn on to the right arm of my pullover. This role required me to stand at the back end of the 'six' when it was 'on parade'. After a further few weeks, the 'Six' leader was repeatedly absent, and I therefore acted as the 'Six' leader. Eventually, he left and a new leader was appointed. This was not to be me but was my neighbour Michael Thornton, who attended rarely, and was in a different Six. I left the Wolf Cubs in disgust and never became a boy scout. I concluded, probably rightly, that I didn't fit well into voluntary team organisations.

Kit building was one of my two most prized hobbies. The other hobby was my Hornby-Dublo electric model railway. This was an oval track with a tank engine and half a dozen wagons. It had very generously been bought for me by my grandmother in consolation for having to leave behind in London my clockwork railway and other toys. I adored both her and it. Unfortunately, production of all such toys had now ceased. I was never able to obtain any track, points or carriages, both of which I wanted desperately for the rest of the duration of the war. However, my great comfort and supporter was Mr Cawthra who lived next door to my grandparents. He was an extremely kindly man in his late fifties who lived with his wife and elder daughter. His younger daughter was very attractive and vivacious and was in the ATS. Between the two terraced houses, Mr Cawthera had actually opened a doorway in their cellar wall between the two basements. This enabled him and his family to share the homemade air raid shelter, which my grandparents had created under their stone steps leading to their cellar. In consequence, he would often come through the door on winter evenings, whistle at the bottom of my grandparents' stairs and politely join them in their living room. He was a fitter at the Bradford Corporation bus depot. He introduced me to model building and engineering, both of which were to become obsessive passions for the rest of my life. As a result of his influence, I soon developed an ambition to become a fitter when I grew up. However, Mr Cawthera's interests were much wider, and he used to create games and then play them with me. One was 'Battleships'. This consisted of sheets of foolscap paper (by courtesy of Bradford Corporation) on which he had drawn a matrix of squares. The two players would then secretly mark crosses on their own sheets to represent different sizes of battleships. The rows and columns were numbered and each player in turn would call out a square, which he suspected might contain one of his opponent's ships. The other far more important interest and activity was the creation and use of a set of tools. He looked at a wooden model aircraft kit that I built by using a penknife. It was unquestionably crude. He examined it uncritically but said that what I really needed was a file, rather than a penknife. He advised me of the type to buy, and the following Saturday, I bought my first workshop tool. Subsequently, he obtained a number of new tools for me by somehow buying these entirely properly at a discount, also by courtesy of Bradford Corporation. All of my birthday and Christmas presents from then onwards included new tools. Most importantly, I obtained a vice, a bevelled wood-chisel, pliers, and a hand drill. With these, my model making was transformed.

My Uncle Rex visited us occasionally on business and stayed overnight. One day, when I came home from school, he was sitting in the living room. There was a brown paper covered parcel in the middle of the floor. I was surprised to see my uncle, and after taking off my coat sat down opposite to him. He smiled and told me to open the parcel. It was a Meccano set. He told me to open the box. I had never seen or heard of Meccano, and I was somewhat puzzled, but having looked at it, I was intrigued. He appeared to be equally surprised at my reaction or lack of one. He then declared that it was a gift for me. I immediately started examining the parts and began working out how they fitted together. I thanked him gratefully. It was a life-changing experience. My previous model making had been creative, but it had little engineering content. With Meccano, my mechanical interest and skill was stimulated and stayed with me for the rest of my life. Perhaps unsurprisingly, Mr Cawthera soon extended my mechanical knowledge and skills even further and provided additional parts and expertise. Perhaps sadly, my grandmother, who encouraged my model making, had allowed me to use a table in the cellar as a workbench on which to fit my vice. It had been used as a dining table in the past, and she considered that it was very old fashioned and of no further use or value. It was a beautiful Victorian mahogany piece of furniture with classically carved legs. Unfortunately, but needless to say, I ruined it. Perhaps fortunately, I would never have had any wish to own it.

In Bradford, one of the most popular events of the year was Guy Fawkes Night, where it was more popularly known as 'Plot Night'. The preceding night there was known as 'Mischief Night'. This was even more popular among boys, particularly since outside fireworks and bonfires had been banned for the duration of the war. Mischief Night allowed boys to go around the neighbourhood carrying out mischievous practical jokes. The most popular of these was to deposit piles of rubbish and horse manure on neighbours' doorsteps. The boys would then knock on the door and immediately run away, hide, and laugh at the residents' response. In contrast, residents occasionally condoned the harmless amusement and gave the boys small portions of 'Plot Parkin'. Parkin was a popular Bradford form of delicious homemade gingerbread. As an alternative to normal fireworks, it was possible to buy 'indoor fireworks'. These were essentially variations of indoor 'sparklers', and there were also small cartons of chemicals which when ignited exuded rather disgusting coils of dark grey worm-like materials. They really were no substitute for 'real' outdoor fireworks.

Belle Vue

Belle Vue Secondary School was at Frizinghall, which was on the opposite side of the city to where Peter Newton and I lived. We were two of the very few boys who did not live on the same side of the valley as the school location. Presumably, the rest of the few Hanson boys who had passed the school certificate had simply moved up to Hanson High School. The most famous pupil of Belle Vue had been J. B. Priestly, the city's then well-known contemporary author and radio commentator. The teaching standards at the school were considered to be comparable to those of Bradford Grammar School, which was nearer the city centre. In order to reach Belle Vue from my grandparents' house, I had to travel into the city by bus and then out of the other side of the city by trolley bus. Both Peter and I used to travel home for lunch each day. School dinners were provided, and these arrived hot in what appeared to be large milk churns and did not have a particularly pleasant smell. The food was regarded generally by most pupils as vile. Juveniles' bus, tram, and trolley bus fares were each a halfpenny, or 'ha'penny' as it was known. This amounted to a total of twenty pence per week. My mother used to round this up and gave me two shillings per week (twenty-four pence). Peter and I used to walk home every afternoon after school, from one side down into the city and up the hills on the opposite side of the city where our homes were. The distance was about two and a half miles. Our route was first down through the once genteel residential suburb of Frizinghall, then across the river, canal, and railway lines and then up into North Wing. This was an extremely deprived residential area and had a fearsome historical reputation for petty crime and gang violence. It was regarded by many people as a 'no go' area. Fortunately, it was always almost deserted during the day, and Peter and I never encountered any problems there. Whilst the walking may have been beneficial to our health and fitness, unfortunately, we also usually smoked a Woodbine cigarette, which we shared between us. However, more importantly, this walking exercise gave us each a bonus of five pence per week.

The price of wooden military model aeroplane kits was twenty-one pence. This, with a little surreptitious help from my grandmother, allowed me to be able to buy a kit more or less every two or three weeks.

The bus route to and from the city centre passed near to my grandparents' house. Buses at that time were painted in drab wartime khaki colour. All were double-decked, had a driver in a cab at the front, and an open passenger platform entrance controlled by a conductress at the rear. All fares and tickets were provided by the conductress, who used to continually walk through the bus to the seated or standing passengers. There was a strap hanging on the lower deck, and one bell push on the top deck at the head of the stairs, which enabled the conductress to signal to the driver when to start and stop. When the conductress was at the front of the upper deck, she had to walk all of the way back to the stairs in order to see whether passengers had finished alighting and joining the bus. Her only view of the platform was through a small convex mirror at the top of the stairs, through which she had to look before ringing the bell. As a ten-year-old boy, I always chose to sit on the seat nearest to the conductress's normal operating position on the platform at the bottom of the stairs. On one occasion when the conductress was on the upper deck, the passengers had finished alighting, and the driver had been waiting for the bell signal for some time I rang the bell. When the conductress came down from the upper deck shortly afterwards, she immediately scolded me. She then decided that I was only trying to be helpful and told me that as long as I was careful I could always 'ring off' for her in future. Apparently, the other three conductresses on the route heard about this, and I was subsequently allowed to 'ring off' for them also. Their regular drivers soon also recognised me whilst I waited at their bus stops and usually acknowledged me with a restrained hand salute from their steering wheels. I was delighted. The other skill that I developed was copied from the actions of bus inspectors who occasionally joined the bus in order to check tickets. They almost always jumped on to and off the platforms of the buses whilst they were starting or stopping. I immediately copied this practice. Health and safety officials of a future age would no doubt have referred me to the authorities as a ten-year-old juvenile delinquent.

Unlike all of my previous schools, Belle Vue was a boys' school, although there was a girls' school next door. I was never again to go to a mixed sex school. In contrast to my previous experience at Hanson School, I enjoyed life at Belle Vue. I was able to learn a whole new range of subjects. Some of these were rarely if ever taught routinely to later generations in schools but proved to be invaluable to me for the rest of my life. I was perfectly at home in mathematics but excelled in geometry. I was the only boy in the class who got a hundred percent marks in the end-of-year examination. I enjoyed English, physics and chemistry, history, and geography. In contrast, I was abysmally bad at French, German, and particularly Latin. I was the only boy in the class ever to get two percent marks for the end of term Latin examination. Intellectually and emotionally, I could never reconcile myself to the pointless use of gender for all objects and subjects in French and German, or the complexity of the cases in Latin. However, I progressed extremely well in English, although I never really understood parsing, syntax, the difference between subjects and objects, or the meaning of participles. My great new loves were art, woodwork, and metalwork classes. Art began with classical art and architecture. We were taught the structure and principles of Roman Trajan lettering and were required to practise them. We were taught Roman and Greek architecture with its classical types and categories of pillars. We were shown the architecture of St Sophia mosque in Istanbul, which ten years later I immediately recognised as the basis of the architectural design of Birmingham University. I practised and reproduced Trajan based lettering many times in later life. Woodwork and metalwork classes were taught by experienced teachers who clearly had been employed previously in industry. Our first exercise in the woodwork class was how to use a craft knife to cut out and cover with wallpaper a cardboard tablemat. In woodwork, the first exercise using wood was making a pencil sharpener. The object somewhat disappointingly turned out to be an exercise in cutting, planning, and chiselling a thin piece of wood squarely and accurately to given dimensions. Theoretically, a piece of sandpaper was then to have been glued to it, in order to sharpen pencils. However, by far the most important part of the teaching was how to use tools correctly and safely, to sharpen them, to look after them, and to use them accurately. Similarly, the metalwork classes were concerned with teaching us skills and practices but actually allowed us to produce a useful object. Our first exercise was to make a door or gate bolt. It involved filing and preparing a mild steel base plate, shaping a square section bolt, and then preparing and shaping retaining guides, and finally riveting them to the plate. The gatepost bolt keeper then had to be formed similarly and riveted to its base plate, and finally, the whole assembly had to be painted black. Fifty years later, I doubt whether any secondary school or its teachers could even begin to teach such skills. Even more unlikely would be the opportunity for ten-year-old boys to sharpen and use razor-edged chisels and hit them with wooden mallets, or use metalworking lathes. However, discipline, largely for safety reasons, very rightly was exceptionally strict. The most spectacular example of this was when one small boy in our class was found to have been holding or playing with his extremely sharp wood chisel incorrectly and potentially dangerously. The woodwork master seized him by the scruff of the neck, laid him face down across his woodwork bench and proceeded beat him with a bamboo cane. Such an incident, although extremely rare, was reminiscent of the Victorian discipline of fifty years earlier. In the modern jargon of the twenty-first century, it would probably genuinely fit one of the universally popular political public relations excuses – 'lessons have been learned'.

All pupils were made members of one of four 'houses'. These were unimaginatively named as 'A', 'B', 'C', and 'D'. Peter Newton and I were both in 'A' House. The school blazer, which was maroon, had the house letter embroidered in bright red on the breast pocket. Wartime clothes rationing was in force at the time. Unfortunately, Peter's parents hadn't enough coupons left to buy him one of the regulation blazers but had obtained a second-hand one in brown. Fortunately, this didn't seem to worry anyone. All boys carried a leather shoulder satchel. This had two shoulder straps, and the obligatory fashion amongst boys was only ever to use one strap over the shoulder but to put one thumb nonchalantly in the strap. One boy had a satchel with one long strap only, and he was ridiculed for being a 'pansy'.

The masters at Belle Vue were all middle-aged, since all fit younger men had been conscripted into the armed services. The school site was on a rather long and rather thin sloping site and was divided into the upper and lower schools. The first three forms were in the top end or higher end of the site. The assembly hall, laboratories, and woodwork and metalwork were at the lower end. Between class sessions, we often had to walk between the sections, and in cold and wet weather, this sometimes resulted in sitting in class in damp clothes. The head of the upper or junior forms was 'Beaky' Wells. Just why he had acquired this nickname was not clear, since he did not have particularly aquiline features. I can only assume that it was derived from the nickname for Justices of the Peace. He was a kind, gentle, and benevolent master, and was regarded with respect and even affection by boys and never with fear. His colleague and great friend was Mr Parry, known universally with great affection by boys as 'Yop'. This was derived from his initials, which were 'EOP'. He was Welsh, large, rotund, amiable, amusing but unfortunately had been gassed in the trenches during the First World War. As a result, he was apt to slobber unconsciously from time to time. Fortunately, shortly after his first lesson to us, Beaky Wells happened to come into the classroom just after this had occurred. He very gently and sympathetically explained quietly and confidentially to us the cause of the condition – and we never ever made fun of it again. Yop was a wonderful history master and initiated and inspired in me a lifelong love of the subject. For this, I have always been extremely grateful. His teaching of mediaeval history was inspirational, and he was an extremely kind man but was rather deaf. I remember a boy called Newsome who burst into tears during class. Yop very kindly tried to find out the cause of his grief, and through the boy's tears came to the conclusion that his dad had died. He tried to comfort him as best he could and even suggested the boy might go home. However, when the boy had recovered sufficiently to become coherent, it emerged that Yop had misheard him, and it was the boy's 'cat' that had died. There was also a splendid chemistry teacher who always wore a pinstriped double-breasted suit and had well Bryl creamed hair. He discovered that I was an Arthur Ransom enthusiast and was trying to sell ones that I had finished reading. Due to war shortages, these were difficult to obtain, and he bought mine at a very fair price. The money was a welcome addition to my aeroplane kit and tools funds.

Our geometry teacher was Percy Shapero, who was a delightful character – middle aged, small, bespectacled, and Jewish. He had the most extraordinary class discipline that I ever encountered. He would wait until the class was seated, and then, beaming through his glasses would raise his hand, and with a very slight lisp address us very quietly as 'boys'. He would then explain, equally quietly, that we were to remain completely silent throughout the lesson, unless we had a question to ask. In the event of even the slightest noise during his class, he would immediately stop, identify the cause or culprit, and then repeat his warning before continuing. It was in his class that I obtained my one and only academic triumph at Belle Vue of a hundred percent marks in his end of year examination paper. There was also a somewhat younger unconventional teacher who kept slipping out during classes, in order to smoke a quick cigarette. Needless to say, he in no way condemned or disciplined boys who he caught smoking. Our English teacher, Mrs Worsnop was one of only two female teachers. She had been recruited due to the shortage of male teachers and was middle aged, matronly, rather rotund, and very dignified, kind, and considerate.

I had no difficulty in learning and writing in her subject, although I always struggled with the finer points of grammatical analysis. Our chemistry and physics masters were both excellent, and I had no difficulties in learning from them.

One of our English masters, a Mr Tompkins, was popularly known as 'Kipper Feet'. He suffered from some condition of his feet, which were splayed, and this was presumably why he was not in the armed forces. He was generally genial, but on occasions could be remarkably and unexpectedly strict and severe. On one occasion, he quite wrongly accused me of cheating in an English test, saying that I couldn't possibly have known how to write in some particular manner and must have copied it. It was definitely completely untrue, as I immediately explained to him. I was also slightly upset, but I then somewhat unfortunately, tried to reply humorously. I said I couldn't possibly need to cheat in English, although I might have to in French. He was enraged. He seized me by the scruff of the neck, dragged me in front of the class, and then proceeded to slap my face repeatedly whilst propelling me from one side of the front of the classroom to the other. He then attempted to justify his behaviour by warning me and the class that cheating was never acceptable – in any subject. Perhaps unsurprisingly, I strongly resented his behaviour, but I just about managed not to cry.

Sport at Belle Vue was somewhat irregular and intermittent. There was a rugby football pitch beyond the end of the bus route to Howarth Road. This was right on the edge of the moor, and both desperately bleak and cold in winter. Clothing, including footwear, was rationed, and we were only able to use second-hand garments and boots which were available from the school sports department. My own gear was fairly ill fitting, and the boots seemed to differ from those of everyone else in that they had leather bars on the soles rather than the almost universal leather round studs. The changing room hut contained benches, rows of coat hangers, and a shower room, the water in which was almost always cold. We were usually still shivering whilst waiting for the bus to return home. I hated the experience at Howarth Road, but that was compensated somewhat by the weekly swimming class at the public baths near the school. I learned the breaststroke but never really mastered the over-arm crawl. However, apart from the occasional opportunity to swim, I never had the slightest interest in any other sport at any later time of my life.

Finally, World War II in Europe ended, and my father was on his way home from Burma. I knew I would be leaving Bradford, hopefully for the last time, and returning to London. To my enormous relief, I believed, at last, a golden future beckoned.

On VE Day, celebrations in Bradford were far more muted than the crowds and scenes of jubilation that occurred in Central London. There were no street parties, probably because food and drink were still rationed. However, on 'VE Night', Bradford was lit up in a manner unseen even before the war. The wartime blackout had ceased, and on VE Day, the corporation bus services continued to run until midnight. The centre of the city was totally floodlit, and most surprisingly in addition to the Cathedral and civic buildings, the front of the Gas Company Showrooms, which were unsurprisingly lit by gas but were the brightest of all. People remained on the streets in the City Centre dancing, singing, and cheering throughout most of the night. Seeing and participating in it was the experience of a lifetime. However, there were two months still to go before the unexpected Japanese surrender. Unhappily, some of the armed forces who had returned from Europe were expecting to be sent to the Far East to fight the Japanese.

A few weeks after VE Day, my mother and I travelled to Newhaven in Sussex to visit my father's eldest sister. When we arrived in Newhaven, my father was still on his way home from Burma, and we hoped and expected that we would soon be able to return to live in London. However, as a result of the wartime bombing, there was a very severe housing shortage. My Aunt Polly suggested that we might live, at least temporarily, in Seaford, which was a few miles further along the coast. She knew of an apartment there, which was owned by a middle-aged spinster friend. There was an excellent daily train service to London, although the journey time was slightly over an hour. Whilst we were in Newhaven, the surrender of Japan was announced, and we celebrated 'VJ' Day. This was a very different experience to that of 'VE' Day in Bradford. The celebrations were in the daytime as street parties, which were provided and attended by their local residents. Flags and streamers were in evidence in abundance, as was food and drink. The Second World War really was over.

My mother and I returned to Bradford, and at the end of October, I looked forward to celebrating Guy Fawkes Night. This because of the end of the blackout restrictions would be the first time that it could be celebrated properly since before the war, The Guy Fawkes traditions in Bradford were completely different from any that I ever encountered elsewhere. Guy Fawkes Night was known as Plot Night, and the night before was known as Mischief Night. Two homemade delicacies were provided, which were known as Plot Parkin and Plot Toffee. Plot Parkin was a gingerbread, and the toffee was baked in a tray and then cut into pieces. On Mischief Night, boys used to go around knocking on householders' doors having first dropped some sort of offensive item such as dog or horse droppings on their front doorstep. They would then knock on the door before hiding behind a hedge or some other doorway. The 'outraged' householder would then open their doors, berate the miscreants, and usually offer each of them a lump of Plot Toffee or Parkin. Needless to say, the following bonfire night was spectacular because boys had collected large quantities of dead timber from parks and other places, and proper outdoor fireworks were once again available. Due to the easing of sugar rationing, the night was complemented by quantities of Plot Parkin and Toffee.

Shortly after Plot Night, my mother and I met my father at Foster Square Station at nine o'clock on a Saturday night. He was in his army uniform as a sergeant in the Intelligence Corps and was accompanied by his large kit bag. He had been demobilised at York, where he had been issued with his final pay, discharge papers, and his 'demob' civilian pinstriped double-breasted suit and a trilby hat. We returned to Beech Grove on the last bus of the day, and the Second World War really 'was' over for us all. For the next few days, I was wonderfully happy. My father began to tell us of some of his experiences, and although the war was not over in the Far East, he had been discharged medically because he had contracted amoebic dysentery and was aged forty. He had been in the Irrawaddy crossing and was the only man to survive in a boat of twelve other men. He then swam whilst under fire to the Japanese-held shore. He subsequently swam for two hours back across the river to escape, despite still being under enemy machine gun fire. Subsequently, he was sent to hospital with amoebic dysentery, before being discharged and repatriated to England. Before his final experience, he had served throughout the Burma Campaign in Imphal and Kohima. On the Monday after he had returned, he telephoned his old employers the Westminster Press in Fleet Street. He arranged to visit them later in the week. He returned to say that he was to start work again as soon as he could find somewhere for us to live in London. In the event, that proved to be impossible immediately, but fortunately, he was able to follow up his sister Polly's suggestion and take up the offer to live in and commute from Seaford. In the meantime, in order to take my now extensive collection of tools to my new home, I found a local carpenter to make me a suitable wooden box. It was beautifully made in pine, was about four feet long, and looked like a small coffin. I was to use it for the rest of my life. However, Christmas came before we were to leave, and I received presents from my father. He bought me some railway books that he had bought directly from the publishers. These were all about 'Pre-Group' Railways, about none of which I had ever heard and had ceased to exist in 1927, before I was born. I had only really been interested in the contemporary London Midland and Scottish Railway. However, the books were a revelation to me and introduced me to what was to become a life-long fascination. In the future, I never had any real interest in any railway period later than the 1930s.

My mother had gone on in advance and followed my father to London in order to retrieve our furniture which had been in store with our ex-neighbours in North Wembley. I followed a few days later, having said goodbye to all of my friends and neighbours. My mother and father had travelled from Bradford Exchange station to London Kings Cross station. This was the normal route. Because I had always been an enthusiast of the LMS Railway, I chose to travel by the more roundabout route from Foster Square to St Pancras. The service, unlike the LNER route, also boasted a restaurant car service. I proudly took advantage of this for the princely sum of half a crown. This was more than two weeks of my pocket money. Fortunately, my mother had given me an extra two shillings for the journey. I was met at St Pancras by my father, who then took me to Victoria Station. When we arrived there, he gave me the money for a ticket to Seaford, and he accompanied me to the ticket window. I duly purchased the ticket, but my father was aghast. He was appalled by my broad Bradford accent. However, he very diplomatically advised me in the gentlest manner possible that I was going to have to change the way that I spoke. He was absolutely right.

Sussex by the Sea

My father had found accommodation in the two-bedroomed upper floor of a semi-detached house occupied by a middle-aged spinster lady. The house was on the outskirts of Seaford on the edge of the rolling South Downs at Hindover or 'High and Over' and the beginning of the cliffs of the Seven Sisters. A gas cooker has been installed in the front bedroom, which then served as a living room. The bathroom was used for water and washing up. The house was about a mile from the terminal railway station in Seaford. Two six-coach electric trains, complete with buffet cars departed from there every morning. One went to Victoria, and the other to the city at London Bridge. They both were joined to similar portions at Lewes and separated when they returned in the evening. The London Bridge train provided my father with a rather long, though comfortable, journey each day to and from his office in Fleet Street. As a newspaperman, he was able to read a selection of daily and evening newspapers that he had obtained at no cost during his working day.

I was enrolled at Lewes County School to and from, which I also travelled daily from Seaford station. However, the school bore no resemblance to any that I had attended previously. Boys came from all over East Sussex and were utterly different from any of my previous school friends. I never saw any trace of aggression or gang behaviour, and the boys and staff were equally pleasant and welcoming. However, they regarded my accent as coming from another planet, and at first, I received the erroneous nickname of 'Scottie'. Sometime later on one occasion, the art master accused me, in a humorous although not unkindly manner of being 'slow and sluggardly'. Perhaps unfortunately, I thenceforth became known as 'Slug'.

The teaching of most subjects and my learning of them continued to be much the same as at Belle Vue. However, history was quite different. The master was a youngish man with rather prominent teeth and a slightly noticeable Manchester accent. As a result, he had unfairly acquired the nickname amongst his pupils of

'Tojo', presumably after the then currently ridiculed Japanese Emperor. At Belle Vue, I had previously been taught history from the Middle Ages, and the 'Drums and Guns' of the eighteenth and nineteenth centuries. In complete contrast, the subject for my present class covered the industrial and social revolutions of the late seventeenth and eighteenth centuries but also the American War of Independence. The master also recommended the excellent definitive history books of Arthur Bryant, and the novels of 'Captain Hornblower' and other books by C.S. Forrester. I read these with immense pleasure. Fortunately, unlike Belle Vue, the only foreign language taught was French. I continued to be abysmal at it. A new subject was music. The master who used to teach this used to bring in his own gramophone records, and this exposed me for the first time to Sibelius' symphonies. Some years later, I acquired most of Sibelius' works on modern LPs.

Because of the distance from home, it was unavoidably necessary for me to eat school dinners, something I had never done before. These were served and eaten in a large canteen. The serving ladies were extremely friendly towards the boys and after enquiring where I came from immediately christened me as 'Bradford'. However, I was introduced to macaroni cheese and other delights of which I had no previous experience. Like all of the boys, I had a very healthy appetite and enjoyed thoroughly all of my new and partly unfamiliar diet. I quickly made friends with a number of boys, although this was largely on a geographical basis. Boys came from all over East Sussex and the catchment area was probably a twenty-five-mile miles radius from Lewes. Therefore, boys tended to choose friends with whom they travelled by train or bus. However, I had one friend who lived in East Grinstead at the opposite end of the county. He and I used to meet occasionally on Saturdays at Eastbourne, which I could reach easily by bus. My greatest pleasure in Seaford was the purchase of a bicycle. I had longed for this throughout the war, when only second-hand bicycles were occasionally available. However, my mother had steadfastly resisted this on the basis of the potential dangers and the universally steep hills that surrounded Bradford. Since none of my school friends lived in Seaford, I was only able to cycle on my own. I did this in my leisure time in and around Seaford but occasionally went to Newhaven. There was almost no road traffic, apart from the occasional bus. I also used to cycle to Seaford railway station every weekday evening to meet my father. I used to wait in the station, in which Charlie Care the foreman was in charge. He was a very friendly local, who also happened to be the Town Crier, a traditional post. There were very few trains and almost no activity in the station in evenings. After a short time, he handed me his ticket clippers and asked me to look after the station for him whilst he went briefly for a little light refreshment over the road at the local pub. On one occasion, he recounted to me that he had first worked as a boy on the London Brighton and South Coast Railway. The summer uniform was a white jacket and light brown coloured corduroy trousers. In wet weather, these gave off a particularly unpleasant smell. It was because their colour was derived from dog droppings. When I told my father this story, he immediately confirmed it. He said that when it rained, boys at his school deliberately moved away from boys wearing corduroy shorts.

My only other school friend Donald lived in Denton, which was about four miles away on the way to Newhaven. Unlike the two-bedroomed upper floor flat in which I was living, his house was detached and quite large. He had a large Trix-Twin Model Railway and a great many Dinky Toys of British warships. I used to cycle to his house quite regularly, but somehow, there was always a strong wind on the three-mile long straight road beside the River Ouse Estuary. Whichever direction I was travelling, the wind always seemed to be against me. However, I always enjoyed playing at his house.

Although I had adapted as best I could to a Sussex accent, my parents were still anxious to rid me of all trace of my Bradford accent. My Bradford elocution teacher John Dale had recommended to me and my mother that I could attend the School of Elocution and Drama in Hove. This was run by Roland Pertwee, the brother of John Pertwee who was a well-known, mainly comic actor. Although it was an hour's journey by rail from Seaford, I could use my season ticket for half of the way. I duly began to attend the school every Saturday morning. I was able to continue taking the Guildhall examinations, which I did successfully. I was also cast in a small junior part in a Pirandello play 'It Is Not Yet Spring' that they presented at a local theatre. I received a favourable mention for my part in it by the local newspaper. However, I really was not particularly interested in the stage or theatre. A severe handicap would have been my inability to quickly learn and remember scripts easily.

West Kensington

After just over a year, my parents and I moved to a flat in London. This was obtained due to Laura Godwin, the sister of one of my mother's friends in Bradford. The flats were owned by her brother-in-law who was an architect living in Coulsdon. The flat was on the ground floor of a four-storey block of terraced flats in West Kensington. The flat was spacious, with high ceilings, and also had limited access to the basement. There was no bathroom, but a bath had been installed in the kitchen and was covered by a removable second-hand kitchen door, which served as a working surface. There was only one bedroom, which was occupied by my parents, and I slept on a 'Put you up' collapsible bed in the back-living room. The block of flats was entered up a short flight of stone stairs from the quiet road in front and had a small-secluded garden behind it. Immediately opposite the front of the house was a gap in the block opposite. It was occupied by a small 'prefab' concrete flat-roofed prefabricated house that replaced the part of the block demolished by a direct hit from a German bomb during the war. After the previous five years of a miserable unsettled existence, the flat in West Kensington was Nirvana. My father could now travel in less than half an hour on the District Line to the Temple, from where he could walk to his office on Fleet Street. My father had arranged for me to go to school, which also could be reached on the underground in approximately the same time.

Almost by chance, my father had found a place for me at a public school. This was the Mercers' School in Holborn, the oldest public school in London. He had entered the narrow school entrance by accident. He had failed to see a small printed notice stating that the school was full and was taking no applications for new boys. However, by sheer chance, the headmaster happened to see him enquiring from the porter and noticed my father's tie. At that time, almost all men used to wear so-called 'Club' ties. The pattern and colour of these were peculiar to each regiment in the army and also to the Royal Air Force and Royal Navy. The headmaster instantly recognised my father's Intelligence Corps tie and invited him to join him in his headmaster's office. It then transpired that they had both served in the Fourteenth Army in Burma. My acceptance at the Mercers' school was immediately assured.

Mercers' School was completely unlike any of my previous four schools. The first difference was that it was hidden. It was entered through a fairly narrow doorway which concealed a covered passageway under a commercial building in the main thoroughfare slightly to the west of Holborn Viaduct. Surprisingly, unlike almost all other public schools, it was completely non-residential. Boys came from as wide a radius as had those at Lewes County School. They commuted daily from Essex and Middlesex for distances of as much as ten miles, with journey times as much as an hour. It was an accepted fact that Essex boys were often late to arrive at school, as a result of train delays into Liverpool Street Station. No boys came from south of the river.

The house names were rather more distinguished than the 'ABCD' of Belle Vue and the 'Seahaven' and other East Sussex regional names at Lewes County. They were 'Colet', in which I was placed, 'Gresham', and 'Whittington', all of which were named after distinguished past city of London dignitaries. The classes had strange names. I went first into a class called 'Shell' and in my next year into 'Remove B'. I never discovered the meaning of these names. All teachers wore gowns, and there were no female teachers. School life was completely different from anything that I had experienced previously. The classes were smaller, and although the boys were fairly friendly towards me, I was always considered to be an outsider. Apart from my strange Sussex accent with a Yorkshire flavour, I was clearly an oddity to all of the other boys who had begun in the first form of the school. The masters generally accepted me, although I got the impression that one or two of them, like the boys, saw me as an outsider and an oddity. They were almost certainly right.

My favourite master was Mr Rossetti, who was our English teacher, and in my second year was my form master. He was in his mid-thirties, always extremely pleasant, kind, and had a very quick puckish sense of humour. He was very popular with all boys, but unlike some of the other masters, he had absolutely no favourites. I made one or two friends, but due to the travelling situation, like boys at Lewes County School, boys tended to make friends with ones with whom they travelled to and from home.

My academic performance continued as it had done in Bradford and at Lewes. Fortunately, once again the only foreign language taught was French. I continued to be abysmal at it. However, I was quite happy in English language, and I was fascinated by 'figures of speech', particularly the obscure or peculiar ones. Mr Rossetti once told me that if I ever got a question on it in the School Certificate exam, I should get a credit. His prediction proved to be right. At the end of each school year, competitions were held in each class for English literature. These consisted of boys reciting or reading and presenting pieces of classic literature or poetry. Perhaps unsurprisingly, I won two or three of these competitions and was awarded first prizes of book tokens. These had to be redeemed at a local bookseller in High Holborn and had to be of a formal nature. I did not hesitate to choose two or three Arthur Bryant history books. A decorative 'Book Plate', an official school acknowledgment of the award was then inserted by the school, and the books were presented formally before the whole school at the end of the school year.

Sport consisted of 'soccer' football in the winter and cricket in the summer. Sports were practised at Grove Park in Kent on Wednesday afternoons and sometimes on Saturday mornings. We travelled by train from and back to Holborn Viaduct station. Inevitably, I was useless at cricket but could run well and was capable of kicking a football. My running had probably been well honed, during the dark days of escaping from enemies at Hanson Primary School. The team position in which I played was what was then known as right wing, from which, being a fast runner, I managed to score a few goals. To my utter astonishment, I was once made captain of the Form House team. As this was for a Saturday morning match, I had no wish for this to continue. Fortunately, it did not. However, on my one and only match, I did score three goals, although I never understood the 'offside' rule. The other sporting activity was swimming. This was a weekly event, after school at a public swimming baths in Soho. We used to travel there by the underground to Piccadilly Circus. This was a sport at which I was reasonably competent and quite enjoyed.

The most extraordinary change that occurred to me during my stay at Mercers' was in my second year. The behaviour of my classmates was something that I had never encountered before and not even heard of. As all of the boys were going through the early stages of puberty and the universally practised activity was masturbation. This took place on every possible occasion and was most commonly shared between friends but could also occur occasionally with boys of the same age in other classes. There was certainly no emotional relationship involved, other than normal schoolboy friendships. Boys had absolutely no interest in girls, nor even knew of pornography. Our activities were in no way similar to the adult form of homosexuality, in which I never ever had the slightest interest. It was merely an activity in which all boys participated. It was clearly a demonstration of the fact that boys were 'growing up'. A classic example was the Friday afternoon swimming class, during which a public pool in Soho was reserved for the exclusive use of the school. The changing cubicles were above and behind the sloping rows of seats surrounding the pool. They had open-topped doors with gaps below them and curtains above them. Each cubicle was for a pair of boys, and boys were simply allowed to choose which ones to use. Inevitably, whoever boys shared with in order to dress after the class had ended, they immediately took the opportunity to masturbate with one another. This was quite regardless of whether they were particular friends or not. It was simply part of the routine. Similar behaviour used to occur when we used to travel back from Wednesday sport afternoons at Grove Park in the empty compartments of the suburban trains to Holborn Viaduct. There was very rarely, if ever any similar contact, social or otherwise with any other forms or classes.

During the post-war period, there was a major labour shortage, and farming was particularly short of labour during harvest time. As a result, schoolboys were employed briefly to help fill the gap. Both at Lewes and Mercers', classes went out to farms to engage in potato picking. At Lewes, it occurred on Wednesday afternoons, when we went by train to local farms, but at Mercers', boys went to a summer camp. This was near Witney in Oxfordshire beside the River Windrush, a name that would achieve notoriety more than half a century later.

My most important experience at Mercers' was the formation of an Army Cadet platoon. This had been arranged by the headmaster with the Honourable Artillery Company. This was the oldest regiment in the British Army, was a Territorial Army unit, and was located nearby at Moorgate. It was closely associated with the Grenadier Guards, with which cadets wore an almost identical distinctive uniform. Our uniform, unlike any other army cadets, consisted of Grenadier Guard's uniform with 'cheese-cutter' cap, the peak of which came down steeply to near the tip of the nose. We were trained by a drill sergeant who was in the Grenadier Guards. The parades were at Artillery House in Moorgate. Because of the absence of adult servicemen during the Second World War, the cadets were constantly trained for and carried out the frequent ceremonial duties, for which the regiment was historically responsible. These ceremonies involved the very rare regimental privilege of marching with fixed bayonets and unfurled Regimental Colours through the city of London. Our training was probably unique among Army Cadets and involved ceremonial parade and bayonet-drill training, and marching at a slightly slower pace than normal infantry regiments. Ceremonial marches were usually to the Mansion House, the Guildhall, and St Paul's Cathedral, as well as marching in the annual Lord Mayor's Show. I was bitterly disappointed that the only ceremonial march and parade that I missed was the wedding of Princess Elizabeth and Lieutenant Philip Mountbatten. This was because I was less than five feet seven tall. However, I had passed both parts of the Army Cadet Certificate 'A'. This was considered to indicate the equivalent competence of a fully trained adult army recruit. It allowed me to wear a red 'star' above my cuff. On one occasion, we were inspected by Lord Alanbrooke who had been in the North African Campaign with General Montgomery. General Montgomery was a governor of the school and on one occasion gave us a talk. He followed this by exercising his right as a governor to give us a day's holiday.

The other summer event at Mercers' was the annual Army Cadet Camp. This was usually at Bisley where the HAC had a 'Hut'. The so-called hut was in fact a brick-built building comparable to a typical golf club, but with additional sleeping accommodation, and was for the exclusive use of the HAC. Most importantly, the week allowed us to shoot regulation army Enfield .303 rifles on the famous Bisley ranges. I proved to be an excellent 'shot'. On one occasion, I was allowed to fire a Bren gun. At the age of fifteen, I found our Bisley week to be a wonderful, privileged experience. In contrast, a year later, the annual camp was at the Royal Marine Barracks at Deal in Kent. There we were given the opportunity to ride an army dispatch rider motorcycle on the grass slopes near the town. When my turn came, I managed to ride about a hundred yards before falling off. I never again attempted to ride a motorcycle, nor ever had any inclination to do so.

My other great interest was my model railway. For the first time, I now had an opportunity to start building a proper layout. Materials were still in short supply, but I had obtained a sheet of building board and some lengths of thin timber and constructed a baseboard. At that time, model railway tracks were almost exclusively of three rails, in which the centre rail supplied the current and the locomotives returned it through the other two rails. I had managed to join the Model Railway Club as a very junior and youngest member. The club was rare and regarded as the leading one in the country. It used to meet once a month in the Ambulance Room in the bowels of Waterloo station. I met there a member who was in his early thirties and had been taken prisoner of war just before Dunkirk. As a result, he had been repatriated at the end of the war with a sizable back pay. He had spent some of this money on a large quantity of what had by then become obsolete uninsulated third-rail track. Instead of using it, he was now in the process of building a modern contemporary two-rail system. He offered to give me all of his old track. I used it to lay what was an alternative contemporary system of 'stud rail', which simply involved inserting pins down the middle of the track instead of a centre rail. This was somewhat less unsightly compared with the previous three-rail system. I was utterly delighted and immensely grateful.

Towards the end of my second year, I had taken and 'passed' the School Certificate, but predictably, I had failed French. Before the end of term, my father had been offered by the headmaster the opportunity for me to repeat the year and take the examination again. Although I had got 'credits' in English language, mathematics, history, and art, and passed in English literature and geography, I would have to repeat all subjects again. I realised that I would never ever be able to pass in French and certainly not to get a 'credit'. Without it, I would be unable to go on to Higher School Certificate, which was necessary in order to enter university. I had absolutely no wish to continue. It was therefore agreed by my father and the headmaster that I should leave at the end of term. I would still be only fifteen years old, and strictly speaking, I should not be allowed to leave before the age of sixteen. However, the headmaster was prepared to overlook the fact, and with very few, if any regrets, I left.

After leaving school, I had not expected to leave home. However, within a few weeks, I had not only left school for the last time but I would never live at home again with my parents. I would only visit them. At the age of fifteen, I could remember living with my mother for eleven years but with my father for only seven. It would be another fifteen years before I had a home of my own.

The Brewing Industry

When I left school, my first ambition was to be a newspaper journalist. My father therefore had arranged for me to go to a secretarial college in Regent Street to learn shorthand and typing. These were regarded as essential skills for a journalist at that time. However, my father, who worked as an advertising manager in Fleet Street, really wanted me to become an auctioneer and estate agent. In contrast, my Uncle Rex wanted me to become a brewer. He claimed that if I became a journalist, I would 'never have a penny to scrape my arse with', and 'why would I want to go to a college which was only full of silly young girls who were going to be typists?' (!!!). Finally, somewhat reluctantly, I capitulated. My uncle decided I was too young at fifteen to become a brewing pupil immediately and therefore arranged a six-month pupillage at Hugh Baird and Sons who were maltsters with their main maltings and headquarters at Greenwich.

My first recollection of contact with the brewing industry was when I was at the age of four. My uncle, Rex Mears, was husband of my mother's only sister May, and he was the head brewer at Hemmingway's, a small brewery in nearby Leeds. My aunt and uncle never had any children. As a result, my aunt became particularly devoted to me. Eventually, I became equally devoted to her. My uncle was part of a large well-to-do family in Wolverhampton, where his father had once owned a brick works and a small brewery, which was subsequently sold. My uncle's two brothers were both head brewers, one in Frome in Dorset, and the other in Alton in Hampshire. My uncle was unquestionably my most wealthy and influential relative. Shortly before the Second World War, he became an allied trader with Kendal's, a sugar and primings merchant. He then moved to Castle Bromwich, a suburb on the outskirts of Birmingham. My uncle, somewhat smugly, used to tell us that he had bought his house by using a local council loan at a low fixed-interest rate, because the council, for some wartime reason were very anxious for people to buy their own property. He obviously became very rich because he then used to visit us in Bradford in his motor car. When war broke out, he quickly became a head brewer again, this time at the Highgate Brewery in Walsall. The brewery subsequently became part of the Mitchells and Butlers 'empire'. In order to live nearer the brewery, my aunt and uncle later moved to Little Aston Park, a very exclusive part of Streetly in Staffordshire. This was halfway between Castle Bromwich and Walsall, where my uncle bought a large house, from which he drove daily to the brewery. Throughout the war, unlike most people, he was able to obtain a ration of petrol, due to his employment in a 'Reserved Occupation'. Due to a 'contact', he also used to buy a new Wolsey saloon car directly from the works at Castle Bromwich each year. He also used to explain subsequently that his 'contact' who was an inspector at the works used to 'accidentally' scratch the paintwork of a car. This would then be completely re-sprayed and then reserved for my uncle. During one of my visits to Streetly, my uncle took me one Sunday morning to the Walsall Highgate Brewery to which he made a routine cursory weekend inspection visit. I was passed into the care of the brewery foreman who showed me around the brewery. I have little or no recollection of the plant, but I was totally appalled by the overpowering smell of beer. I found it difficult to imagine how anyone could work in such an unpleasantly smelly environment. However, I then understood why my uncle's tweed suit always smelled strongly of beer. Nevertheless, I agreed, somewhat reluctantly, at the age of fifteen to begin a brewing career.

As a result of my future career decision, one Sunday evening in November my father took me from our home in West Kensington to the Old Kent Road. His objective was to find lodgings for my pupillage at Greenwich. After visiting a couple of basement tenements, which my father decided were unsuitable, we moved on to New Cross. After knocking on a few front doors of small terrace houses in a side street, we found a lady, who must have taken pity on me. She offered a room for me to share with one other lodger in the attic. The house was gas-lit, and we inspected the bedroom, which appeared to be satisfactory. The lady then volunteered the information that her husband worked for the local council and that he had to leave early each morning. (It was subsequently revealed that he was a street sweeper – a perfectly respectable, though somewhat humble occupation.) My father then left me, having agreed to pay eighteen shillings per week, on the understanding that I would only need breakfasts and evening meals from Monday to Thursday and would come home for weekends. The fellow lodger with whom I shared the attic bedroom was a kindly young baker. He used to go to work at half-past four each morning and tended permanently to smell of baking flour. The following morning, I was collected by my uncle who was in London at the time. We reported to the head office of Hugh Baird and Sons in Greenwich High Street. There I met Herbert Lanham, the head maltings and purchasing manager, who would be supervising my pupillage. He explained that I would be joined by another pupil – Dick Peach, whose family owned a rival malting company. We would learn all about and work in all parts of the barley buying and malting processes, including the malt-roasting plant further down Greenwich High Street. Subsequently, he always addressed Dick and me as 'Mr Bradforth' and 'Mr Peach'. The only precedent that I could think of for this at the age of fifteen was that of midshipmen in Nelson's Navy a hundred and fifty years earlier.

Life as a pupil was a completely new experience for me. Dick Peach and I were shown around the malting floors, where the growing malt was turned by hand, using huge wooden hand shovels three times a day. I was subsequently required to do the turning and also loading and emptying the water steep, usually at six o'clock in the morning and loading and emptying the kilns. Another activity was receiving and despatching two-hundred pound sacks of barley and malt using two-wheeled handbarrows. The attraction of the early morning efforts was going for breakfast with the workmen to a small cafe around the corner from the maltings. Bearing in mind that food rationing was still in place, bacon, eggs and beans were something of a luxury. Now, being a 'grown-up', I felt I was able to swear and smoke cigarettes in public. Before the introduction of the 'Clean Air Act', London was subject to 'smog', and Greenwich, being beside the Thames, was particularly affected by it. I can recall walking back to my lodgings in the evening and frequently, quite literally, being almost unable to see my hand in front of my face. Buses crawled along at less than walking speed following the conductor who was shining a torch on the kerbstones on the pavement.

My first work was 'turning' malt which was growing on the malting's floors. After being steeped in cold water, the barley was laid out about a foot deep on the floors and turned every eight hours by labourers wielding large wooden shovels. As part of our training, Dick and I also spent time in the laboratory and listened to the buying and selling correspondence, as dictated by Mr Lanham.

His letters always began with the unique phrase 'Dear Sirs, Yours of the nth inst. to hand, we note…'. Twice a week, Herbert Lanham, Dick Peach, and I went up to the Corn Exchange in the city. We left the office at about ten o'clock, and the first port of call was a pub a couple of hundred yards from the office in Greenwich High Street. The pub was closed, but Mr Lanham knocked on a side-door and we were ushered into the empty bar. After Mr Lanham had consumed a quick glass of whisky, we moved on to the bus stop for our journey to Wapping. There we entered the underground to travel first to Whitechapel, and then to Mark Lane (later known as Tower Hill). At Mark Lane, we entered the Corn Exchange, which was a large concourse without a roof (which had been demolished by an air raid during the London Blitz). It was filled with traders buying and selling grain, which in our case was barley. Mr Lanham was recognised immediately by traders who came up to him in turn with small sample packets of barley. Mr Lanham would open these carefully and pour the contents into the palm of his other hand. He would ask whether the barley was 'dried in stack'. He would first hold the emptied contents of the packet to his eye, sniff the contents, and quite often carefully select and pick up a single barleycorn between his thumb and smallest finger. He would then present the corn to the potential seller and quietly issue the dreaded word 'mould'. After buying as much barley as he required, we would then retire to a pub around the corner for lunch. Mr Lanham always addressed Dick and me as 'Mr Peach', and 'Mr Bradforth'. When we reached the pub, Dick and I were asked what we would like to drink. As I was only fifteen years of age, I made the inexcusable error of asking for a glass of cider. Immediately, I was suitably admonished, and it was pointed out to 'Mr Bradforth' that he was due to enter the brewing trade. I then somewhat sheepishly asked for and subsequently drank slowly my very first half-pint of draught bitter.

Birmingham

After I had been working in my pupillage at the maltings for three months, my uncle announced that he had obtained a brewing pupillage for me in Birmingham. The general practice for pupils was to pay a premium, usually of some hundreds of pounds, to the brewer who would be teaching and supervising the pupil. However, my uncle had found a brewery that not only did not require a premium but actually paid a modest wage to the pupil. This was therefore regarded as an 'Improvership' rather than a pupillage. I was to receive one pound weekly, which I discovered subsequently was subject to income tax. Because the tax was sixpence a week and the Inland Revenue could not handle amounts of less than one shilling, that amount was deducted from my wages on alternate weeks by the pay clerk. To put the value of money into perspective, it should be recalled that the average labourer at that time rarely received more than two pounds per week.

When I left my maltings pupillage, I was now sixteen years old, and for the first week stayed with my aunt and uncle in Streetly. During that time, I was taken to Dares Brewery in Belgrave Road, a slum area of Edgbaston, popularly known as 'The Burma Road' due to the large population of immigrant Indians residing nearby. I was introduced to the head brewer, a Mr William Glew, popularly known as 'Billie' or more covertly and unsurprisingly as 'Sticky'. He was a small forty-year-old bespectacled and rather meek and mild man, the antithesis of what I had expected to meet as a head brewer. I subsequently commented rather naively to my uncle that I thought it would be impossible not to like and 'get on' with him. It was agreed that my first priority was to find lodgings locally, since the journey from Streetly to the brewery involved a bus and tram journey of over an hour. It would also be impossible for me to get to the brewery for an early morning mash. The character of the second or assistant brewer could not have formed a greater contrast to Mr Glew. 'Paddy' Lyttleton, who had a brother who was a brewer at Whitbread's, was in his mid-twenties and had recently come out of the Royal Air Force, in which he had served as pilot during the Second World War. He still wore his RAF greatcoat. He was a caricature character with a wide moustache and a typical 'gung-ho' manner and attitude. However, he was able to recommend suitable lodgings out at Moseley, a respectable suburb slightly further tram ride out than Edgbaston. The brewery was a perfect size in which to learn the brewing trade. In addition to the brewhouse, it had a boiler house, bottling plant and stores, a cooperage, garage, and the inevitable engineer's workshop. The brewery had a maximum output of about six-hundred barrels per week and was an ideal size in which to learn every practical aspect of brewing. The main draught beer was 'Dares Bitter', which was claimed to be the palest beer in the country. There were a number of Dares bottled beers, as well as Bass, Worthington, and Guinness, all of which came in wooden casks.

I settled in to my new lodgings the next Sunday night. In contrast to my 'digs' in New Cross, Moseley was a very respectable suburb of Birmingham and the lodgings were a large detached house in its own grounds. As well as regular periodic visits by a number of commercial travellers, it was occupied by a number of permanent residents. These included a university lecturer, a civil service tax inspector, and the family of a civil engineer who along with his family had spent the Second World War in Changi Jail in Singapore where they had been imprisoned by the Japanese.

My first day at the brewery began with the issue of my first white coat, a tour of the plant with Mr Glew and introduction to all of the staff and workers. During one of these introductions, I was greeted by a small worker from the Racking Room. He was exceptionally friendly and had a beaming smile. He shook my hand and welcomed me enthusiastically in a language of which I was unable to understand a single word. It transpired that, like a number of other labourers, he came from the 'Black Country' between Birmingham and Wolverhampton and had a unique dialect that was peculiar to the area. It was a dialect, along with that of the more common 'Brumigham' that I subsequently learned to understand and even mimic but at the time was completely alien to me.

The Brewers' Office on an upper floor was small, narrow, and extended over the brewery yard. From its window could be seen the whole of the brewery site, and to the right over the brick boundary wall a small residential square of squalid back-to-back tenement houses. In the middle of the square was a collection of communal brick 'privies' and a cold-water tap. These were apparently the total sanitary provisions for the square. They provided a source of some amusement to Paddy Lyttleton who observed and reported regularly on the comings and goings of the identifiable characters of the (usually female) residents. There were two desks in the office, one of which I was to share with Paddy Lyttleton. There was also a small sink next to the door, which was intended for the examination of beer samples but also provided facilities for washing glasses and our lunchtime crockery.

I rapidly became familiar with the brewery, around which I was taken by Paddy Lyttleton and found particular interest in the bottling stores, engineer fitter's small workshop, and the cooperage. The heads or foremen of these departments were extremely friendly towards me, and I rapidly learned a great deal from all of them, including the brewery foreman. Paddy Lyttleton was also very friendly, but his somewhat robust sense of humour was demonstrated when he invited me to take a deep smell of the hop aroma through the manhole cover of a conditioning tank that had just been emptied. It was of course full of carbon dioxide, a deep breath of which had the effect of me being hit on the back of my head with a hammer. However, Paddy left his employment after I had been at Dares for only a couple of months. For reasons of economy, the Dares directors decided not to replace him, but that as an 'improver' I should take his place. This change inevitably meant that I had to spend more time with Mr Glew.

A feature of the staff and workers that impressed me most was that they had nearly all served in the armed forces throughout the First or Second World Wars, with a few exceptions of which Mr Glew was one. A feature of Mr Glew, which I discovered fairly rapidly, was that he seemed unable to answer clearly many of my basic questions about the brewing process. He would refer me to 'look it up' in a brewing textbook that languished in the office. I discovered subsequently that his previous employment at a brewery in Burton-on-Trent was as a 'Mashing Clerk'. This was basically the equivalent of a Mash Tun Room Foreman, who would have only limited knowledge of the rest of the brewing process. Eventually, I became completely disillusioned by Mr Glew's lack of knowledge and usefulness, and this no doubt contributed to my Uncle Rex arranging for me to 'move on'. In the meantime, Mr Glew arranged to go on his summer holidays. Since there was no one else available, the directors decided that I could fulfil the role of 'Deputy Brewer' in Mr Glew's absence. I would be able to report to Mr Aubrey Dare, who had returned recently from Australia. Aubrey Dare was another 'larger than life' character. Unlike the traditional gentlemanly brewery director, his conversations were peppered with expletives, the most common of which referred to the 'bastard' this and that and were delivered in a pronounced Australian accent. In actual fact when Mr Glew went on holiday, so did all of the other Dare brother directors. I was then left bizarrely in sole charge, at the age of sixteen, of a six hundred barrel a week brewery during the peak summer output.

One of the behavioural features of almost all workmen and foremen in the brewery was their apparent insincerity towards senior staff. They would politely and even enthusiastically agree during discussions with any of their seniors but immediately afterwards would contradict and often contemptuously abuse them with their peers. At the time, I considered this to be dishonest and perhaps a characteristic of 'Midlanders'. However, after entering the army some years later, I realised that this was common practice between all ranks and their superiors. The other conversational comments that were used repeatedly were endless joking references to 'piles', 'crabs', and 'the clap'. I realised many years later that these references were used only by World War I veterans and related directly to the appalling hygiene conditions in the trenches. These conditions, which had affected over a million men, were only revealed graphically in full when they were broadcast on television to the general public one hundred years after the end of the First World War.

I particularly enjoyed visiting the coopers' shop. The cooper always wore a heavy leather apron with a large hole in its middle. I subsequently discovered the purpose of this was to avoid removing his apron when relieving himself. However, somewhat surprisingly, he allowed me to use the cooperage tools and also made for me a small oak one-gallon cask to fill with Dares Bitter and take home as a present to my father.

I was especially interested in the bottling process, and I also used to visit the bottling stores as frequently as possible. There, along with other things, I was allowed to use the foot-operated bottle-crowning machine. This activity involved picking up each full bottle with the left hand, placing it vertically and firmly on the filling piston, pressing the foot pedal, waiting for the bottle to be crowned, and then placing it on the moving discharge bottle conveyor. This required skill and coordination, which I learned slowly. Failure meant that bottles instead of being crowned were shattered, the contents wasted, and the possibility of the operator being cut. Health and safety legislation was a long way off into the future. Whilst all of the beer for bottling came through pipes from the brewery, Bass,

Worthington and Guinness were delivered by lorry from its brewers. Bass and Worthington came in fifty-four-gallon hogsheads, and Guinness came in hundred and eight gallon Butts. All of these had to be manhandled up on to wooden stages in the stores in order to be matured before bottling. It involved a level of sheer brute force and physical effort that fortunately, I was too young to be asked to practise. Up until the 1960s, the palates of Bass, Worthington and Guinness were completely different from their final modern filtered and carbonated equivalents. They were 'naturally conditioned' in their oak casks and the flavours were much stronger and distinctive from all other beers and stouts. In consequence, they were an acquired taste enjoyed by something of a select minority of drinkers. I rapidly joined this group of connoisseurs and now regard the present-day products as a pale shadow of their former superiority and exclusivity.

The morning mash at the brewery occurred before the local tram service began; therefore, I needed to have my bicycle sent from London by my parents. The cycle was a 'utility' model, which was the only specification that was allowed immediately after the Second World War. During the war, new cycles had been virtually unobtainable. Like all utility model, the 'sit up and beg' frame, handlebars, and wheels were all painted matt black. Despite this, the cycle was my pride and joy, because I had to wait until the end of the war to obtain it. Since I now had to traverse a steep hill to Moseley every day, what I wanted most of all was a Sturmey-Archer three-speed gear. Teddy Rich, the brewery engineer, offered to help me to fit a gear, and I duly bought one. Teddy was a wonderful tutor and friend. He had been in the Royal Engineers during the First World War and unfortunately had been gassed. Apparently, he had been out in No-man's Land repairing a telephone line, and although he had been wearing a regulation gas mask, he had torn it slightly whilst crawling through the barbed wire. As a result, it failed to protect him. Teddy showed me how to strip down, build new wheels, replace the handlebars and brakes, and virtually to create the equivalence of a brand-new cycle with chromium-plated fittings. The knowledge and skill that I gained proved invaluable to me for the rest of my life, for which I am eternally grateful. Similarly, Teddy taught me as much about plumbing as I ever needed to know. The great advantage of living in Birmingham at that time was that it was known, quite rightly, as the 'City of a Thousand Trades'.

After my move to Birmingham, I joined the local Royal Warwickshire Army Cadet Corps. After leaving school, I had continued in the Cadet Force and had risen to the dizzy heights of lance corporal. I wore two stripes on each arm surmounted by a flaming grenade, as was the custom in the Grenadier Guards. I also wore a stiff 'Cheese-cutter' hat instead of the conventional cloth beret. When I applied to join the local Royal Warwickshire Cadets in Birmingham my previous training and experience must have impressed the local commanding officer. In a remarkably short time, I was promoted first to sergeant, and then uniquely, and unprecedentedly, to the warrant officer rank of company sergeant major. I immediately went out and bought a three-foot long cane with a chromium-plated knob, which was decorated with the Royal Warwickshire regimental symbol at its head and a chromium-plated base tip. I was entirely familiar with the necessary 'stick drill' that was displayed by all Brigade of Guards senior NCO's and warrant officers. Few other cadets, adult regular soldiers or ex-servicemen would have been likely to possess this knowledge. The rank of company sergeant major was normally awarded exclusively to adults who had served previously in the army, and as far as I was aware, this had never been awarded to a juvenile cadet. I loved every minute of it.

On one of my drill nights, my Uncle Rex invited me to come out to his home in Streetly for dinner. I arrived there on my refurbished Coventry Eagle cycle, after the nine-mile uphill journey from Birmingham. Fortunately, it was summertime and not raining. My uncle's guest there was Bert Cox, who was head brewer of Mitchells and Butlers, the biggest brewery in Birmingham. Mitchells and Butlers were the largest customers of my uncle, and he and Bert Cox were close friends socially. I suppose the visit must have had some bearing on the fact that shortly afterwards my uncle announced that I had been offered a pupillage at Mitchells and Butlers brewery at Cape Hill in Birmingham. This would include the opportunity to attend Birmingham Brewing School, which was part of Birmingham University at Edgbaston.

Cape Hill

After eighteen months at Dares Brewery, I entered my pupillage at Mitchells and Butlers Cape Hill brewery. In contrast to Dares, it consisted of two main breweries with a total maximum output of twenty thousand barrels per week. Number Two Brewery only brewed draught mild ale. This was produced only in quantities of a thousand barrels per brew and to a maximum of nine thousand barrels per week. The breweries at Cape Hill had a joint capacity that was thirty times larger than the maximum output at Dares. When I arrived at Cape Hill, I was taken from the reception in the administrative offices into the brewing offices in Number One Brewery by a junior clerk. These six offices were entered from an outside iron staircase to the first floor and then inside the building to a second floor. Along a long corridor, these brewers' offices were located on the left, and on its right by windows that offered a dreary panoramic view of the Cask Wash House roof. Whilst waiting at the end of the corridor to meet the head brewer I saw two white-coated middle-aged brewers further along the corridor outside the office of the third brewer. I then heard one of them ask the other in a noticeable Black Country accent, "Who is that young bugger, waiting to see Bert Cox?" After a short wait, I was invited into the office of the head brewer by his secretary, a middle-aged man in a brown double-breasted suit. I discovered subsequently that no female employees worked in the offices along the Brewing Corridor or in the brewery. All office staff worked in a large building on the opposite side of the brewery yard. Clerical staff in the main office sat on tall stools at high Dickensian sloping desks, usually with a pint glass of draught mild ale perched precariously on top. Clerical workers, along with all other brewery employees received a daily beer allowance of two pints of draught mild ale.

    Bert Cox was a genial man in his early sixties. As head brewer, he always wore a double-breasted business suit – and never a white coat. He welcomed me warmly and explained the terms of my proposed pupillage. After my initial employment as a pupil, I was to be offered a six-year contract, during which I would attend Birmingham University Brewing School for the first three years at a modest salary. I would then work for three years as a shift brewer at a full salary. Promotion at Cape Hill was entirely on service and seniority. He explained that there were twenty brewers and that I had extremely fortunate prospects. He then went on with a somewhat remarkable revelation. He had been a shift brewer for twenty years before reaching the higher echelons of daytime brewer. He had hated every minute of shift brewing, until he eventually became a day brewer, and finally head brewer. In contrast, I would therefore be uniquely lucky. He explained that the next senior brewer to me was a whole ten years older than I was. Therefore, I would only have to do ten years before I came off shift work. After only ten years as a day brewer, I would eventually become head brewer for at least a further ten years. For the next six months, before my two years conscription into the army, I was to be paid a wage of twenty-five shillings per week. Until I joined the army, I would be allocated as a pupil to Number Two Brewery but only on daytime shifts and not on nights.

Beer consumption in Birmingham and the Midlands consisted overwhelmingly of draught Mild Ale. Many of Mitchells and Butlers' hundreds of pubs did not even sell draught Bitter Beer, and Number One Brewery produced only a few hundred barrels per week. In contrast, Number Two Brewery had a maximum capacity of nine thousand barrels per week, which consisted entirely of draught mild ale. This output was produced in one thousand barrel quantities, or 'lengths' as they were known, every twelve hours. The brewery was modern, immaculate, and clearly a showcase. However, it was a leisurely environment in which to work. The day-shift cycle began with a Monday afternoon of only three hours, before teatime in the Brewers' Mess at Number One Brewery and then home. This also occurred on Wednesdays. Two Shift Brewers worked there permanently, along with a third brewer from Number One Brewery. The Number One Brewery brewer was one of five whose shift cycles included three weeks at Number Two Brewery every sixteen weeks. This working pattern was the most complex one I ever encountered. However, it had the unique benefit of involving an average working week throughout the whole cycle of only thirty-seven hours. It also included every four weeks a 'long weekend' from Thursday lunch to Tuesday afternoon. As a pupil, I attended only from 'nine to five' on five days per week, and never worked on nights. Nevertheless, I was still able to meet all of the seven shift brewers during my stay as a pupil.

The two permanent shift brewers at Number Two Brewery were Walter Harper and Joe Hacket. They were both middle-aged and charming. Neither of them had previously been brewers, but had been recruited during the Second World War temporarily to replace younger brewers who had been conscripted into the armed forces. They treated me in a most kindly and almost a 'fatherly' fashion. Joe Hacket had been in the army during the First World War. He always arrived at Number Two Brewery in a business suit, with a fawn raincoat folded neatly over his left arm. He would raise his brown Holmberg hat politely, followed by the classic words, "Good day, gentlemen – dry underfoot today." This was clearly a routine reference to life in the trenches. Walter Harper was an ex-brewing chemist, gardener and an enthusiastic opera lover. The concepts of Hi-Fi and FM radio had just begun, and Walter initiated in me a lifelong interest in all of these. Later, when I returned from my national service, I met Charlie Smith, a Mash Tun Foremen at Number One Brewery. He was an electrical enthusiast and helped me to build my own 'state of the art' amplifier, FM Tuner, tape recorder, record player, and very large twelve-inch loudspeaker enclosure.

Number Two Brewery was probably one of the largest single brewing plants in the country, having been built as a then 'state of the art' modern plant in the 1920s. It consisted of two very large red-bricked tower blocks, connected by a 'bridge' corridor at third floor level. One block contained the brewing plant and solitary brewers' office, whilst the other block contained the collecting and fermenting vessels. The output of any single production cycle of one thousand barrels at Number Two Brewery was twice the size of the maximum weekly output at Dares Brewery. During the two years of experience encountered in my three pupillages, I had therefore managed to span the full scale and extremes of the brewing trade. However, unlike my previous experience at Dares of wandering freely around all departments, I was confined to the Brewhouse of Number Two Brewery for the rest of my pupillage. On the Cape Hill site, there was of course a bottling plant, boiler house, engineering workshop, transport department, cooperage, also two maltings, a wine and spirit warehouse, a railway with two locomotives, and even a fire station. Despite the valuable opportunities that experience in these departments would have offered me, I was never invited or allowed even to visit any of them. Most surprisingly, I was most definitely prohibited from visiting Number One Brewery, in which in addition to draught mild ale all of the many other beers, ales, and stouts were brewed. The plant had a maximum weekly output of eleven thousand barrels, which was more than that of Number Two Brewery. Brews were of a bewildering range of complexity and quantity. I subsequently discovered, when I finally worked in Number One Brewery as a shift brewer, that it was incredibly labyrinthine and ramshackle. It had been extended piecemeal over the years from the original small brewery, little larger than Dares Brewery. However, as I eventually learned, it was probably one of the most complex and intensively worked breweries in the country, and the ultimate challenging experience for any shift brewer. In contrast, life at Number Two Brewery was a very leisurely occupation, with its one-thousand-barrel mash either at nine o'clock in the morning or evening. This routine was interspersed by breakfast, lunch, or tea in the 'Brewers' Mess'.

The exclusive Brewers' Mess was a square oak-panelled room located below the Brewers' Offices in Number One Brewery. It contained a large square dining table surrounded by twelve oak Windsor-backed armchairs. It had a single high window overlooking the Number One Brewery roofs and a large electric clock over the door. It had an adjoining small kitchen from which meals were served by a permanently employed lady cook. There was a rigid hierarchal order with which chairs were occupied. The side with its back to the door, and most importantly, under the clock, was only ever occupied by the Number One Brewery shift brewer on duty. The right-hand side was occupied by the Number Two Brewery shift brewer. The side under the window and facing the door was for the second brewer and two bottling brewers, whilst the two maltster brewers occupied the left side. As a pupil, I was allowed to sit next to the Number Two Brewery shift brewer; although for no reason I ever discovered Joe Hackett never used the mess.

In anticipation of my conscription for national service, I decided that I needed to have dental treatment. I had heard dark tales about the primitive resources and practices of army dentists. I had small points of decay on two of my back teeth, and it was very difficult to obtain a dental appointment. John Knox the fourth brewer put me in touch with a local dentist who he knew. At the time, dentists who had been practising for over thirty years were not required to have Dental School qualifications but were allowed to practise if they had served an apprenticeship. I obtained an appointment, and the dentist confirmed that two of my back teeth had caries, popularly known as 'decay'. To my utter astonishment, he said that he would remove them rather than drill and fill them. Sitting in a dental chair with the dentist hovering over me, I felt somewhat threatened and failed to disagree. He removed my two teeth effortlessly – and completely unnecessarily. The two teeth were the only ones I ever lost during the rest of my life. I never forgave the dental charlatan or John Knox.

Before I left Cape Hill to join the army, I was summoned to see the head brewer, Bert Cox, in his office. He greeted me in a friendly manner and revealed that he had been in the army throughout the First World War. He said that he was pleased with my progress and that everyone was satisfied by my performance. He commented that he knew that my pupillage salary had not been sufficient to cover my cost of living. He then wrote out a note, rang for his male secretary, and asked him to go 'over the road' with it to the accounts department and collect some 'personal business expenses'. When his secretary returned, and after he withdrew, Bert Cox put fifty-pound notes in my left hand, shook my right hand, and wished me goodbye and 'good luck for my next two years in the army.'

Social Birmingham

I had first lived permanently in Birmingham at the age of sixteen and found Birmingham residents, popularly known as 'Brummies', very different from those I knew in Middlesex, Yorkshire, or Sussex. Above all else, there appeared to be no obvious 'class' or status distinction, either in behaviour, dress, or most notably in regional accent. People could have broad 'Brumigham' or 'Brummie' accents and range in occupation from labourers to millionaires. Middle class citizens often tended to try and modify and soften their accents, but they were almost always readily identifiable as 'Brummies' or Midlanders. However, in the outer suburbs such as parts of Edgbaston, Harborne, Sutton Coldfield, and Streetly, there were clearly significant numbers of prosperous middle and upper class citizens. One of the major industries was car manufacture. One of the subtle measures of social status was what car a person was 'running'. It was almost always the first topic of conversation when people met and were introduced for the first time. It immediately identified their probable financial and social status. Another subtle indication of status was the practice of 'dining out'. Food was still partly rationed at that time and people tended not to invite friends or guests to dinner at their homes. Instead, the more affluent citizens would 'dine out' on a Saturday evening at one of the restaurants usually fairly local but occasionally some distance away. The cuisine and price of the meal would subsequently be a topic of conversation, which once again subtly indicated the wealth and status of the diners. The Midland economy clearly was booming, and the most notable feature was a complete absence of unemployment. In fact, there was a significant, if not serious, labour shortage. Within a few years, major industrial employers and Birmingham Corporation would actively advertise in the West Indies and Caribbean to pay for the passage of immigrants and wages in advance to come to live and work in the Midlands. The most famous of these was those who arrived on the ex-troop ship the Empire Windrush.

My own introduction to Midland society was when I first lived temporarily with my aunt and uncle in Streetly. The village was devoid of and remote from any form of social entertainment. Television had not reached the Midlands, and there was almost nothing in which I could occupy my leisure time. Following my uncle's helpful suggestion, I visited the local youth club one evening. It was a salutary experience. I spent a couple of hours sitting on a chair in the local church hall watching thirty or forty young people socialising and dancing with one another. At no time was there any attempt to involve me in their activities, in which in any case I would have had no ability to participate. After returning home, I reported my experience to my uncle. He rather jocularly gave me what subsequently proved to be an invaluable piece of advice. At the time, I thought it was rather patronising and unsympathetic. He said that when I moved to live in Birmingham, I should attend ballroom dancing classes.

Apart from cinemas and theatres, there were a number of large ballroom dance halls in Birmingham. The largest of these was the West End Ballroom in the centre of the city and the equally large Tower Ballroom beside Harborne reservoir. The West End held dances on Wednesdays and Saturdays, and the Tower on Saturdays only. I also discovered that there was a dance 'school' at the south edge of the city, which held classes on a Sunday evening. As soon as I moved into lodgings in the south of Birmingham, I began to attend the school. It was located on the third floor of a rather unprepossessing Victorian block of commercial buildings. It occupied a modestly sized room with a ballroom floor and a gramophone. On my first visit, I feared a repetition of my previous experience in Streetly. However, after sitting as an onlooker for half-an-hour, a brief teaching session began. All of the 'pupils' were required to stand on the dance floor, either with a partner or a dance instructor. My instructor was a middle-aged lady in a 'party' dress, and she took me by the hand and showed me how to hold her in the correct pose. The chief instructor then demonstrated the basic sequence of steps for the dance concerned and required the pairs of dancers to repeat them. Finally, he turned on the record player to the currently universal classic 'strict tempo ballroom dancing' music of Victor Sylvester and his band. The dancers then performed the steps that had been demonstrated. My teacher was splendidly patient, and I suppose rather motherly, in response to my young age. I was faintly amused and rather surprised that she had a slight limp. As a result, the inside of one heel of her dance shoes had worn away, presumably because she couldn't avoid her heels scraping together. However, she was a very good and patient teacher, and I rapidly learned the steps that had been demonstrated and was very grateful for her help. Somewhat surprisingly, after a few weeks, I became quite competent at all of the three main ballroom dances. These were the waltz, quickstep, and slow foxtrot. I continued to attend the weekly classes for some months. Once I had become confident, I began to attend the public dance halls once or twice a week.

Almost all public dance halls at that time allowed only classical ballroom dancing. Other forms such as jazz, 'jiving', and 'rock and roll' were strictly prohibited. The universal convention was that dance tunes were played in threes, followed by a brief interval after which partners were normally changed. The three dances were invariably three waltzes, quick steps, or slow foxtrots. Very occasionally, three tangos would be played. The standard procedure was that all of the patrons occupied the spaces beside and around the dance floor, whilst the band occupied a stage on one side of the floor. The unique benefit for male dancers was that they could view all of the female partners in the hall and select their potential partner in advance. By manoeuvring into a strategic position near to their intended partner, they could ensure that they would be the first to ask for the next dance. In contrast, female dancers had no such opportunity, except on the very rare occasions of an 'Invitation Waltz'. Then, for one dance, only females were allowed to invite any male dancer of their choice to dance with them. If the female dancer's invitation was accepted by the potential partner, they would then go on to the floor for the next three pieces of dance music. At the end of any three tunes and dances, a fairly comprehensive assessment could be made of one another by the partners. During each pause between the tunes, the partners might or might not continue to hold one another around the waist. If they did, it was a clear signal that they were enjoying one another's company. If they did not, it was almost certain that they would not dance together again.

One of the unusual features of Birmingham was that alcohol-licensing regulations determined by the 'Watch Committee' prohibited public sale of alcohol after ten o'clock at night. In contrast, there was a remarkably efficient public transport system. Normal bus services finished at around eleven o'clock. This was the time by which most dances finished. Very few, if any, young dancers owned cars and were entirely dependent on public transport. At midnight, a remarkably comprehensive all-night Corporation Bus Service to all points on the city boundary began from the city centre. This continued 'on the hour' and returned on the half-hour throughout the night. The result for male dancers was that they could ask any girl of their choice whether they could 'see them home'; confident that wherever the girl lived, the male partner could subsequently get to his home without difficulty.

After a few months, I had apparently become a very competent dancer. Consequently, I had absolutely no difficulty in selecting any partner of my choice. Finally, just before I was due to be called up for my national service, I met a particularly attractive and personable young girl who was the same age as me. To my complete surprise, she asked me if I would become her permanent partner and enter competition dancing with her. Competition dancing was the ultimate level of ballroom dancing and involved dedicated commitment and significant costs of teaching lessons and formal costumes. She would have made a wonderful Birmingham girlfriend and housewife. However, with my national service beckoning within a few weeks, I very reluctantly and sadly declined.

National Service

Unlike almost every other eighteen-year-old at the time, I was looking forward and could hardly wait to be conscripted for my national service in the army. Because of my cadet training in the HAC, where we were trained by the Grenadier Guards, I pondered the possibilities of applying to join the Guards' Brigade. However, it was only in the Welsh Guards that I would just be able to scrape in, just above their minimum height restriction of five-foot eight-inches. I also considered applying for the Royal Horse Artillery. However, both they and the Guards were stationed permanently in London, and I really wanted to get the opportunity to be sent abroad. I therefore joined the Royal Artillery and was sent to be trained in field artillery at Oswestry in Shropshire. There were four regiments at Park Hall Camp in Oswestry; two were simply reception units in which recruits stayed for two weeks. There they were issued with uniforms and kit, examined medically, assessed mentally, inoculated against various diseases, and taught how to stand to attention, and turn right and left. Most importantly, they were issued with two pay books, cryptically referred to as 'AB64' parts one and two. The 'Part One' was essentially an identity record of the name, to be carried at all times, and concerned details of number, and rank of the soldier concerned. It also recorded personal details such as any physical distinguishing marks or features and religious denomination. Fortunately, I was aware of the implications of the religious reference. Sundays in the army were normally days of rest. However, on Sunday mornings, troops instead of enjoying a leisurely breakfast and relaxation were required to attend church parades at which they were then either marched to the church of their religion or given services in the camp. I knew of these requirements, but also that if I registered as 'Non-conformist', I would be excused all such parades. Needless to say, I registered as 'Non-conformist'. This was possibly also the most accurate personal description that could have been applied to me. In the intelligence tests, I was graded as and 'SG1', apparently which categorised me as being in the top five percent of soldiers. As a result of this, I would automatically be required, to attend the War Office Selection Board Centre to establish whether I was eligible to be trained to become a commissioned officer. As I had attended a public school and had the highest possible Army Cadet Corps qualifications, I felt confident that I would succeed.

After two weeks in their reception unit, recruits were 'posted' to one of the two training units, the 17th and 64th regiments. These were in the same camp and were where they would spend a further six weeks. I was somewhat relieved to be posted to the 64th. The 17th Regiment had a fearsome reputation for strict discipline and very hard work, compared with the 64th. One of the two batteries within the 17th Regiment was '24 – 'Irish Battery', who wore green cloth tabs on the shoulder epaulettes. This was the most dreaded group of all and unequalled until I was posted subsequently to '55 – 'Asten' Battery in Tonfanau. However, after two weeks in the 64th, I, along with the other 'SG1s', travelled to Barton Stacey, a camp in Wiltshire where, along with about twenty or thirty other recruits, I was tested for four days. We received many tests and were required to take part in various group exercises. To my astonishment and utter despair, I failed to be selected. It was one of the biggest disappointments of my career and indeed my life. I then returned very dejectedly to Oswestry.

Battledress uniforms and equipment were the basic dress of all soldiers at that time, and most surprisingly, an enormous amount of effort was deployed on fitting and tailoring them. Each unit had their own 'Regimental Tailor', all of who were civilians. The initial baggy tunics or 'blouses' were carefully shaped to a slimmer and more flattering shape. The length and precise waist size of trousers were altered similarly. These extensive alterations were repeated subsequently for 'Second' and even 'Third' 'Fittings'. In contrast, the dark blue berets were the responsibility of the recruits, who were required to shrink them by soaking them in hot or cold water. Boots, belts, gaiters, and other equipment were entirely the responsibility of the recruits. In this, I was at a very considerable advantage. Because of my Army Cadet Service with the HAC and Grenadier Guards, I had in-depth experience of these dark arts. In particular, I knew how to polish army boots and the brass components of webbing equipment. Army boots were heavy ankle boots, of which the leather was known as 'Zug' leather. This presented a very hard and durable waterproof surface to the boot. Unfortunately, the surface of this hard leather was heavily dimpled, and this was an anathema to the tradition of 'spit and polish', which at that time was almost universal throughout the army. In order to transform the toecaps to a smooth surface, this required skilful conversion of some hours of hard painstaking work. The conversion method was first to flatten the dimples of the toecap by using a hot iron. The cap was then pressed laboriously and repeatedly with the back of a toothbrush. When the surface eventually became smooth, the boot was ready for polishing. This was achieved with a cloth, which was dipped into 'Kiwi' black shoe polish and then pressed hard, spat on, and rotated in 'little circles' with the forefinger on to the then smooth surface of the toecap. During the dipping and rubbing process, it was necessary to spit repeatedly on to the surface of the toecap. In order to achieve the standard of shine required, the process would take many, many hours for each toecap. This traditional 'spit and polish' procedure was of course a wonderful way in which the off-duty time of recruits and other soldiers could be occupied. I, uniquely, but perhaps unsurprisingly, had brought into the army my already highly polished Army Cadet boots and also a tailored greatcoat. I used these of course on all important inspection parades.

The use of 'Blanco' and the polishing of the brass fittings of khaki 'webbing' equipment were also a vital skilled and time-consuming art. The 'Khaki Yellow No. 3 Blanco' was a round block of hard paste, which when wet could be spread with a brush on to the webbing equipment. Despite its title, the Blanco dried to a flat light green khaki colour. It was applied daily, by using a wet brush, sponge, or piece of rag. Cap badges and the brass buckles and sliding parts of 'webbing' equipment were also required to be cleaned daily. These were always cleaned only in 'Bluebell' polish, a rather finer consistency than the more popular 'Brasso'. Brass items were initially cleaned with small torn-off strips of, usually coarse, cardboard on to which a small quantity of Bluebell was poured. This was then rubbed continuously until the blackened residue was finally dried up and exhausted. Subsequently, the items were cleaned in the same manner but using a soft yellow cloth. Battledress uniforms had to be ironed each night with an electric iron, which was shared by the occupants of each barrack room. These activities occupied recruits for many hours in the evenings and more briefly once soldiers became more experienced in the skills. All of the materials and cleaning equipment had to be bought by the recruits.

After two weeks in the 64th, I contracted severe influenza and was sent to Chester Military Hospital. The regime there seemed to be based on what must have been fashionable during the two world wars. All inmates had to wear loose-fitting bright blue trousers and jackets. These were made from a very coarse, though fairly soft, woollen blanket material. The cotton shirt was white with a badly fitting collar, around which was worn with a bright red woollen knitted tie. Grey tennis shoes were worn on the feet. This red, white, and blue ensemble may have been intentionally patriotic, but it was the extreme opposite of the obsessively 'smart' uniform dress in the rest of the army. The reception of patients consisted in showing them to their beds in wards of some twenty or thirty soldiers. The first treatment was somewhat surprising. After recording the inmate's details, they were first supplied with a bottle of Guinness. Shortly afterwards, the male nurse returned to administer a large dose of liquid paraffin, a rather unpleasant concoction that was a very powerful laxative. I was fortunate not to have to suffer the more common treatment of having an enema. This procedure consisted of inserting a large brass funnel into the patient's rectum and pouring in a quantity of what appeared to be soapy liquid. A few minutes later, a rather rapid visit to the latrines became necessary. The meals were very little different from the rest of the army, but dinners were usually accompanied by a bottle of Guinness. After a few days, I was returned to my unit at Oswestry, where apparently there had been fear of a serious influenza epidemic.

The daily routine of training at Oswestry consisted of standard infantry marching and rifle drill with which I was totally familiar. It also involved periodic guard duties and 'fatigues' every few days. The guard duties were usually from six o'clock at night to six the next morning. The real problem with guard duty was that it required time-consuming preparation beforehand and then rarely used to allow for more than three or four hours' sleep during the night. The guard duty involved parading with rifles, and in best uniform, and being closely inspected by the 'Orderly Officer', a junior commissioned officer allocated for the day to carry out general duties. The 'Guard Commander' was a sergeant in charge of the guard. During the inspection, the orderly officer selected what he considered to be the most smartly turned out member of the guard. This gunner was nominated as 'stick man' and was relieved of all of the two-hour outside guard duties. After marching to the Guard Room, each gunner was allocated to a 'stag', as it was popularly known, which consisted usually of two men. The 'stag' were then marched to the locations at which they would stay for the next two hours until relieved by the next 'stag', and then marched back to the Guard Room. In winter, standing outside in the cold during the night for two hours was not a pleasant experience. Usually, each guard had two stags during the next twelve hours. The next morning, the night-time guard was relieved by the daytime guard or military police. Members of the guard then continued with their normal daily routine. All gunners and NCO's carried out guard duties once every two or three weeks.

All SG1's were also given training as technical assistants popularly known as 'Tech Acks'. This involved the role of calculating the location of targets and the necessary deployment of the guns. Barrack square training was on 'Twenty-five pounder' field guns. These required a six-man crew. The NCO, almost always a sergeant, who was in charge was 'Number one' and stood behind the gun. He gave all orders, and by means of a large steel 'handspike' locked into the rear 'trail' of the gun, he directed it by lifting the whole gun and pivoting it to the correct direction on the circular firing platform, on which the gun was attached and deployed. He also gave all orders. The 'Number three' who was, the aimer, sat on a small round wooden seat beside the barrel and controlled the elevation of the gun and any necessary slight adjustments to its direction. When given the appropriate order, he fired the gun. The role of the number two was to open and close the breech. Shells were loaded by the numbers four and five, who first placed the shells on to the loading tray which had been dropped open behind the breech. The number two then rammed the shell home into the barrel with his wooden metal-tipped rammer. This was followed by the brass cartridge case containing the propellant. The number two then smartly closed the breech. The order to fire was then given by the number one and firing lever was then pressed by the number three. After the shell had been fired, the gun recoiled, and the number two smartly caught the breech lever handle as it passed him, thereby allowing the recoil of the gun to open the breech and automatically ejecting the empty brass cartridge case. This whole procedure could then be repeated four or five times per minute. When the gun was being fired, the number two always knelt close to the breech, on one knee, with the ramrod held smartly horizontal under one arm. Numbers one, four and five stood to attention one side or to the rear of the gun. The whole cycle of the procedure was carried out with parade-ground precision. I was trained as a number two, which I regarded as the most skilled and 'glamorous' of the roles and enjoyed myself thoroughly.

The gun was towed by a small lightly armoured four-wheel 'Quad' vehicle, which had sufficient room inside for the gun crew and driver. A hole in the roof allowed the number two, whilst the vehicle was travelling, to stand up and observe and give road signals to following vehicles and guns. On our return a few weeks later from the firing camp at Trawsfynnyth, I was required to stand up all the way. Along the beautiful green mountain valleys between Dolgelly and Llangollen, I was provided with a moving panorama of wonderful scenery. As a direct result, I fell deeply in love for the rest of my life with Mid Wales, North Wales and the Cambrian Coast.

After six weeks and having failed my War Office Selection Board Officer Selection Test, I was posted to the 59th Light Anti-Aircraft battery of the 55th Training Regiment, commonly known as 'Five-Five'. The regiment was located desolately at Tonfanau on the remote shores of Cardigan Bay and was regarded as a 'Borstal' type camp and dreaded by most trainees. Shortly before I was posted there, two recruits had committed suicide. There tended to be a hierarchy of artillery regiments. Seventeen pounder Anti-tank, Twenty-five pounder Field, and 40mm Bofors Light Anti-aircraft regiments tended to be regarded as top of the 'active service' list. In contrast, Medium 5.5 inch, 7 inch Heavy, and 3.7 inch Heavy Anti-aircraft regiments tended to be regarded as pedestrian, 'safer' and have older gunners in their ranks. At Tonfanau, there was also a 27th Heavy Anti-aircraft and Radar training regiment, and this was definitely looked down on by soldiers in the 'Five-Nine'. The battery into which I was posted also carried the battle honour of 'Asten Battery', which it had apparently gained during the battle of the Ardennes during the Second World War.

I, along with three other 'Failed War Office Selection Board' gunners, was sent from Oswestry to become light anti-aircraft gunnery instructors. These other three national servicemen were all from the 17th Training Regiment at Oswestry. One of these, Peter Rich, was a slight, dark Cornishman and became my closest friend for many years to come. I later became the 'best man' at his wedding. All four of us had been categorised as 'Failed, Watch'. This allowed us to reapply and to present ourselves to the Officer Training Board after six months' further service.

When we arrived on the single wooden platform of Tonfanau railway station, we were accompanied by a couple of dozen new recruits. We were met by a sergeant, who ordered us loudly to form up in three ranks. The camp was on the opposite side of the railway line, and we were marched, carrying our kit bags into one of the wooden huts of the camp. The hut was already occupied by a dozen or more newly enlisted raw recruits, who apparently were about to start their basic training. Both I and the other three arrivals were dismayed, if not appalled, at the prospect of repeating our recently completed basic six-week training. To our enormous relief, the sergeant returned shortly to tell us that he had not realised that we were on an NCO's training course. He then took us to another hut.

In the other hut, we met two new fellow gunners, who apparently were to be on the same course. They were both in their mid-thirties, and we also soon became great comrades and friends. They were both so-called 're-enlistment' recruits who had served previously in the armed forces. Ron Jeffery and 'Jigger' Lees had both been regular soldiers for three years before the Second World War. Ron had been in India, and Jigger had been in Aden. We were, in the coming weeks, entertained by their accounts of life in the regular army of the 1930s. Jigger was tall with fair 'frizzy' hair and very amiable. In future weeks, he would often laughingly call us 'silly little Lance-Bombardiers'. He had spent three years of his service in Aden. He said that if he ever got posted to Aden again, he would desert. In contrast, Ron was dark, shorter and of slightly heavier build and had a somewhat ironic sense of humour. Like all ranks in pre-war India, he had a 'batman'. Ron once told us the disgraceful story of hitting his batman with a piece of bacon, because it had not been cooked sufficiently. He had then callously told the batman to see his 'Holy man' to get cleansed. In the twenty-first century, such a story would not only be offensive and unrepeatable but regarded as almost criminal. Finally, they told us the 'Old Soldiers'' aphorism, ' – I 'ates all wogs; and wogs starts at Calais'. Little could I imagine that more than sixty years later this would become the inspiration and major philosophy behind Brexit.

Our training was for us to become Junior NCO gunnery instructors with the rank of lance-bombardier. For this, we were provided with a short bamboo cane, often known as a 'swagger stick', which was always held horizontally under the pit of our arm. We also had to be trained 'stick drill' in order to incorporate this into our foot-drill, in which we thrust our stick horizontally under our left arm when standing or saluting and in our right hand when marching. It was an unusual skill, usually associated with commissioned officers and almost never with junior NCO's. Our gunnery training was for the 40mm Bofors Light Anti-Aircraft gun, each of which had a crew of seven men.

Our gunnery instruction was carried out by an 'Assistant Instructor of Gunnery' from the School of Artillery. Nobody, of any rank, ever argued with an 'Ack-IG'. This one was a regimental sergeant major, who uniquely wore officers' uniform. He was surprisingly restrained and polite, unlike the usual stereotype of a non-commissioned warrant officer. During classroom breaks, he would elegantly extract a cigarette from a silver case and light it with his silver lighter.

We also had to become drill instructors. I, of course, was in my element following my cadet sergeant-major experience. We were all promoted to lance-bombardiers and a few months later were promoted to full bombardiers with two stripes. The 'holding' of two 'stripes' by national servicemen was extremely rare in all other regiments. National service gunners were never promoted to sergeant. Peter Rich and I became the only two men in the regiment to qualify to be rifle marksmen. For this achievement, we received an additional pay of 'one and sixpence' a week for the rest of our army careers. We also shot for the regiment at an annual divisional competition at Altcar, which was north of Liverpool, and each of us won a 'Young Soldiers' cup as a prize.

The battery sergeant major was in his early thirties. He uniquely carried 'wings' on the breast of his blouse-tunic, having been in the Parachute Regiment during the Second World War. He was commonly known as 'Busty' Gadsden. He was in fact not overweight but had a very well-built physique. He always carried a two-foot wooden cane with a chromium-plated metal head and tip. It appeared to me to be homemade and did not compare with the three-foot Malacca one that I had carried in the cadet force. However, 'Busty' was extremely good-natured, and quite popular, and was very understanding and tolerant towards his national service NCOs. His parade-ground drill was excellent, unlike most sergeants, sergeant majors and other warrant officers that I encountered in the Royal Artillery. I liked and admired him greatly.

A number of the sergeants appeared to have had very limited educations. As a result, they were required to attend weekly education classes in the camp 'Education Centre'. In these classes, they were apparently taught the basic skills of reading, writing, and arithmetic. The centre was run by a sergeant and private who were in the Education Corps. These sergeants, uniquely, were often national service men who had gained university degrees. Their 'clients' at Tonfanau were mainly from the Heavy Ack-Ack regiment, and one of whom was rather unkindly known as the 'screaming skull'. He had obviously served for some time previously in very hot climates or theatres of war. His face was extremely gaunt and very, very deeply lined and tanned. His orders and commands were extremely shrill, and his 'scream' could be heard above those of most other sergeants. He was probably only in his late thirties.

Perhaps unsurprisingly, one of the duties of anti-aircraft gunnery training NCOs was to give instructions not only in foot drill and gun drill, they also had to give lectures on and demonstrate the mechanical workings and complete dismantling of their guns and also ballistics theory and flight trajectories of projectiles and aircraft. 'Classes' consisted of troops of thirty or forty recruits. A particular problem was that at least half of the 'audience' had absolutely no interest whatever in the subject matter but simply welcomed the opportunity not to be on the barrack square. Needless to say, I enjoyed this challenge thoroughly, particularly in how best to handle the most disinterested members of the 'audience'. During the 'lecture', my basic technique was to single out the least responsive recruits, bring them to the front of the audience, and then order them to demonstrate what I had just been teaching. It proved to be remarkably effective in obtaining their immediate and future attention. It also provided an effective incentive to other potentially disinterested members of the audience to pay more attention to my 'lecture'. Possibly, one of the biggest benefits to me in giving lectures in the future was the composition of my current audience. The recruits ranged from college graduates to ex-Borstal inmates. Since I proved successfully to be able to lecture to them, I would be capable of lecturing to any group of people in the future.

The nearest towns to Tonfanau were Dolgelly, Barmouth, and Machynthleth. However, Aberystwyth was the largest town on the Cambrian Coast, and a three-ton lorry was provided every Saturday as free transport for Permanent Training Staff. Aberystwyth was another world. It had shops, a cinema, a seafront and beach, and most importantly, a dance hall. I, along with my fellow NCOs, used to travel there on Saturday mornings. Needless to say, I managed to meet there my first and only Welsh girlfriend, who lived in a very small village a few miles outside the town. Like all locals, she spoke Welsh, and she had not learned to speak English until the age of twelve. Happily, she introduced me to what was popularly and irreverently known locally amongst servicemen as the 'National Welsh Sport' practised by local girls. To be fair, considering that there were no cinemas, television or other amenities in the remote rural areas of Mid-Wales, this was hardly surprising since there was little else to do. After the end of the dances in the dancehall, we illuminated used to spend a couple of hours in an empty cottage next to her house, from which I returned shortly before midnight, having been picked up by the 'three-tonner'. Fortunately, this passed through the village on its way back to camp.

One of the benefits of the remoteness of Tonfanau was that all permanent staff was allowed Long Weekend Leaves. These lasted from 4 pm on a Thursday to 8 am on a Monday. I used to travel home to my parents in West Kensington and used to arrive there from Paddington at about 4 am. I returned at 10 pm on the Sunday night mail train via Euston and Crewe. One of the techniques that I developed was to sleep on the luggage racks of the trains from Whitchurch to Machynlleth, where we would arrive at 6 am. On one weekend, the Festival of Britain was in full swing; along with my father, I visited the main site where the new Festival Hall had been built, and alongside which was the old shot tower and the 'Skylon'. We also visited Battersea and the at that time famous Roland Emmet miniature railway. The tiny open-air carriages contained four-seat compartments in which couples of passengers faced each other. Whilst sitting in one of these I commented to my father that I rather doubted whether the famous cartoonist Roland Emmet had much to do with their design. The young lady facing us smiled and leaned forward; she explained that Roland Emmett was her husband and was sitting next to her. I immediately pulled out a couple of picture postcards of the train, and he kindly signed them for me.

All regiments periodically received notification of 'special' courses on to which they were required to send a representative. The most bizarre activity on which I was randomly and very reluctantly sent was a two-week course to become a basketball referee. I duly became a 'Second Class Referee' for army basketball events. Mercifully, I was never required to perform in this role. Finally, I was put in charge of 'Continuation Training', which was provided for those recruits who were intended to be posted to active service in the Far East. Both Korea and Malaya were 'Active Service' theatres of war. The commonly known 'Con Troop' involved a great deal of additional training such as anti-tank and field firing. In Oswestry, the 'Con Troop' there was regarded with great dismay. Gunners were required to carry a rifle at all times, including when sleeping at night, when they were required to lay beside it. Apparently, in the Korean War in winter, British troops who were sleeping on frozen hillsides warmly wrapped in blankets had been surprised, overrun and killed. Consequently, 'Con Troop' recruits were taken for an overnight exercise on a nearby freezing Welsh mountain where they were allowed to sleep only under a single blanket. The purpose of this training was to prepare them for the Korean War in winter, to where they might be posted. Somewhat bizarrely, they might alternatively be posted to Malaya where the jungle was hot and humid all of the year round.

I could not have enjoyed my first nine months of conscription more. My only regret was that I was unable to get the opportunity to be posted abroad. No national service instructor had ever been 'posted' out of the 55th Training regiment, and I was due to spend the remainder of my service on the remote shore of Wales. However, just before Christmas, I was summoned to see the commanding officer. He was totally surprised, and concerned, and apparently very annoyed to inform me that I was to be posted to the 32nd Medium Artillery regiment in Scotland. He said that it was unprecedented, and there was nothing he could do to prevent it. I pointed out that when I had failed to be accepted by the Officer Selection Board, I had been categorised as 'Failed, Watch'. This entitled me after six months to re-apply for selection to be candidate. My commanding officer said there was nothing he could do about it, but he was puzzled as to why I had failed on the first occasion. He then concluded that the Board had decided that I would be more useful to the army as a non-commissioned officer in a Training Regiment than as a subaltern. If that was the reason, he and they were almost certainly right.

In due course, I went on Christmas leave from Wales to my grandparents' house in Bradford. Whilst I was there, I met my dear school friend Peter Newton who was now serving his national service in the RAF. We were both in uniform and had a drink together in a local pub in Bradford Moor. It was the last time we would ever meet. I returned from leave to Scotland, to where I had been issued with a travel warrant to a station called Auchendinny. I arrived at Edinburgh, only to discover that the station at Auchendinny had been closed some years earlier. I was therefore picked up by truck and taken to Glencorse Camp, which lay just outside Edinburgh on the edge of the Border Country. To my astonishment when I arrived at the camp, I found that the regiment was due to be posted abroad. Perhaps unsurprisingly, there was only one national Service lance-bombardier but no 'full' bombardiers in the regiment. Most NCOs had been in the Second World War, a few of whom were in the regiment in the North African Campaign. Astonishingly, one gunner had even been in the First World War. However, he was due to be discharged finally in a few weeks' time. I became even more puzzled to discover that none of the other soldiers were from Light Anti-Aircraft regiments. Whilst I was at Glencorse, King George VI died. I heard this on the radio in the barrack room and went in to the Orderly Room to tell the sergeant major. I felt it was an opportunity of a lifetime to announce such an event. I announced proudly, using the traditional proclamation, but with the second part completely wrongly, "The king is dead – long live the king."

One of the duties of the regiment was to mount ceremonial guard at night at the entrance to Edinburgh Castle. For this task, we were provided with rifles, the bayonets and fittings of which, astonishingly, were chromium plated. The Guard Room was mediaeval dungeon-like and bitterly cold. The snow was deep in Edinburgh at the time, and the steep narrow cobbled sloping entrance to the castle had cast iron plates to protect the cobbles from the wear of metal cart-tyres. All cars were stopped at the entrance in order for the guard to check their identity. During the night, only senior army officers were allowed entrance by car, and as a result, the whole eight-man guard had to be 'turned out' for 'inspection' on each occasion. Inevitably, after the 'inspection', the wheels of the visiting heavy staff car would spin, and the vehicle would be unable to restart on the slippery slush-covered iron plates. Guards were then required to sling their rifles over their shoulders and push behind the visiting vehicle. Unsurprisingly, the rear wheels of the vehicle sprayed them and their uniforms with a shower of cold slush. When on the following morning I commented unfavourably about this practice to the incoming relieving Black Watch corporal, he laughed unsympathetically. He raised the hem of his kilt and pointed out sceptically that it was 'nothing' compared with freezing slush being sprayed 'up your kilt'.

During the next few weeks, various rumours circulated, one of which was that we were to move to Barnard Castle in County Durham. This was known as a bleak and rather remote town in the North of England. It seemed to me to be a much less desirable posting than Tonfanau. However, within a month, the regiment was posted to Hong Kong. The Korean War was raging at that time, and most observers assumed that Hong Kong was simply a temporary staging post on the way to Korea. Before leaving Glencorse, I had explained to the battery commander that I was due shortly to be entitled to re-apply for a commission and asked how I could do this in Hong Kong. His response, somewhat dismissively, was that it was unlikely that I could do so, and why should I want to miss the opportunity of such a wonderful posting as Hong Kong. Although I felt somewhat disappointed at the time, in actual fact he was absolutely right.

On the Saturday night before we were to leave Glencorse, I went to the local village dance. At the end of it, we were surrounded by local girls sadly wishing us goodbye. It seemed reminiscent of films of the world wars. I ended the night being kissed goodnight simultaneously and passionately by two young girls, one in each arm. It was a unique experience. We left the camp the next day and arrived at Liverpool by special train at 4 o'clock on the following morning. After spending the rest of the night on the cold concrete floor of a room on the dockside, we boarded the twenty-thousand-ton ex P&O luxury liner, the 'Empress of Australia'. There were already a thousand other troops on board, mainly the 7th Royal Tank Regiment, and as we paraded on deck, the ship departed. Somewhat astonishingly, a brass band, surrounded by waving civilians, played on the quayside. We were now following the advance party of the regiment that had departed from Southampton a month earlier on the 'Empire Windrush', which was later to become famous, or perhaps infamous for its previous use as an immigrant ship. However, at that time, it had become a troopship. It was smaller than the 'Empress' and was likely to have a much rougher sea passage on the way to Hong Kong.

Shortly before the ship departed, we were all issued with a large off-white canvas roll with a length of rope wrapped around it. These, we were informed, were our hammocks, and we were allocated to 'F2' Deck. This, we discovered, was at the 'sharp end' near the bows of the ship, three decks down, and below the waterline. It transpired that as a troopship the deployment of army 'passengers' was on the 'Mess Deck' system. On descending to Deck F2, we found a number of fixed benches and tables to which we were each allocated a place. As a 'haven of rest', we were provided with hooks which were fixed to pillars above and around the tables. We were all told to claim tenancy of any pair of hooks that we could find which were fixed to the various pillars that were not occupied.

Sleeping at night involved 'slinging' hammocks to the appointed hooks, but some troops preferred to lay on the hard mess tables. The ship, although an ex-luxury liner, was not fitted with stabilisers, which at that time either were not in use or hadn't been invented. I found sleeping in a hammock a completely comfortable experience, particularly in the rough seas that we encountered frequently. The hard canvas hammocks were not provided with 'hammock sticks' and consequently wrapped themselves tightly around the sleeper. The only lighting during the night was from dim red emergency lights installed on the ship's sides. However, on waking during the night, I discovered that the bowels of the ship in which we were travelling were overrun by a huge infestation of cockroaches. The mess tables and in particular the blankets of those sleeping on them were particularly badly infested. Somewhat curiously, from my rather highly raised position with my hammock only connected with the rings at its ends, I rarely found myself visited by any cockroaches.

Food had to be collected in steel cans and tureens from the galley, which was four decks above. This was then brought down to the 'mess deck' by gunners selected by the NCO in charge of their table and shared out appropriately. To be fair, the food and drink were certainly up to the contemporary army standards of the time. However, the food was rarely hot enough, and the possible absence of any morsels that might have disappeared on the way from the galley could never be completely discounted.

During the day, we were paraded on deck, but we were not allowed to wear boots. Needless to say, foot drill, as well as other activities was extremely limited. We therefore had a great deal of spare time. There were a number of Royal Navy sailor ratings on board, some of whom during leisure hours set up crown and anchor boards. I had never encountered this game before and watched discretely from a distance. The rules of this gambling game appeared to include the unusual way of operating, which allowed any player to remove their wager from the board at any time before the dice were shaken. I observed carefully the rolling of the dice, which were placed and shaken under an upturned enamel mug. I soon realised that the dice could be either rolled over, or simply rattled around without being turned, in which case the operator knew the next outcome. This choice was obviously being manipulated by the operator, who decided whether to attempt to retain the previous display of the dice or to change them. This in turn depended on how much betting money had been placed on which of the symbols on the board and therefore which were liable to win or lose. Having observed this closely, I attempted to place one or two bets and only not retrieving the bet when I knew the coming results. Some of the operator's fellow naval ratings soon detected my efforts, and after observing a number of threatening glances from them, I withdrew from the competition. For the rest of my life, I very rarely gambled, and on those necessary social occasions, only very cautiously.

When we reached the tropics, we were able to watch films in the evening. These were projected onto a screen erected on the Aft Well Deck. We also received hygiene lectures from a young captain in the Royal Army Medical Corps. In particular, he warned us of the dangers of contracting venereal diseases in Hong Kong. He described remarkably graphically how we should make use of the so-called Prophylactic Aid Centres, popularly known as PAC's, which were located strategically in various parts of Kowloon. He described what these centres contained and illustrated graphically how the users should scrub their genitals with the brushes and soap provided. They should then apply the issued prophylactic cream to the affected organ. I was astonished to discover later that the cream contained mercury. An attendance slip, on which the soldier's details and time of encounter were to be recorded, was then to be left in the post-box within the centre. If the 'customer' failed to carry out these procedures and was subsequently discovered to have contracted venereal disease the result would be twenty-eight days military detention and total loss of pay.

Travelling with us on board was also a number of 'married families'. These were wives and children of regular soldiers and officers. We normally had no contact with these passengers, but on one occasion, two women ventured accidentally on to a middle deck used normally by troops for parades. On seeing troops emerging from decks below, one of the wives was heard to say that she didn't realise that soldiers were actually living down below the waterline in the 'bowels' of the ship.

During the voyage, the ship called at Tangiers, Port Said, Aden, Colombo, and Singapore. At each of these ports, we were allowed to go ashore, usually for about six hours. As a nineteen-year-old, unlike most of his fellow national servicemen who had never travelled further afield than Bognor Regis, it was the reward of a lifetime.

Hong Kong

After six weeks of our voyage from Liverpool on the 'Empress of Australia', we arrived in Hong Kong. We were on parade on deck as we sailed through a beautiful wide green-lined channel, which we were informed was known as the 'Gateway to China'. We also learned that Hong Kong, Kowloon, and the adjacent New Territories were occupied by a population of approximately two million Chinese citizens. The numbers were increasing continuously due to the many Chinese who were illegally fleeing to Hong Kong from mainland China. There were also twenty thousand British troops in the colony. Unfortunately, there had been riots recently, and one of our duties would be 'riot prevention'. I felt slightly uneasy about the disparity in numbers between the residents and us. I had been appointed as NCO in charge of the ceremonial 'Escort to the Battle Axe'. This long silver-plated axe was carried over the shoulder of the tallest gunner in the regiment as we marched through Kowloon from the ship to Gun Club Hill barracks. A photograph of the event subsequently appeared in the London Daily Telegraph. The battle-axe had apparently been captured during the Eighteenth Century at the battle of Martinique. Since the battle had been exclusively a naval one, I always found this somewhat puzzling. The battery now carried the grandiose title 'Seven-four – the Battle Axe Company, Three-two Medium Regiment, Royal Artillery', which was proudly announced and preceded the first words of command on all ceremonial occasions.

Our uniform in Hong Kong during the summer months consisted of 'bamboo green' shorts, cellular tunics, and a fairly wide-brimmed floppy cotton 'bush' hat. During the daytime, we rarely wore our tunics, except when on guard duty. On such duties during the daylight hours, our sleeves were rolled up to above our elbows. However, we normally worked stripped to the waist in what was commonly described as 'Buff Order'. We wore normal heavy black leather army ankle boots and woollen socks, above which were woollen 'hose tops' puttees. Under the top folded portion of the hose tops was attached a tape, which was tied around the calf of the leg in order to hold up the hose top. Sewn to the tape was a red and blue swallow-tailed chevron representing the Royal Artillery Colours. The top of the hose top was then folded over to conceal the tape. We then had to fit puttees. These were jungle green woollen strips of cloth, which were about six inches wide and three feet long with another two feet of inch-wide green tape sewn to one end. The puttees were wrapped tightly and carefully around the junction between the top of the ankle of the boot and the hose-tops. The tape was then required to end exactly on the outside centre of the top of the leg. Considerable practice and skill were required in order to achieve this result. However, most importantly, the whole assembly actually provided a very practical, comfortable, and supportive arrangement to the ankle and lower leg. In order to fit this elaborate costume arrangement precisely, we were required to measure carefully all of the dimensions of the various folds and creases by using the length and width of our Army Pay Books.

After a short time of operating in 'Buff Order', we all developed a dark tanned skin, the colour of which was indistinguishable from that of the local Chinese residents. This transformation had been regarded for many years as sign of army veterans who had been overseas long enough to get what the classic phrase described as 'get your knees brown'. The only time that 'Buff Order' proved to be problematical was when firing a rifle. With no possibility of surreptitiously concealing any padding to protect the shoulder, the effect of the recoil could be quite painful. The brass butt plate of the rifle was unpleasantly hot, but in order to fire, it needed to be pressed hard into the bare shoulder to minimise the effect of the 'kick' when the trigger was pulled.

Gun Club Hill Barracks were a classical example of colonial architecture. The long white buildings, which surrounded the drill square, contained two levels of barrack rooms above the ground floor, each of which contained long shaded verandas. On arrival, all soldiers were issued with four thin six-foot long planks of wood, and one large and one small off-white linen sack. These items were the bedding materials required for the steel two-tier bed frames in the barrack rooms above. The bags then had to be filled with straw and the planks placed in the iron bed frames. The large bag was the mattress and the small one was the pillow. Despite the rather austere appearance, the bedding was eventually discovered to be quite bearable. Unfortunately, the planks tended to have slight splits and fissures along their length. After a few days, these would become occupied and infested with bed bugs. However, soldiers found that by taking the planks on to the concrete verandas outside and bouncing the ends of the planks vigorously on the concrete floor, the bugs were ejected and could be trodden on. This became a regular procedure for the next few weeks. Later, it was discovered that the troop storekeeper had a steel bed with diamond-frame wire springs, which he had boasted that he believed was immune from infestation. However, a few weeks later, even he took his bed out onto the concrete, only to discover that at the joint of every 'diamond' spring was a recess that contained a solid mass of live bugs. The other feature of the barracks was that on every daily morning parade, the battery sergeant-major read out Garrison Standing Orders. Amongst other items, these always warned against the penalties of contracting VD without having submitting a PAC 'chit'. In practice, all soldiers when off-duty were only allowed to leave the barracks if they first presented at the Guard Room their Pay Book, a packet of condoms, and a blank PAC slip. Because of these regulations, one of the gunners, who happened to be a Quaker, refused ever to go out of the barracks.

The other bizarre routine was the weekly 'Free From Infection' parade, popularly known as the 'FFI'. This was carried out by the junior Troop Second Lieutenant. The troop was required to parade naked whilst each man was inspected under his arms, crutch, and between his toes for fungal infection. Infection occurred commonly at the top of the legs. In order to detect this, the inspecting officer would insert his 'swagger' stick into the soldier's crutch and delicately move it from side to side. The infection, which was common and widespread, was 'Tenia Pedis', the same organism as that of 'Athletes Foot'. The cure for this condition was to paint the infected area with 'Gentian Violet', a very vivid purple triarylmethane dye. Whilst this was undoubtedly very effective, it was nevertheless somewhat embarrassing to the patient, since all soldiers' daylight parades and activities in Hong Kong during the summer were performed in shorts and stripped to the waist. Similarly, this condition and its treatment were often to be seen on English civilian schoolchildren who were the families of soldiers. The other main reason for the 'FFI' inspection was to detect any obvious extreme symptoms of venereal disease. Despite all of the advice and injunctions with which we had been regaled on board ship, cases of 'VD' were not uncommon amongst troops. Chinese young women on the streets in Kowloon and Hong Kong were young, slim, beautiful, and always very elegantly dressed in full-length delicately embroidered silk sarongs. I, along with most soldiers found them irresistibly attractive. I found them so attractive, in contrast to the few English families of fellow soldiers, that I gained the ambition of one day having a Chinese wife. In the meantime, however, the 'short time' services of these young women were widely available for what to us was the trivial sum of the equivalence of less than a pound in English money. This was probably less than a quarter of the weekly overseas pay of a private soldier. It was therefore perhaps unsurprising that at the age of nineteen I had little hesitation in taking advantage of these services whenever possible.

After a month in Gun Club Hill barracks, the regiment moved up to a camp in the New Territories near the then small village of Yuen Long. This was about twenty miles north of Kowloon a few miles short of Chinese Border. It could only be reached by a very roundabout and hilly route around the rocky east coast and inlets of the New Territories. In some places, the road was surrounded by large paddy fields on each side. These were usually occupied by Chinese workers wearing black sarongs or jackets and with conical Chinese 'Coolie Hats'. They worked all day up to their knees in water, into which, we discovered later, was emptied all of the villagers' human waste. This may have explained the rather unpleasant odour, which seemed to surround these flooded fields. Early each morning, the workers could be seen on the road to Kowloon wearing wooden-soled sandals or in bare feet and with long bamboo poles across their shoulder at each end of which was suspended a large basket. The baskets contained produce that appeared to be cabbages. They were carrying these all of the way to Kowloon markets. Instead of walking, they appeared to trot and periodically transferred the pole from one shoulder to the other. Apparently, this was to relieve each shoulder in turn of the weight of the two basket-loads. Presumably, the sight that they presented could have been seen at any time during the previous few hundred years. Sadly, we learned a few weeks later that the medical officer who had graphically regaled us with warnings about our lives in Hong Kong was killed in the same location by an army truck whilst attending to a road accident. My knowledge and ability in all foreign languages was and always would be abysmal and almost non-existent. The language in Kowloon, as on Hong Kong Island, was Cantonese. However, all of the Chinese films were in Mandarin. In the New Territories, the language was Hakanese. All of these were completely different languages and apart from Mandarin varied throughout China. To make this even more confusing, Chinese words each had five tones, which conveyed completely, and sometimes embarrassingly, different meanings. My vocabulary was, unsurprisingly, somewhat limited. It consisted of the Cantonese for 'how much?', 'too dear', 'yes', and 'no'. I must also have picked up in the New Territories either another word, or a different intonation of Hakanese. This was greeted with apparent amusement by residents of Kowloon. The Hakanese speaking residents of the New Territories were considered generally by those of Kowloon and Hong Kong Island as what might be the equivalent in Britain as 'poor country bumpkins'. However, in my experience, they may have been poor, but they were invariably very kind and generous toward British servicemen. On an occasion a few weeks after we had arrived in the New Territories, a fellow bombardier and I were alone in the open country in an open jeep during a battery exercise. We had stopped beside a remote deserted paddy field to eat our 'packed lunch', which consisted of corned-beef sandwiches, which, in true 'cookhouse fashion', were about an inch thick and somewhat indigestible. An old Hakanese man wearing a 'coolie' hat and riding on a bicycle with a basket on the front came alongside us. He was offering to sell bottled 'fizzy' drinks for a few cents each. These were almost certainly 'bottled' by him and of which we had frequently been warned by medical officers that we should always avoid. We indicated somewhat forcefully and clearly that we didn't want any such products and attempted to dismiss him. However, he persisted, and after repeatedly refusing, we decided to offer him our discarded sandwiches in order to dispose of them. His response was astonishing. He was overwhelmingly grateful and insisted on giving both I and the other bombardier a bottle of his 'fizzy' drinks. I suppose that this was some sort of Chinese tradition in always returning hospitality. I was really quite 'touched' by his kindness, which was somewhat in contrast to our dismissive attitude. However, we did not drink his gifts. Forty years later in Singapore, I was astonished to discover that Hakanese residents there were considered to be 'foreign' wealthy landowners and investors. The only possible explanation seemed to be that they had somehow become rich by selling their New Territories properties during the subsequent massive urban and commercial development and expansion of Kowloon.

Like troops in pre-war India, all ranks had their kit and laundry cleaned by batmen. These were local Chinese civilian 'boys' and usually worked for five or six soldiers. I shared a thirty-year-old local who we called Charlie. On one occasion, he offered to accompany anyone who would like to see 'the sights' of Kowloon. Four of us took up his offer, and we were taken to an area that was officially 'out of bounds' to soldiers and occupied only by Chinese residents. We were taken into a house where I was entertained by an attractive young Chinese woman and had my very first 'good time' with her. Afterwards, when she discovered that it was my first 'good time', she was highly amused and said that had she known she would have provided her services free. However, she restrained herself from returning my money.

The camp in the New Territories was located in large colonial houses behind one side of the main road at Ping Yuen and Pak Yuen, small hamlets just south of the very small village of Yuen Long. Beside our quarters were some mature trees from the branches of which there were hanging what appeared to be large nuts. The cases of these 'nuts' when opened revealed a white fruit that I had never before seen or heard. They were lychees, and they were delicious, especially when taken straight off the trees. I would always enjoy these in the future, even though from tins. The regiment's living quarters and the parade ground were about a quarter of a mile apart and were joined by a rough pathway between them. This pathway, which had to be traversed daily for parades and meals, was either very rough and dusty, or very wet and muddy, depending on the day's weather. Inevitably, these conditions soiled uniforms and boots when having to go on parade. Another bombardier and I decided that this was highly undesirable. We completely unofficially organised working parties to try and lay an acceptable stone surface. Unfortunately, a couple of months later, before we could finish it, the regiment moved a few miles inland into single storey barrack huts besides a local military airstrip. The strip consisted of a single runway, which was occupied by a Royal Air Force squadron of the then new Meteors and Vampires. These took off and landed three abreast during the day and night. The screams of the jet engines were impossible to ignore.

On one occasion, I was sent in charge of half a dozen gunners to 'Mount Snowdon'. This was a large hill, nearly one-thousand feet high very close to the Chinese mainland border, which it overlooked. On it, the Royal Artillery was in the process of building an observation post commonly known as an 'OP'. This was rather naively believed to be hidden from the 'enemy' on the other side of the border. The post was in the process of being constructed by digging a large hole in the ground, which was subsequently to be roofed and covered over with soil and turf. Whilst we were there one of the gunners was stung on the head by a large hornet. In response to his agonising reaction, he actually had to be held down on his back by two other gunners. He eventually calmed down, and when he returned to camp, he was able to receive medical treatment. At the end of the day, before leaving the site, I discovered that an insulated cylindrical two-gallon tea urn was missing. After fruitlessly searching for it, I concluded that it must have accidentally either have been kicked or fallen down the hill. Fearfully anticipating a major hostile enquiry with me as the NCO in charge, I could see that this might not add favourably to my military record.

The hilltop was quite small, and the urn was fairly heavy. It proved impossible to see any trace of the urn by simply looking down the slopes, on which there were numerous small shrubs. After sending the gunners down the slopes, it became obvious that the boundaries of where it might have rolled were almost impossible to judge. I therefore organised the gunners to spread out around the sides of the hill and watch carefully. I then began to roll various round, fairly large stones in different directions down the slopes. The gunners then had to check where the stones finally lodged. After a surprisingly short time, much to my relief, one of the gunners reported that he had found the urn in a bush. My fears of a possible adverse disciplinary charge disappeared.

On one occasion, the troop was deployed on an exercise, and the four guns of the troop were laid out in fairly open country nearby. The commanding officer visited the site in order to inspect our progress. He immediately, very officiously, started issuing what he clearly regarded as important commands and criticisms. Among them was his instruction that the site required anti-aircraft protection. He pointed imperiously to a nearby tree and said that he wanted a Bren Gunner to be deployed in the branches. It was quite the most absurd, stupid, and ignorant order that I ever encountered in the army. First of all, a Bren gun was a most ridiculous weapon with which to attempt to use against aircraft, or with which to climb a tree, and secondly, the boughs of a tree were the worst possible place from which to get an all-round view of the sky. The possibility of being commanded by such an idiot in a real-life conflict, perhaps in Korea, did not bear thinking about.

All troops were entitled normally to an annual fourteen-day 'Long Leave', usually to spend at home on a family holiday. However, in Hong Kong this was clearly not practicable. As an alternative, troops were allowed to go on a ten-day cruise on a troop ship to Japan to Kobe, Kure, and Yokohama. Unfortunately, this option required a visa from the United States Authorities who at that time were occupying and in control of Japan. I twice attempted to do this, but on both occasions, I was unsuccessful. However, an alternative routine was that one troop at a time was allowed to leave the rest of the battery in order to go to a 'Leisure Camp' at Big Wave Bay on the south coast of Victoria Island. Victoria

Island was more commonly known as Hong Kong Island. Big Wave Bay was an isolated location close to a golden sandy beach and a beautiful warm blue sea. There were few, if any, civilians near. As a result, the whole troop turned the rather minimal facilities into a male nudist colony, for which the local climate and sun were ideally suited. For ten days, we enjoyed the isolation and the sun. Unfortunately, I had recently developed a mild Tenia infection under one of my armpits and was therefore displaying the usual Gentian Violet 'trademark'.

During our stay, I ventured once, during our visit to go, fully dressed, into the city of Victoria, latterly more commonly called just 'Hong Kong'. After encountering a rather beautiful female resident Chinese girl and enjoying her company and services for longer than I should, I realised that I had missed the last bus back to Big Wave Bay. The distance to the camp was about nine miles, and not being able to afford a taxi, I prepared to walk. The girl was most concerned and actually offered to pay for a taxi. I was not only greatly touched but deeply embarrassed and firmly but gently refused. It was one of the kindest and most generous gestures that I can recall. It simply reinforced my ambition, one day, to have a Chinese wife. In the event, it was a moonlit night, and the walk back was really quite pleasant. There were no guardroom restrictions at the campsite, and I was able to re-enter quite unobtrusively.

A feature of barracks and camps in the New Territories was the presence of an insect that until then we had not become familiar. It was a two-inch long brown flying beetle, commonly known as a 'Shit Beetle'. It appeared to be completely harmless but had an extraordinary resilience. When flying around the barrack room, it would periodically get hit by the large slowly rotating ceiling fans, hurtle across the room, hit a wall violently, then the floor, and finally simply take off and fly away apparently unscathed. One of the duties of bombardiers was to act as 'Orderly Sergeants'. Due to the failure to promote national servicemen to the rank of sergeant, bombardiers were repeatedly required for the duty. One of these duties was to wake up all barrack rooms at six o'clock in the morning. They then had to issue the regulation daily medical prescriptions of anti-malarial and salt tablets. Unsurprisingly, most soldiers were reluctant to swallow these on waking. My technique was to order all troops to get out from under their sheets, sit upright on the end of their beds, and put their bare feet on the rather cold concrete floor. They were then ordered to swallow the medication, although no water was available. Needless to say, none of this enhanced their enthusiasm for the treatment or my popularity.

Medium Guns were usually deployed up to ten miles behind the front line. In contrast, Field Guns and Light Ack-Ack units normally operated on the 'front line'. It was therefore essential to be as efficient as possible with their technical operation and rapid deployment. The 5.5-inch guns of a Medium Artillery regiment were completely different to any of the ones with which I was familiar. Unlike my previous highly trained experience and training on 'Twenty-five pounder Field Guns' and '40mm Bofors Anti-Aircraft Guns', I was completely unable to find either manuals or training for 5.5" Medium Artillery. However, I was told I was to become a 'tech ack' sergeant. The 'tech ack' was a mnemonic abbreviation for 'Technical Assistant'. This was a clerical task behind the guns involving calculations, which depended on arithmetic and the manual use of five-figure logarithmic tables. These were used in order to calculate ranges and issue instructions on the direction and elevation of fire. I found this incredibly boring, and despite the guaranteed opportunity to be promoted to sergeant, I really did not want to occupy such a role. I regarded it as the militarily useful equivalent of a battery clerk. As a result, I managed to fail the course. I was also 'stripped' back to the rank of gunner.

I was put on to 'Mail Duty'. This involved taking the regiment's personal mail to Kowloon each morning and returning with the mail from England in the late afternoon. I accompanied a driver in a small fifteen-hundredweight truck. We had to spend the middle of the day in Kowloon before returning to camp with the mail from England. This was a splendid duty, and one of its benefits to me was the opportunity to learn to drive. The trucks, like all army vehicles, had what were known as 'Crash' gearboxes, rather than automatic ones. In order to change gear, this involved the rather skilful exercise of 'doubling the clutch' every time that the driver changed gear either up or down. I managed to master the skill, but it never seemed to me to be a very easy exercise. The driver often used to leave the vehicle in the secure area and go our separate ways during part of the day. On a couple of occasions, I went to the local cinema. All of the films were Chinese and the language was Mandarin, but the cinema tickets were ridiculously cheap and watching films was better than walking around Kowloon all afternoon. On one occasion when I was leaving the cinema, I met a young Chinese girl who invited me to her home in 'Tin Town'. This was a large collection of shacks, made, literally, out of packing cases and with corrugated iron roofs. She became my regular 'girlfriend' during the rest of time as a Mail Orderly. However, much to my relief, I was eventually posted back to Gun Club

Hill to the 72nd Light Anti-Aircraft' Regiment that had arrived recently from England.

My three months in the 72nd Light Anti-Aircraft Regiment were amongst the happiest of my army career. Many of the soldiers there had been trained by me at Tonfanau back in Wales. Despite the fact that I had been a full Bombardier, with something of a reputation for strict discipline, none of my new fellow-gunners ever took any advantage of my demotion. The sergeant in whose gun-crew I had been posted was a tall genial Welshman, who inevitably had served in the Second World War. He apparently knew of my history and background and knew also that I was the only soldier in the regiment that was a qualified 40 mm Bofors Gunnery Instructor. His opening words to me were, "Well – you know what you are doing, boyo – you will be my number seven." The role of a 'number seven' on a Bofors gun was by far the most interesting of the seven-man gun crew and certainly required the most skill, knowledge and ability. In contrast, the 'number one' was normally a sergeant and had little to do except stand behind the gun, identify targets, and give orders. My troop commander was Captain Johnson who had served in Korea and had been wounded in the leg. As a result, he usually carried a walking stick, limped slightly, and unlike all other ranks, he always wore long full-length trousers. He was very kind and caring, and after I returned to England, I discovered that he had written to my parents to say how pleased he was for me to have been posted to his regiment. The battery commander was Major Boycott, whose ancestry, unsurprisingly, could be traced back to Ireland. He was an extremely able commander and had been an instructor of gunnery at the School of Royal Artillery. Instructors at the school, unlike my own training, were expert on every one of the many different guns used in the various regiments of artillery. This was a very rare and highly respected role, and no one from commanding officers downwards in Royal Artillery Regiments ever argued with an 'IG'. Beside this, my own expertise in only the 40mm Bofors paled into insignificance.

One of our regimental activities in Hong Kong was the periodic regular practice of 'Riot Drill'. For this exercise, 'Riot Squads' were formed by each of the four troops in the regiment. This was always practised in the early hours of the morning, usually near the city centre in Kowloon. We all carried rifles with fixed bayonets and ammunition pouches. Our training instructions from the troop captain were simple and clear. We were to march into position and form two ranks in 'line abreast'. On encountering the rioters, the troop would be ordered to halt, and the front rank would be ordered to kneel down. The officer in charge would then read the British 'Riot Act' to the facing crowd. If they did not disperse, he would then select one or two rioters at the front of the crowd and instruct two or three of the kneeling gunners to fire their rifles only at these selected rioters. The troop captain then amplified these instructions, prior to firing, by explaining that the aim of the soldiers was not to kill the selected target rioters but to wound them, preferably ensuring that they shed as much blood as possible. It was also desirable that the victims should need to scream alarmingly in pain, since this was believed would deter the rest of the crowd. The theory was that because only one or two men in the front rank would actually fire, the crowd would be unable to identify which of the troops actually fired. This always appeared to me to be a rather unrealistic belief. Finally, the troop captain added a cynical piece of army humour. This was the mock instruction that we were only allowed to open fire without orders if we were absolutely certain that it was definitely our comrades and rivals in 'B' Troop coming the other way.

In a very short time, I was promoted back up to full bombardier, and became, somewhat reluctantly, a 'Number One', despite not becoming a sergeant. One of the regiment's first exercises was to travel to a remote part of the New Territories to the east of Kowloon. This was a remote barren, sloping hill area overlooking a number of small rocky islands. We were to practise field and anti-tank drill. This was very unusual for anti-aircraft regiments and was practised only rarely and involved using telescopic sights and armour-piercing ammunition. I had specially asked for and drawn a pair of 'barrel sighting tubes' from the troop stores. Apparently, no one else was familiar with these, or had thought this necessary. These tubes were required so as to set up the precise accuracy of the gun. In order to carry out the adjustment procedure, one tube had to be inserted in the breech and the other inside the conical flame-guard around the muzzle of the gun. The gun was then trained on a distant target, which could then be viewed through the barrel from the pinhole in the middle of the other tube at the breech end. I knew from past experience that an essential supplement to these items was a long piece of torn or knotted rag to be attached to the muzzle tube. This ensured the presence of the muzzle tube could be seen, which was otherwise invisible inside the conical flame-guard at the end of the barrel. After completing the adjustment procedure, I removed the rag and returned the tubes to the towing vehicle of my gun.

Shortly afterwards, the young NCO in charge of the gun next to me asked to borrow the tubes. I refused, somewhat churlishly, on the traditional basis that I had signed for them and that he should have thought of it and done the same. Shortly afterwards, the battery captain arrived and ordered me to pass over the tubes. When firing commenced, each gun in turn was directed to shoot at small areas on individual rocks that were pointed out by the officer in charge. After my gun had finished firing, the gun next to me did the same. Its first shot seemed rather strange and fell short of its target. At the same time, what appeared to be shrapnel flew off the gun. The muzzle end of the gun was seen to have lost its conical flash-guard, and the last foot of the barrel muzzle had peeled back just like a banana. Needless to say, the muzzle sighting tube, lacking a piece of warning rag, had been left in place. Major Boycott arrived to comment that the last time this had happened at a firing-camp in England two men had been seriously injured. A court-martial would now be necessary for this present incident.

On another occasion, the commanding officer had decided to test the operational security of units by carrying out inter-troop exercises. Apparently, my troop had been chosen to test the security of 'B' Troop, who were on a three-day exercise on the hills outside Kowloon. A group of four men from my troop were to attempt to infiltrate their campsite and bring back some sort of token trophy. I and four other gunners were chosen to carry out this 'raid'. We went in a fifteen-hundredweight truck to a location about a quarter of a mile away from where 'B' Troop was deployed. It was dark; we had blackened faces and crawled close to the area where the guns were deployed. We managed to crawl right inside the perimeter, close to where the gun crews were sleeping. After an hour, I decided reluctantly that it was impossible to remove any significant item of equipment. We therefore returned undetected to where we had left our vehicle. To our amazement and horror, the vehicle had disappeared. After searching fruitlessly for about half an hour, we reluctantly walked the five miles back to Gun Club Hill Barracks. I could envisage a court-martial being a possible outcome. However, when we arrived, the troop commander informed us that the vehicle had been 'abducted' by 'C' Troop, who had been given the task of surreptitiously shadowing and observing our progress and performance. Ignition keys were rarely if ever used in army vehicles, but I suppose that we should have disabled our vehicle by removing a spark plug or some other essential component. However, it had never occurred to me at the time.

One of my great prizes in Hong Kong was the purchase of my first Rolex Oyster watch. At that time, these were a very rare and very expensive luxury item. However, in Hong Kong they were widely available at a fraction of the European prices. There were, of course, many fakes. Nevertheless, I managed to buy a genuine one in a luxury jewellers shop in Kowloon. After the traditional haggling, I paid less than half of the price of an equivalent one in England. I subsequently took it to the Rolex shop in London who confirmed that it was genuine. Another luxury item was the surprising availability of Harris Tweed jackets, which also proved to be genuine. These could be made to measure and tailored overnight. In England, these jackets were exclusive, fashionable, and rather expensive items. I bought three, made to measure, for less than the cost of one in England.

I enjoyed myself thoroughly for the rest of my stay in Hong Kong. In the meantime, my previous battery was posted to Korea. In actual fact, I was too near to demobilisation to have gone with them had I remained. Shortly before I was sent back to England, I was summoned to see the commanding officer. He offered to promote me immediately to sergeant if I would sign on to serve for one more year. I explained that I was due to go to university when I returned to England. He ruefully, though I thought rather gallantly, said that if he had such a choice at my age, he would have to opt for the university. In fact, he was quite right. At that time, only two or three percent of the population ever got the opportunity to go to university, although ninety percent of those were male. In contrast, anyone could join the army.

My nine months in Hong Kong were amongst the happiest days of my life. I returned reluctantly to England on the 'Asturias', another twenty-thousand-ton ex-liner. Life was somewhat easier on the Asturias than on our way out on the Empress of Australia. The ship operated on the 'mess deck' system, in which like a normal cruise liner, food was eaten in a dining area and sleeping was in bunks on the decks below. During the six-week voyage at Christmas and New Year, an unfortunate event occurred whilst we were travelling up the Red Sea. Two Scottish Highland infantry regiments were also travelling home and managed to throw a piano overboard as part of their Hogmanay celebrations. As a result all troops on board had a shilling deducted from their pay for 'barrack room damages'. Finally, I returned to England and was stationed in Woolwich for ten days whilst awaiting discharge. I was once again reduced to the rank of gunner before returning home to my parents in Kensington. My army service was then transferred to five years in the Territorial Army. I was posted to a Territorial Army Light Anti-Aircraft regiment, which was originally a Royal Warwickshire infantry regiment. Coincidently, it was in the same drill-hall in the middle of Birmingham in which I had been a cadet sergeant major. Once again, I was the only man in the regiment who was a qualified gunnery instructor on 40mm Bofors guns, with which the regiment was armed. Shortly after I arrived, I was promoted to full bombardier once more. I suspect that I was one of the only national serviceman ever to be promoted three times to the rank of 'full' bombardier.

Shortly after returning to Birmingham, I was horrified to discover that I was suffering from 'crabs'. These were small lice that lived in and around pubic hair follicles. They were painless and harmless but a very distinct embarrassment. Recalling the repeated joking references to them and their cure by World War I veterans, I immediately went to the nearest pharmacist and asked for some 'Blue Unction'. He was a rather elderly and looked at me with slight amusement. He said that the medicament was now called 'Blue Ointment', and he then provided me with a small tube of it. I returned to my lodgings and found that the treatment was immediately effective. The essential blue ingredient apparently was mercury. The event was my last live legacy from Hong Kong. However, despite having contracted the 'crabs', I had mercifully escaped both of the other two First World War afflictions of piles and 'The Clap'.

During service in Hong Kong, all troops received an extra 'Overseas Allowance' in addition to their normal pay. As a bombardier, I also received more than the average national serviceman. I had therefore saved money during my service and had accumulated over a hundred pounds, which had been paid into my 'English Post Office Savings Account'. One of my first actions after my return to Birmingham was to buy a brand-new Raleigh Lenton 3-speed cycle for £22. I immediately added a second sprocket to the gear, and a two-speed 'Derailleur' gear, the operating-lever of which was used to switch between the two sprockets. This gave me a unique six-gear arrangement and benefitted from the advantages of both types of gear, whilst avoiding their inherent limitations. I never ever heard of anyone using the same configuration, and this vehicle became my 'pride and joy' and served well for almost all of my personal transport needs for the next ten years.

After I had started at Birmingham University, the commanding officer of the Territorial Regiment first said I was to be promoted to sergeant but shortly afterwards reversed his decision. He explained that he didn't want me to join the Sergeants' Mess, as he wished me to become a commissioned officer. Once again, my ambition to wear three stripes surmounted by a gun was frustrated. Instead, having served for over two years in the Territorial Army, I decided that it was time to leave. I therefore accepted the alternative offer to transfer to the 'Special Reserve', which only involved being called back into the regular army in the event of a 'National Emergency'. Shortly afterwards, the 'Suez Crisis' occurred, but fortunately, I was not 'called up'.

Finally, I had left all association with my military service, having failed miserably in both of my alternative ambitions of becoming either a sergeant or a subaltern. Perversely, I had also on this occasion, turned down the opportunities to become either or both. In retrospect, those were probably among the most sensible decisions I ever made.

Swinging Birmingham

When I returned to Birmingham after my national service, both Birmingham and my perception of its society had changed. I had left the city as a callow 'green' virgin and returned with more worldly experience of life than the majority of males of my age group. The city itself had changed. Considerable rebuilding of war-damaged areas had taken place, but new buildings and roads were still being constructed. In particular, I returned to what seemed to me to be a completely different social life. Although the 'Swinging Sixties' had not yet begun, following the newly readily available contraception and 'the pill', promiscuity among young people was certainly widespread. However, this behaviour was of a distinctly social nature. After attending public dances, the majority of females would be 'taken home' by their chosen partners. Invariably, whilst finally bidding one another 'goodnight' at or near the girls' homes considerable 'groping' and similar activity by both parties would occur. Such behaviour was almost universal, obligatory, and regarded as completely harmless and normal. Public dance halls and their regular attendance would continue to be a major feature of young social life for at least the following twenty years. The form and nature of the dancing bore almost no resemblance to the 'Strictly Come Dancing' television programmes of the following century. Most importantly, it provided a wonderful opportunity for young people to meet intimately an almost unlimited number of similarly aged young people of the opposite sex. It was a unique and irreplaceable social phenomenon that disappeared by the end of the century.

I returned to my pre-national service practice of attending a couple of public dances each week. I very soon acquired a regular 'girlfriend'. She was an extraordinary choice. Her appearance and dress were completely different from any other dancer that I ever saw. She was slim, had rather aquiline features and completely unfashionable hair and dress. Unlike the majority of girls and women, who invariably had short hair, her very straight dark brown hair was down to her shoulders and appeared to be permanently fixed in place. She always wore a well-tailored suit. I first danced with her at the Tower Ballroom, purely out of curiosity. She had almost no conversation, but as I immediately discovered, she danced extremely well. Somewhat to my own surprise, I offered to 'see her home' after the dance, and equally to my surprise, she accepted. I continued to dance with her for the next three years. She worked at the Kunzle Factory as a chocolate packer and lived in a council house on the outskirts of Harborne. To my astonishment, she had visited Switzerland twice to look after children in an orphanage supported by Kunzle. Although her name was Evelyn for some reason, I always referred to her to my friends as 'Tiger Lil', although never to her face. To my eventual horror, I finally discovered that when I had first met her she was only just sixteen years old. However, there was never any danger of our relationship becoming permanent or serious. She claimed to be engaged to a boyfriend who was a regular soldier in the Coldstream Guards, who was stationed at Caterham Barracks in Surrey. He came home on leave periodically, during which time she was unable to see me. I was somewhat relieved by this 'engagement' and had no wish to encounter her 'fiancé'.

During the next three years, I only had two other 'regular' girlfriends. When I went to Birmingham University seven months after returning from Hong Kong, I had little or no interest in the relatively small number of female students, most of whom were eighteen-year-old school leavers. However, as a university student, I met many nurses and student nurses. When I was in my second year, I met a First Year Dental Student who persuaded me, somewhat against my will, to buy a ticket to a Dental School dance. I met her there and perhaps inevitably, she became my permanent girlfriend. She was blond, very slightly short, but with a good figure, and very vivacious and attractive. Her name was Odile, but I always for some reason somewhat dismissively referred to her as 'Liz'. She had two equally attractive younger sisters and two older brothers. One of these was a Wing Commander in the Royal Air Force. Her mother was a widow who owned a number of dental practices, and the family was clearly very wealthy. Inevitably, Odile was highly intelligent, extremely perceptive, and had a wonderful and fascinating personality. However, at the end of her second year at Dental School, she failed her exams. Inevitably, she blamed me for her failure. Fortunately, she was accepted almost immediately by Leeds University Dental School and continued her studies there. I visited her at Leeds on a couple of occasions. On the first occasion, she was staying on the outskirts of the city. It was winter, and there was snow on the ground. We were unable to find privacy in the house in which she was staying, so we conducted our amorous activities in a nearby dark snow-covered field. The event conformed to the classic comic music-hall joke of 'lying on the cold ground with only a thin woman between me and the snow to keep me warm'. On the second occasion that I visited her, life was much more pleasant, and Odile was living in a basement flat near the centre of Leeds.

I always found Odile very attractive, and I was extremely fond of her. She was, without question, the only female that I had met that with whom I would really have wanted to spend the rest my life. However, I had categorically and repeatedly refused to countenance marrying her. Needless to say, I always enjoyed her company very much, and we always got on extremely well. Nevertheless, I realised that although she was highly intelligent and a thoroughly pleasant, good natured, and thoroughly likable character, she was not only highly intelligent and perceptive but could always also be very manipulative. I concluded that if I married her, I would probably spend the rest of my life analysing her motives and trying to counterbalance them. In particular, I took a chauvinistic view that I did not relish the prospect of having a wife who would always earn more money than I could as a brewer. I also had what I suppose was an equally prejudiced and irrational reason, that her family were all Roman Catholics. Her surname was of Irish origin. Odile once told me somewhat derisively that I had 'The map of Ireland' all over my face. At the back of my mind, I recalled having been told that my great grandfather was Welsh but had an Irish Catholic wife, with who he had eight sons. When his wife died, he took the sons to the nearest Protestant church and had all of them baptised. I did not want my children to become Roman Catholics.

The other girlfriend that I had for nearly a year was a repertory actress. I had met her on a sole visit that she had made to the West End Ballroom. Her name was Janet, and she lived in Moseley but was permanently travelling around the country in Repertory Acting Companies. Inevitably, she was periodically and fairly frequently out of work, or what was euphemistically known in the profession as 'resting'. During these periods, she would live in London at an establishment known as the 'Theatre Girls' Club'. This was a large house in Greek Street in Soho, which was strictly regulated. No males were allowed inside the premises other than to call for or return inmates after 'taking them out'. 'Girls' were able to live there very cheaply for as long as necessary and they were able to visit London agents in order to find their next work. Most importantly, from my point of view, they also received complementary tickets for matinees of many shows in London theatres. I was taken on one such occasion to the Lyceum to see the pantomime 'Cinderella'. The stars were Max Bygraves, a leading popular singer of the period, and a very young Julie Andrews. She was beautiful, vivacious, and her voice and diction were perfection. It was a wonderful introduction to seeing her at the beginning of what was to become a worldwide star career.

Another feature of my relationship with Janet was communication. Long before the advent of mobile phones, the only practical form of verbal communication whilst away from home was the public telephone box. When Janet was 'playing' in other parts of the country, we would write to each other and exchange the telephone numbers of nearby public telephone boxes. We would then specify a date and time at which we might communicate. Provided that there were no queues at the nominated boxes at the time arranged, I would then pay for the agreed call. However, after a few months, by mutual consent we agreed to remain merely friends.

The only other student that I ever 'took out' was a medical student called Bogenna. I had been informed that she had no boyfriend to take her to the annual Medical Ball. On discovering this, I invited her, more out of curiosity than gallantry, to allow me to take her to the ball. There were only half a dozen female medical students in each year, despite the fact that there were at least forty or fifty male medical students in the same year. However, no male students had invited her. Bogenna was Polish, an attractive and formidably intelligent girl and had a fearsome history. During the Second World War, she and her mother had walked some hundreds of miles out of Poland to safety from the invading Germans and Russian armies. I once met Bogenna's mother, who was charming. She was giving a birthday party for Bogenna at which she had prepared a dish which I had never seen before nor seen since, even in Poland. It was a multiple sliced stack of sandwiches with different fillings between each layer. The crusts had been cut off the slices. The pile was then compressed for some time and finally cut into thin slices vertically in the opposite plane. It was quite delicious. After taking Bogenna out once more, she apparently decided that she was beginning to like me more than was good for her. She therefore announced that our relationship should end. I was slightly disappointed but faintly relieved.

One of Bogenna's few fellow female medical students was called 'Lally', which was a diminutive of 'Lalita'. She was blond, rather short, pretty, and in my opinion utterly delightful. She was the daughter of a local G.P. I fell completely and unreservedly in love with her. As a result, I continued to observe her from a distance but never made any advances towards her. I considered that with my experience and liaisons of the previous couple of years, I was totally unsuitable to become her 'boyfriend'. Therefore, I suppose gallantly, although rather stupidly, I refrained from ever asking to 'take her out'. Instead, I persuaded one of my dental student friends to take her out, which he duly did. However, he eventually found another girlfriend, to whom he became engaged but never married. She terminated the engagement when he failed his final dental exams. Undeterred, he retook his exams and soon became engaged to another nurse who he eventually married. Despite all of these events, my feelings towards Lally never changed. Shortly after qualifying, she married a fellow doctor and presumably lived 'happily ever after'. I perhaps naively considered that I had made the right decisions and might even have done her a favour and had gallantly saved her from a 'fate worse than death'.

Birmingham Brewing School

When I returned finally to Cape Hill from Hong Kong, I was presented with a Contract of Employment by Mitchells and Butlers. It provided a modest salary for three years whilst I was at university. The sum was slightly higher than the then current government 'Student Allowance'. This was to be followed by a salary of five hundred pounds a year following my return as a shift brewer. The attached conditions were remarkable. Among them, I was required to live within half a mile of the brewery, other than with '…the express permission of the directors'. Furthermore, I was not allowed to own stocks or shares in 'any' brewery company 'including' Mitchells and Butlers. Viewed with hindsight from the twenty-first century, it may seem surprising that a contract of employment could set the same fixed salary for six years ahead, without any clause for adjustment. Inflation at the time was a significant factor.

My three-year full-time attendance at Birmingham University Brewing School enabled me to become a 'fully qualified' brewer. The first-year syllabus consisted only of physics, chemistry, and botany. These were necessary because I had left school without gaining the Higher School Certificate. Fortunately, the classes were shared by other first-year students, all of who were studying either medicine or dentistry. Many of these students were to remain my close friends for the rest of our family lives. In contrast, the second year provided me with knowledge that proved invaluable to me for the rest of my active working life. Apart from a weekly brewing lecture, all of the classes were in the various engineering departments. These subjects – mechanical engineering, electrical engineering, heat engines, machine drawing, and geology were the hallmark of excellence of Birmingham University. The two subjects that some brewing students found most difficult were heat engines and machine drawing. Heat engines required the application of complex mathematical formulae to evaluate the performance of all types of engines such as steam boilers and engines and turbines, internal combustion engines, and gas engines. Mr Emory was the tutor for both of these subjects and apparently was 'teetotal'. Bizarrely, he appeared to have a 'soft spot' for brewing students, who he regarded as not 'proper' engineers or 'normal' university students. The weekly session in the heat laboratory involved measuring and analysing the performance of one of the many full-size industrial machines that were installed there. Students had to fill in very detailed pre-printed laboratory record sheets. The completion of these sheets involved complex mathematical calculations which had to be entered on to the sheets by the groups of students. However, these printed sheets were simply repeated each year, and the previous year's brewing students frequently passed them on to the next year's students along with their calculations and results. Unfortunately, one year the students had simply adapted or copied the previous year's analysis results adjusting them slightly in order to conceal their origin before submitting them to Mr Emory. His response was surprising. Mr Emory pointed out to them that the results they had presented, though interesting, were for a machine that no longer existed, since it had been scrapped a few months earlier than the alleged records.

The drawing office contained large imperial-sized drawing boards, to which students were required to bring their own tee-squares and drawing instruments. On our first visit to the drawing office, Mr Emory's first instruction was to tell us all to go away and wash our hands before touching a drawing board or picking up a tee-square or pencil. In future, we would all be required to bring a soap and towel with us. Our first drawing was of a large nut and bolt holding together two pieces of metal. This seemed to be an embarrassingly simple and obvious subject to draw. The trap that emerged when we had produced the results was that the nut and bolt could only be fitted one way around. Half of the students managed to get it wrong. The most important aspect of machine drawing was that it taught me how to apply the then new British Standards both to machine drawing and subsequently to architectural drawings. As a result of the knowledge I gained, combined with my future studies, I was able to apply this profitably both in my work and domestically. It benefitted me immeasurably, and during the next fifty years, this knowledge provided me with many, many thousands of pounds of real wealth. I had even toyed with the idea of returning to Birmingham University and becoming an engineer. However, my limited mathematics ability and the sheer potential financial costs deterred me fairly easily.

My great friend and fellow brewing student David Barnard and I had decided that there was a gap in the curriculum, in that we had no lectures on statistics.

We therefore asked permission from Professor Hopkins for us to attend classes in the economics department. Economics was currently regarded as a 'soft', not 'proper' subject in which, unlike the engineering departments, there were a large number of female students. Female students were not of great interest to the other ninety percent of male students, who preferred the company of nurses from the many surrounding nurses' homes. However, we were allowed to attend these classes in which somewhat bizarrely the Irish lecturer recommended the Penguin paperback book 'Facts from Figures' by Moroney as the only essential textbook. In fact, he was quite right, and what could have been a somewhat daunting subject was in fact very understandable. Perhaps fortunately, David and I were not eligible or allowed to take the end-of-year examination. However, I found the book to be invaluable and continued to use it at many years to come, both at work and at every university that I subsequently attended.

During the three years at the university, the only drawback was that I was receiving a modest salary and an occasional small pay from the Territorial Army. Unlike my contemporary students, I was unable to obtain more lucrative work during vacations. However, I partially overcame this handicap by obtaining, along with a fellow brewing student Dave Priest, a part-time job during term-time at the Theatre Royal in the middle of Birmingham. We were employed as stagehands, more commonly known as 'scene-shifters', in a Christmas pantomime. This allowed me to enter, experience, and enjoy the wonder-world of the stage, and my very close subsequent personal relations with members of the acting profession. My role as a stagehand was to be a 'brace and weight boy'. This involved connecting and disconnecting a six-foot-long wooden brace with a two-way iron hook at one end to twelve-foot tall pieces of canvas and wood painted scenery, known as 'flats'. The 'boy' held the brace upright in one hand, and in the other hand, he held a forty-pound round iron weight. The 'flat' was swiftly slid into its marked position by a hand called a 'flat pusher', and the 'brace and weight boy' followed closely behind. The 'boy' then twisted one side of the curved hook into a ring at the back of the 'flat' and dropped the weight onto the iron foot of the brace. Speed and coordination were required for these activities, and 'boys' were quickly berated by the 'flat pusher' if they failed in either. The show that was running at the time was 'Old King Cole', a Christmas pantomime starring Vic Oliver, a radio comedian and talented pianist, who incidentally was married to one of Winston Churchill's daughters. He was staying somewhat unconventionally in the same room at the nearby Midland

Hotel with the 'Principal Boy' and also the 'Good Fairy'. I was fascinated by the difference in character between these two women. The 'Boy' was tall, elegant, sophisticated, and rather 'up market'. She always spoke beautifully but ignored stagehands. In contrast, although the 'Fairy' spoke beautifully on stage, I was surprised when I first encountered her close to. The spotlessly white fluffy fairy-like lace dress when viewed closely behind stage was absolutely filthy. On my first meeting with her, she came off stage and leaned against the iron radiator by which I was standing. She then turned to me in a friendly manner and issued the immortal words in her natural broad cockney accent "Christ – it's bleedin' cold out 'ere." The other character that I found unusual was the part of King Cole's 'Chancellor'. He was portly, rather dignified, and in his mid-fifties. Although his was a relatively small part onstage, he always recited the prologue, unseen in the small 'Prompt Box' located offstage. Having had some previous small experience of the acting profession, I had always been impressed by actors' ability to memorise their parts. In fact, repertory players performed one role each week, whilst learning their new lines for the following week's play. In complete contrast, the 'Chancellor' used to enter the 'Prompt Box', carefully take out his spectacles, open his script, and solemnly read his few lines from it. He would then put his spectacles away, fold up his script, and walk away in a dignified manner. In fact, he had remarkably few lines to present onstage in the rest of the pantomime. Absurdly, although the incident was trivial, I learned an important lesson from it. 'Never waste time learning or doing anything that is unnecessary– unless you have to.'

The shows that followed the pantomime season were all classical operas. It was an amazing experience for me to view these from behind stage. The first opera was Wagner's Tannhauser played by the touring company of the Royal Opera House at Covent Garden. During the prelude, the dimly lighted stage was filled with dancers from the Royal Ballet. Before and after their entrance on stage, they crowded around and almost completely filled the areas where the stagehands stood. The dancers were all so scantily and transparently dressed that it was difficult to imagine that they were not completely naked, and that this was not some salacious Soho performance. I, along with the rest of the hands, found this unusually interesting. It also may have helped to reinforce my interest in classical opera and ballet.

After returning to Birmingham, I had lived in various lodgings. These were more popularly known as 'digs' and could vary from the luxurious to the slovenly. I had been fortunate in returning to a house on the fringe of Edgbaston, immediately next to the Bristol Road. The Bristol Road ran from the centre of Birmingham, less than a mile away, to Selly Oak where the university site was located. Mrs Parkinson, the lady who owned the house, was a widow in her fifties or sixties. There were two more permanent residents, who were middle-aged, and who had been there for some time, and both always wore pinstriped suits at all times. One of them was a Liverpudlian manager of a local large grocery store, and the other, a middle-aged bachelor who had been in the Northamptonshire Regiment in the Second World War. There was also a continuing succession of 'guests' who stayed periodically, usually for a few days at a time. These included travelling salesmen, variety artists, actors, and opera singers. Every three months, two travelling salesmen came to stay for a week. They were selling advertising space in the then widely circulated Kelly's Directory. They were both Mancunians and had served together in the Royal Navy as Royal Marines on a cruiser during the Second World War. Their exploits and stories of how to sell products and services face-to-face to customers or clients were an education and inspiration to me. It would actually benefit me considerably in the future. On one occasion, singers from the Covent Garden Royal Opera House came to stay for a week. They were all rather large but very friendly and entertaining. On another occasion, at the same time as the two Kelly's Directory salesmen were staying, the comedian Kenneth Williams also came for a week. Although he later became known as a comedian, on this occasion he was playing at the Theatre Royal in Birmingham as the Dauphin in 'Joan of Arc' alongside Alec Guinness. He was clearly homosexual and quite unable not to act flamboyantly at all times. This usually involved humorous jokes and anecdotes about other actors, during which at some stage, he allowed his trousers to become undone. In one of these recollections, he recalled staying in an Edinburgh boarding house. One of his fellow actors was a rather dignified male actor, who on leaving the lodgings was accosted by the landlady from an upper floor window. She requested him to '– not leave your piss pot under the bed, as the steam rises from it and rusts the springs'. The actor concerned politely raised his hat and assured the landlady that he would conform to her request. Despite these anecdotes and antics, Kenneth Williams really was very funny, and I and the two ex-marines were equally but cautiously and patronisingly amused.

    Out of a hundred students, only my fellow brewing student Dave Barnard and Bob Halford, a dental student, had been in the army. Both had been commissioned. Needless to say, they were my best friends. All of the other students had come straight from school. Bob Halford was on the Students Union Committee, representing dental students and proposed that I should join the committee to represent brewers. I accepted the invitation and was appointed as a member. It was my first exposure to committee meetings. Inevitably, it revealed to me that there were always members who took the opportunity of meetings as an ego trip to 'take the stage' and waffle and perform in front of a captive audience. After attending a couple of meetings that I found excruciatingly boring and were of no relevance to brewing students, I retired quietly. Unfortunately, I was to suffer many more such meetings in the future. However, I perhaps unkindly allowed myself to take my own ego trip. Each year, a photograph was taken of the committee. The professional photographer had a traditional camera for recording long groups of people. It had a clockwork mechanism that allowed it to rotate. The photographer would point the camera at one end of the group, and the camera would rotate slowly to the other end. I took up a position at one end of the group and then performed an old Victorian trick. As soon as the camera had photographed me, I walked behind the group to the other end. When the camera eventually reached this end, it photographed me a second time.

Despite not being required to return to Cape Hill during vacations, I was not allowed to obtain holiday employment. I therefore decided to return to Wales for a short break. On the first vacation, I went by train and then on foot to North Wales. My 'luggage' was my 'Valise', a large webbing pack, which was worn in the army, but only on route marches, punishment parades, or movement between camps. In order for this to look 'smart' whilst in the army, I had lined mine with plywood boards on the inside, and these kept the pack in a rigid geometrical shape. Because I had fallen in love with North Wales, the route that I intended to take was to walk from Trawsfyneth to Caernarvon via the summit of Mount Snowdon. Trawsfyneth was at that time a remote single street village close to the artillery firing range that I had visited during my training at Oswestry. However, I decided to walk from there to Harlech, which was on the coast about ten miles away to the south. The walk went beside the lake, which a few years later was to house a hydroelectric power station. During the ten-mile walk, I never encountered another human being. After reaching Harlech and visiting the historic castle, I headed north along the coast about another ten miles to Porthmadog and the Ffestiniog Railway, which had only recently reopened. I visited the railway and then travelled by bus to the side of Mount Snowdon. I set off to walk up to the peak via what was known as the 'Pyg Path'. This was on the opposite side from the popular route and railway up the mountain, and at best was only a narrow footpath, and at worst narrow and precipitous. Perhaps fortunately, I met a group of hikers on the ascent, and this reinforced my confidence. However, they found my attire, and in particular, my rigid army pack something of a curiosity. I descended from the summit by the popular route, which was simply a pleasant downhill walk, before going on to Caernarvon, where I visited the castle. I then returned to Birmingham by train.

Perhaps surprisingly, bottling and packaging were not subjects that were taught, or even referred to during the three-year course at the Brewing School. This might possibly have been because bottling managers were rarely brewers, but more importantly, there were no textbooks on the subject. During the summer vacation after my second year, Professor Hopkins, the head of the Brewing School, introduced an unprecedented innovation. He arranged for brewing students who wished to do so to attend a two-week course at the Guinness School of Bottling. The school had been created recently by the Guinness Company on the premises of a small independent bottling company at Preston in Lancashire in order to train their sales representatives and independent bottlers. The bottling company continued to operate as an independent bottler and supplying the local area with all types and makes of beer. The school was run by an ex-technical college lecturer. My fellow students Dave Priest and Nigel Bass from Birmingham and four students from various breweries attended the course. It was an extraordinary and very enjoyable two weeks. Lectures were held in what had been the boardroom of the company, and we were seated on comfortable chairs on either side of a large long mahogany table. On the first morning, the tutor introduced himself, and then referring to us as 'gentlemen' stated that it was most important to carry out the initial induction procedure. He asked us all to write down what was our favourite bottled beer. He then handed our answers to his assistant who immediately left the room. After a brief introduction to the history of the Guinness Company and the reasons behind the creation of the school, we were somewhat rudely interrupted. His assistant had entered the room with a large two-wheeled barrow stacked high with wooden beer crates each containing two-dozen bottles of beer. He referred to the list that he had been given and then dropped two crates behind each chair. Our tutor explained that these were for consumption on our morning breaks, lunch, and afternoon breaks. Neither coffee nor tea were ever offered on these occasions. His next request was to ask us to submit our expenses. He explained that 'Uncle Arthur', as he subsequently always described the Guinness Company, would cover all lodging, travelling, and out of pocket expenses to, from, and during the course. He was absolutely right. 'Uncle Arthur' was an extremely generous host. One student, who travelled twice from and to Southampton by car, was able to pay to purchase the old Austin Seven that he had bought specially for the occasion.

I was the only student who had any previous experience or knowledge of bottling. Nevertheless, quite apart from the hospitality, I found the course both interesting and informative. However, during the second week of the course, students were taken into the bottling plant where they were given the opportunity to operate practically on the bottling line. The plant was of a very similar size to that at Dares Brewery on which I had learned to operate some seven years earlier. The problems and skills required were those with which I was well familiar. Within a few minutes, beer was swilling around the floor on which the crowning machine was being operated by the students. Fortunately, I had long since acquired the skills necessary to avoid this. Nevertheless, I learned subsequently that for all practical future exercises, machines and bottles were specially filled with water, and not beer.

Eventually, after passing the final exams back at the Brewing School, I left university and obtained full-time employment as a brewer. Unlike my contemporaries, it was eight years since I had entered the industry. Since leaving the army, I had been obliged to continue serving in the Territorial Army. This was not an onerous duty, and not only provided me with a small additional income and two weeks paid annual camp but also allowed me to obtain a civilian driving licence. Nevertheless, it would be another ten years before I owned a car. Whilst at university I had acquired many new friends. Some of them had served their national service, or if they were dental students, many were about to do so. Of all of my friends, I was the only one who had not left the service either with a commission, or as a sergeant in the education or Intelligence Corps. However, I was unique in having been a full bombardier three times.

Nevertheless, it was clear that I could always claim in the future that I was socially handicapped as a result of my failure in early life.

The Diploma in Malting and Brewing that I obtained from Birmingham University was not awarded until at least a year after the end of the three-year course. Students were required to pass an oral examination held by one of the head brewers of a large brewery. My oral examination was held by Danny

Wallace who was head brewer at the very large Ind Coope Brewery in Burton on Trent. He had a reputation of being somewhat strict. However, when I visited him, he welcomed me in an extremely friendly manner. He took me all around the brewery and bottling stores, asking me technical and practical questions that I had no difficulty in answering. Finally, he took me to the cooperage. At the time, almost all draft beer was delivered in oak casks. Coopers were the most highly skilled workers in breweries and had to serve a seven-year apprenticeship in order to qualify. All casks were made out of Memel Oak, the character and dimensions of which changed continuously throughout the life of the cask. The effect of this was that the capacity of a cask was constantly changing, due to the shrinkage of the wood. It was therefore a continuing task for coopers to keep changing the oak staves in order to repair and restore the full legal capacity of the casks. It was part of a head brewer's job to order and purchase all new timber. I had never heard of it being the role of a junior brewer. However, Danny Wallace handed me a couple of timber staves and asked me to compare them. Although I had spent a great deal of time in the cooperage during my time at Dares Brewery, I really had no idea of what to look for in choosing timber. Danny then explained that he hadn't really expected me to know that one of the staves was 'shivered' and should therefore be rejected. It was a term traditionally used by seafarers in the phrase 'Shiver my timbers'. Nevertheless, Danny said that I had passed the exam and done very well. In actual fact, I was never again required to judge the quality of oak cask timber. However, the knowledge proved to be invaluable to me in future years. Whenever I sat drinking in ancient pubs, which had exposed half-timbered ceiling beams, I could identify confidently which of the timbers were shivered.

Cape Hill Shift Brewer

When I returned to Cape Hill to take up my role as a full-time shift brewer, I was allocated initially to Number Two Brewery under the supervision of Walter Harper. However, after a few weeks, I was transferred to Number One Brewery, which I entered for the first time. My first mentor was Claude Smith. He was arguably the 'golden boy' of the seven shift brewers, since he was very slightly older, but by only by a few months, than his contemporaries Bill Hadley and Ted Grant. It was therefore considered, somewhat bizarrely, that eventually he would be promoted to become head brewer because of this 'seniority'. In reality, as I discovered subsequently, this made him overly cautious at all times. This was in contrast to Bill Hadley who was the only honours graduate, and Ted Grant who was the nephew of a previous somewhat notoriously unpopular 'Victorian' head brewer. The other two shift brewers were Bill Plowman and Geoff Woolons, of whom Bill was older and Geoff was slightly younger than him. Neither was considered eligible for the post of head brewer, although it would not be relevant for at least another twenty years.

The roles of the senior brewers at Cape Hill may not have been typical of large breweries. Bert Cox, the head brewer, never during my seven years at Cape Hill was ever seen in any of the breweries. Neither was he ever seen in a white coat. Indeed, he was very rarely seen in his office or anywhere else. All contact with him was through his secretary, whose job apparently involved keeping all records of all brewery activities. Mark Homer second or chief under-brewer also rarely, if ever, appeared in any brewery. However, like all other brewers, he always wore a white coat. His office was next to that of the head brewer to which it was connected by an internal door. His role was to prepare and monitor all brewery operations, forecast demand, and produce the weekly Brewing Program, upon which all brewing operations depended during the coming and present weeks. Equally importantly, he monitored and approved daily all operations, mandatorily recorded in the shift brewer's 'Pocket Book', which was carried at all times by the shift brewers in operational charge of all breweries. He had a rather mixed reputation. Before the Second World War, he was known to be a martinet, and there were many anecdotal stories of his past behaviour. However, following the end of the war, he had apparently joined a somewhat philanthropic movement called Moral Rearmament, after which he became a picture of benign tolerance. Bill Houghton was the third brewer and was directly in charge of all actual brewery operations, although he also rarely if ever appeared in any brewery. He was tall, very competent, and always extremely pleasant, friendly, and tolerant. He always, like all other brewers, wore a white coat. The fourth brewer was John Knox, a tall jovial Scottish extrovert. His role was totally unclear, although he apparently used to assist and deputise for the third brewer. He was somewhat obsequious and usually finished telephone conversations with his seniors with the immortal words, "Yes, sir. Right away, sir." Finally, there was Ronny Russell – an extremely amiable and pleasant brewer who very occasionally worked as a shift brewer. This was usually due to illness or shortages amongst the regular shift brewers. He was the most senior brewer to have served in the Second World War.

Claude Smith was the most 'senior' of the shift brewers, although there was no official hierarchy. Claude was very friendly, but he had a rather superior manner, presumably because he was considered to be the 'Crown Prince' who, many years in the future, would eventually become head brewer. Claude gave me an initial tour of Number One Brewery, which had an extremely complex constantly interchangeable plant. It consisted of a set of five mash-tuns, seven coppers, two hop-backs, eight collecting and fermenting rooms containing more than a hundred vessels, and two racking rooms. Any and every one of the dozen different types and quantity of brew could, and did, pass into through and out of all of this plant via any combination of routes and vessels. New brews were started every three hours at any time throughout the working week. During any shift usually, there would be at least fifteen beer brews being moved and processed, and fifty or sixty collecting and fermenting vessels to be inspected. The shift brewers were required to control and record all brews throughout the plant, using a 'Pocket Book', which was designed to fill exactly into the right-hand thigh pocket of their white coats. In addition, they had a small 'shield-shaped' pocket stitched specially to the coats above the right-hand pocket in order to carry a piece of white chalk. In every shift, the brewers were required to initiate, monitor, control, and collect all of the brews being processed, and record in the 'Pocket Book' the full details and progress of every brew. Apart from their white laboratory coats, shift brewers' 'standard' dress was a shirt, collar and tie, a very old and dilapidated pair of trousers, and equally distressed old shoes, all of which they changed when coming on or off shift. Shoes, trousers, and coats could be exposed during a shift to any combination of water, wort, beer, yeast, caustic soda, bleach, and sulphuric acid. As a result of these hazards, brewers were able to claim a 'clothing allowance' of twenty-five pounds of annual Income Tax Relief for the purchase of 'special protective clothing'. However, I did not own a pair of old worn-out shoes. I therefore ordered and purchased at a discount from the brewery stores a pair of industrial shoes. The structure and leather, and quality of these shoes were identical to that of regulation army boots, with which I had so recently been familiar. The only difference was that they were brown, had no ankles, and were reinforced with internal steel inside their toecaps. The result was that they were quite noisy, and I suppose somewhat unsurprisingly, I acquired the nickname of 'twinkle toes'. However, I regarded the clatter of these shoes to be very beneficial. I had on a previous occasion, whilst accompanied by the fermenting room foreman, accidentally discovered a worker smoking a cigarette. Needless to say, he was immediately 'sacked'. After I acquired my 'twinkle toes' shoes, I never again stumbled unexpectedly on any miscreant workers.

The mashing process was extremely traditional, and the process was entirely mechanical and manual and in the control of the shift brewer, with the mash room foreman in attendance. These foremen always wore white aprons, in contrast to the brewery foreman who wore a brown warehouse coat. Mashing consisted of mixing freshly crushed malt with hot liquor (treated water) to a mash at a predetermined temperature. The mashing temperature was one of the 'Holy Grails' of the Cape Hill brewing process. The brewer was required to achieve a 'mashing temperature' of precisely 'one fifty-one and a half' degrees Fahrenheit. This involved judging the correct mixture of hot and cold liquor (the 'striking temperature') and the mixture consistency as the mash entered the mash tun. Even a deviation of a quarter of a degree in the resultant mash was regarded as unsatisfactory by higher authority and would be marked with a 'red circle' when the pocket book was inspected by Mark Homer, the chief under-brewer'.

The overall control routine called 'taking tuns' involved a constant very fast walk from one room and floor to another, up and down ladders, and in some cases in and out of vessels. In the fermenting rooms, brewers were accompanied by the fermenting room 'charge hand' who carried a copper sampling can on the end of a long brass handle and a short ladder to enable the brewer to climb up to the inspection thresholds of high vessels. The brewer carried the fermenting book and a glass sacharometer. He also had to chalk any necessary processing details and instructions on slates attached to the processing vessels and record details in the books and documents used by departmental foremen. There were three 'charge hands' whose characters and characteristics varied considerably. The time required was usually between thirty and forty minutes and depended only partly on the number of vessels to be examined but also on the agility and performance of the 'tun man'. Billy Bates was regarded as the 'speed king', and brewers always hoped he would be on their shift. In contrast, Tommy Barnes was a pleasant but asthmatic geriatric and usually would take almost twice as long. Charlie Deddicot in contrast had been in the Royal Navy and always clumped around the fermenting rooms amiably in his leather ex-wartime sea boots up to his knees in a most steady, solid, and reliable manner.

Every possible movement throughout the brewery was the direct responsibility of the shift brewer. As an exercise in 'multi-tasking', there has never been in my subsequent experience, nor have I ever observed any management exercise, or process control, to compare with it. This also explains why I was never allowed to enter Number One Brewery in the previous six years. It is unsurprising that few brewers over the age of forty ever worked in Number One Brewery. Most essentially, the 'shift brewer in charge' had to enter, on time, the necessary details of each brew in the Excise Book in the Excise Office. There were two excise men, one of whom, Mr Jordan, was popularly known as 'Jordy'. He had been an observer in the Royal Flying Corps in the First World War. He was most amiable and used to walk around the various vessels with his spectacles half way down his nose and reciting aloud the details he was writing down in his Excise Book. He once related to me that as a flying observer in scout planes during the war, unlike pilots who wore flying-helmets, observers were issued with regulation army steel helmets, popularly known as 'tin hats'. It was standard practice for observers to sit on their steel helmet rather than wear them on their heads. He explained that bullets from enemy aircraft usually came from below rather than above the plane. In contrast, the other excise officer was in his late twenties and was the only complete alcoholic that I ever met in the brewing industry. As well as part of his brewery duties and a plentiful supply of beer, he would visit at night the adjacent Wine and Spirit stores to which he had a key and imbibe sherry. He rarely concealed his problem, and once demonstrated to me that in a morning whilst attempting to write in the Excise Book, he could write all numerical data with one hand but required both hands in order to write number eight digits.

The most demanding shift of the whole brewing cycle at Number One Brewery, in contrast to Number Two Brewery, was 'Nights'. This was a sixty-hour week consisting of six consecutive nights starting on Sunday from ten o'clock at night until eight o'clock the following morning. This sequence was worked in turn every four weeks by the five Number One Brewery brewers. However, the whole nineteen-week, very complex brewers' cycle averaged out to a thirty-six-hour week. I took careful account of this fact when I subsequently applied for positions at other breweries. The most difficult night was, for some reason, on Mondays. It was then that I learned the art of meal timing. The brewer could either eat early, when he was not hungry, or very late when he was 'starving'. I was to discover twenty years later, that a similar problem affected firemen. Occasionally, as a result of the retirement of older brewers, a number of middle-aged, experienced brewers were recruited. For some reason, none of these, along with the two permanent shift brewers at Number Two Brewery, were regarded as being eligible for eventual promotion as Day Brewers. A couple of years after I became a shift brewer, a forty-year-old brewer was recruited to work in Number One Brewery. He left his work in the middle of a nightshift some months later – traumatised, and never to return. However, after a few weeks of supervision by the other shift brewers, I was finally 'passed out' to work my own shift, which I continued to do for the next three years.

Geoff Woolons was a Yorkshireman and became my closest friend among my fellow brewers. He had been in the Parachute Regiment and had served in Palestine during the terrorist activity immediately after the Second World War. He was the youngest of my fellow shift brewers, and I was extremely fond of him. He, like all of the other brewers, owned a motor car – a Ford Anglia. On a number of occasions, I was taken with his wife and two young daughters for picnics beside the River Severn. The two children repeatedly demonstrated the fact that I was incapable of either catching or throwing a ball. It was a handicap that remained with me for the rest of my life. Every few months, Geoff and I were on night shift at the same time, with one of us at each brewery. Sunday and Wednesday nights were both quiet brewing nights. On these occasions, we somehow gained a reputation for creating an unusually substantial number of empty pint Albright bottles, and leaving them for collection outside the Brewers' Mess. We also tried to explore the extremely difficult technique of how to handle and consume a 'yard of ale' from the novelty antique glass item displayed on the wall in the Brewers' Mess. However, eventually we only practised with water, in order to prevent any unnecessary loss of genuine ale.

One of the essential features of work as a shift brewer was the requirement to do frequent arithmetic calculations in order to instruct necessary dilutions of the wort at various stages in the brewing process. Whilst most of the other brewers carried out these calculations effortlessly and reliably, I was prone to make the occasional mistake. Such errors were regarded by the senior brewers as inexcusable. My solution was to use a slide rule, in the manipulation of which I had become highly skilled whilst studying engineering at university. Unfortunately, conventional slide rules were about ten inches long and couldn't possibly have fitted into the breast pocket of a brewer's coat. I therefore acquired a somewhat esoteric but equally accurate version known as having a 'pi-displaced' split scale, which was only five inches long. This fitted inconspicuously into the breast pocket of my white brewing coat and enabled me to check my calculations reliably. I discovered subsequently that Ted Grant, a fellow shift brewer, used a similarly convenient small circular plastic calculator, which he had acquired as a bomber navigator in the RAF during the Second World War.

Despite having been with the company for some years, neither I nor any other shift brewers were ever given the opportunity to work in or visit the Bottling Plant or other parts of the site. However, I enjoyed thoroughly my three years as a shift brewer and was seriously dismayed at the thought of having eventually to work from 'nine to five'. After a short time as a shift brewer, I became interested in work study. This had become a major national issue, promoted and publicised widely by the government and the newly established 'British Institute of Management' commonly known as the 'BIM'. They had produced a number of informational and educational booklets on this and associated subjects. They also created an examination and qualification that was regarded as equal to a university 'ordinary' degree. I started to attend management classes at Aston Technical College, which later became Aston University. I eventually obtained there a Diploma Certificate in Management. I had always had a keen interest in engineering and had enjoyed thoroughly my second year at Birmingham University in mechanical engineering, electrical engineering, heat engines, machine drawing, and geology. In order to reinforce these subjects, I also enrolled at Handsworth Technical College where I studied for a National Certificate in engineering. The staff at the college had, unlike those at Birmingham University, all been practising engineers in most parts of the trades and industries that existed in Birmingham. Their past practical experience was invaluable in their teaching, from which I benefitted greatly. In particular, I found that the precise measuring techniques, lathe work, and the qualities and heat treatment of metals to be invaluable in future years. The syllabus also contained a great deal of mathematics in what to me were obscure and rather abstruse spheres. In particular, I struggled with the concepts of 'compound angles' such as 'sine A plus sine B equals?'. The understanding of differential calculus continued also to evade me. Rather sadly, after two years, I eventually gave in and abandoned the course.

Partly as a result of my 'extramural' activities, I began to see how they could be applied to brewing and began to chart all of the mains and pipework of the two breweries. This was unbelievably complex and had never been attempted before – even the engineers department had no record either simple or comprehensive of many parts of the pipe layouts. As a result of my efforts, which were viewed with mild interest by the other brewers, they acknowledged that it was a unique first attempt. However, as a result, one of my few triumphs at Cape Hill was the advent of the 'Suez Crisis'. For a number of months, fuel oil became unobtainable. The seven coppers at 'Number One Brewery' were heated and boiled by oil burners, whilst the three at Number Two Brewery were heated by steam coils supplied with steam from the nearby coal-fired Boiler House. There was a serious potential danger that the brewery production might have to have to be restricted. I had discovered in my survey of the piping network that there were two four-inch copper pipes, otherwise known as 'mains' that connected Number Two Brewery to Number One Brewery, which was a quarter of a mile away down the hill. No one had any idea when or why these pipes had been installed, and apparently, I was the first person to rediscover or be aware of them. The chief engineer confirmed that they could indeed enable mild ale to be brewed in Number Two Brewery and pumped from the hop backs down to the Fermenting Room of Number One Brewery. My 'discovery' enabled full production at the two breweries to continue until the end of the 'Suez Crisis'. Shortly after the crisis, Mitchells and Butlers were granted the Royal Warrant and were allowed to display the Royal Coat of Arms on the cab doors of all of their lorries. I felt quite proud to be working for such a distinguished company.

My only other enterprise whilst at Cape Hill was the invention of a pipe coupling. I had dreamed up the idea whilst at university on how to produce a simple hygienic method of connecting three inch 'mains' or pipes. These were used extensively throughout the collecting, fermenting, and conditioning rooms. These copper pipes had threaded brass collars with two large lugs on their perimeter. The pipes were either male or female 'handed' at each end. A 'grommet' of thick string was used to seal the joints. The pipes were constantly being coupled and uncoupled in order to run wort or beer into different vessels. The lugs were hammered and battered violently with heavy rubber mallets to couple and uncouple them. The frequent leaks that occurred were remedied by a further beating of the lugs. I had decided that this was not only remarkably primitive and labour intensive but was also potentially unhygienic. I therefore designed a hygienic universal union with a neat 'snap' coupling, which required no hammers or spanners to join it. I had it provisionally patented, and I designed and had it manufactured it as the 'Superex' Sealed Union'. Its design, development, and manufacture gave me a wonderful unique opportunity to visit a number of small engineering companies in Birmingham. I learned a great deal of basic manufacturing knowledge from this experience. I had the union tested at Birmingham University Engineering laboratories, and it performed faultlessly. Unfortunately, it suffered from two fatal disadvantages. Although the hygienic round-section rubber seal was simple to insert in vertical pipes, it was difficult to insert in horizontal pipes. Since most of the pipes in breweries were horizontal, this made it impractical for the frequent coupling and uncoupling required for pipes in fermenting rooms. Secondly, it was much lighter and more compact than the clumsy threaded unions that were currently in use. If these were to be replaced, it also therefore required the pipe to be replaced by a slightly longer one. My enterprise, perhaps fortunately, for my future careers therefore failed. However, I was somewhat amused some years later to be shown a 'brand new' design of stainless-steel union by the brewery engineering firm APV. It was clearly a close copy of my original 'Superex' sealed union.

One of my best friends in Birmingham was Brian Lee, a fellow Brewing School student who had become an assistant brewer at Davenports, the smallest of local breweries. The owner was so-called 'Baron' Davenport who had sold all but four of their public houses in Birmingham. He had reinvested the money in small delivery vans, which were the size of large 'milk floats'. From these, Davenports provided a weekly 'home delivery' service at a competitive price to any customers who required them. The beer was all bottled, always in specially designed bottles, and supplied in unique wooden crates containing half a dozen bottles. This effectively prevented empty bottles or crates being returned to other breweries. Brian and I subsequently used to exchange part of our beer allowances in order to provide him with a wider variety of beers. On one occasion, I was curious as to how Davenports could provide 'home delivered' beer at such a competitive price. I measured the contents of a bottle and discovered that it was less than the conventional volume of a 'pint'. The other probably unique feature of the brewery was that it backed on to the Birmingham to Worcester Canal and from which malt was delivered. However, the narrow-boat barges were all unloaded manually by prisoners from the local Birmingham Winson Green Jail. Whilst at Brewing School Brian had lived in what were probably the most luxurious lodgings of any student. It was in Metchley Park, a most exclusive part of Edgbaston close to the university. The house backed on to the canal, and during his stay there, Brian built a small rowing boat out of a sheet of 'eight foot by four foot' marine plywood. Dick Stockland was one of my many Dental School friends, and he and I used to join Brian in exploring the canal. After leaving Dental School, Dick bought himself a genuine canal 'narrow boat', which provided a wonderful leisure activity. The house in which Brian was living was occupied and owned by the widow of a judge and their three daughters. Brian later married the youngest of these, and they and my future wife and I remained life-long friends. Soon after I left university and began my fully paid employment, I had decided that it was time to prepare for having a home of my own. I therefore decided to take out an Endowment Life Insurance Policy for two thousand pounds. This should enable me to be able to use it in due course to obtain a mortgage. At the time, new two-bedroom bungalows in Harborne were no more than two thousand five hundred pounds. However, as this was more than four times of my then current salary, it presented a distant prospect. Uncle Rex was shocked and said that a young man of my age should not to be entering financial commitments so soon. I should be saving my money in the bank. However, an insurance agent visited me to record my personal details for my application for my Endowment Insurance Policy. One of the questions he had to ask was how much alcohol I drank on average. I replied that I only drank beer, on average about four or five per day. He looked somewhat surprised and decided that he would record 'Occasional beer drinking'. It was a masterly interpretation of the English language. With only a slight stretch of the imagination, it might be possible to interpret the dictionary definition of 'occasional' as ' intended for particular occasions' as appropriate. The daily routine of brewers always involved particular occasions.

An unfortunate event occurred on one occasion when I was returning home after lunch from my morning shift at Cape Hill. I was cycling along my normal route through an exceptionally quiet residential part of Edgbaston. At the bottom of the long gentle hill of Rotten Park Road was a road intersection where I turned left onto the equally residential main road. Both roads were deserted. As I turned left, I heard a shout coming from behind me on the main road. At first, I ignored it and continued pedalling. After a few hundred yards, a very young policeman on a bicycle caught up with me. He officiously told me that I had failed to stop at the intersection and that he would have to report my offence. I explained that there was no traffic, which he then pointed out was irrelevant. A few days later, I received a letter from the chief constable of Birmingham, no less. It stated that '…in contravention of the Road Traffic Act, I had committed an offence. On this occasion no further action would be taken, but it would be kept on Police Record.' It is to my eternal regret that I never kept this unique document as a trophy or had it framed.

In my second year as a shift brewer, I went on annual holiday leave to the Scilly Isles with my ex-Brewing School friend Dave Barnard. He had just left a brewery in Ulster and was waiting to take up his new post at Whitbread's Brewery in Chiswell Street in London. Our visit to the Scillies was preceded by the delivery of my monthly beer allowance. As a shift brewer, I was entitled to have my beer allowance delivered monthly, normally to my home address. The allowance amounted to the equivalent value of the price of a four and a half gallon cask of mild ale. Bizarrely, married brewers were entitled twice that quantity. The arcane logic behind this rule I always found difficult to discover. However, I had arranged my allowance for that month to be four dozen pint bottles of 'Albright Ale' to be delivered 'c/o The Harbourmaster, St Marys, Isles of Scilly'. The 'allowance' was delivered in two huge wooden cases. Dave and I duly collected the heavy crates from the quayside. We covered the two cases discreetly with my green army 'Poncho' cape and staggered with them between us back to our lodgings. Dave then explained to our landlady that we had collected some 'advance excess luggage' and politely asked whether we could store it somewhere. We were duly offered an outside garden shed for the purpose. The most notable event of this, my first proper annual holiday, was that at mealtimes in our lodging house I was seated beside an attractive young woman called Shirley. She was the same age as me. Dave had explained to me that she was an Olympic long-jumper, who had just won a Bronze Medal for the British national team in Helsinki. Although Dave had a keen interest in sport, I had absolutely none and simply noted it mentally as 'well done'. However, I discovered that her name was Shirley and that she lived in Croydon. It occurred to me that it might be worthwhile meeting this young woman on my regular 'long-weekend' visits to my parents in London. I subsequently met her in London and on one occasion introduced her to the delights of Wagner's Valkyrie at the Covent Garden Royal Opera House. She managed to survive this ordeal. She also came up to Birmingham to spend a weekend with me in my flat in Edgbaston. The sequel to these events was that Shirley and I decided, one Saturday lunchtime in a teashop in Barnes, to get married. I returned to Birmingham, where I revealed this to one of my great dental friends 'Coke' Lloyd. His nickname was not in any way associated with drug taking, but the fact that apparently his head looked like a coconut when he surfaced in a swimming pool. His response was immediate. He told me that I would be an absolute fool not to marry Shirley. It was the second time in my lifetime that I ever took any notice of anyone else's advice. The previous occasion was my Uncle Rex's advice, over ten years earlier, that I should become a brewer. Six months later, I married this young woman. It was a rather short courtship, and Shirley's father took me to his local pub and enquired whether there was any biological reason for our haste to get married. However, I explained that in order for me to receive a married persons' income tax rebate (of £37) we needed to get married at the beginning of April. My long-time Birmingham ex-university dental student girlfriend Odille was not amused by my engagement. However, her widowed mother who had feared the prospect of her daughter marrying me was no doubt greatly relieved.

My marriage had serious implications for my brewing career. I was living in a flat just on the borders of the respectable part of Edgbaston. It was half of the ground floor of a detached Victorian House, sharing a toilet, and with a bath hidden beside the sink in a narrow passageway that served as a kitchen. As an aftermath of the Second World War, all housing at that time was still in very short supply, and there were still large bombed areas in Birmingham. Mitchells and Butlers provided two or three semi-dilapidated flats for a small number of married junior brewers, all of who had small children. However, I was advised that no accommodation would be available for me in the foreseeable future. The other contemporary change was that of the Chairman 'Bob' Butler. He was the model of an old-time benign employer. Each Christmas all brewers were called to the boardroom, where married brewers were presented with a turkey and unmarried ones received an equivalent cheque. He had been summarily replaced by Alan Walker, who was commonly believed to be a 'financial wizard' but was also a 'hatchet man' from the insurance industry. He soon began to display his talents. Bob Butler retired, and Peter Butler the new young managing director left the company abruptly, as did Clive Orham, the very talented assistant bottling manager. Apparently, both Peter Butler and Clive Orham who was the deputy bottling manager had views that differed from those of Alan Walker. Finally, Alan Walker stated that all future home beer allowances, which at that time were based on their total volume, rather than their money value, would include any increases in excise duty. In other words, when the excise duty went up, the allowance would be reduced. Such excise increases had been commonplace during the previous years. Ironically, and unprecedentedly, the next budget statement of excise duty announced a reduction instead of an increase in the duty. Inevitably, Walker did not increase the beer allowance correspondingly. Similarly, turkeys which were normally given to all married brewers at Christmas apparently were not considered to be necessary or appropriate.

My normal personal transport relied almost entirely on my trusty Raleigh Lenton bicycle, but Shirley had no such facility. However, at Birmingham University Edgbaston campus, there was a large totally enclosed cycle shed for students, The 'shed' was part of the Student Union building, I was aware that at the end of each academic year, students were required to remove all of their cycles after the beginning of the vacation. Any cycles that were not removed by their owners were taken away and scrapped by the janitors shortly before the beginning of the next academic year. There were usually five or ten cycles left by students each year. Presumably, their owners were unable or unwilling or unable to pay to take them home to other parts of the country. I visited the premises in the middle of the vacation and selected an excellent BSA Ladies Cycle with a Sturmey-Archer four-speed gear. I took it back to our flat, stripped it down, reassembled it, and then gave it magnanimously to Shirley. We were now a two-cycle family. I realised that the specification of her four-speed cycle was not up to my six-speed model. However, I chauvinistically considered that as a World Class Olympic Medallist, she should have no difficulty in keeping up with me.

Colin Allport, the second brewer at Davenports, was slightly older than Brian Lee and me. He and his wife lived in a brewery house. Shortly after Shirley and I were married, he invited Brian, Margaret, Shirley, and me to dinner. The house was fairly modern and had a pleasant dining room. When we all sat down to dinner, our host had a bottle of red wine on the table and poured us each a glass with which to accompany our meal. The meal and wine were excellent, as we afterwards commented. On the way home, we four guests were discussing the very hospitable and enjoyable evening. However, we were all appalled by the ridiculous 'pretentious behaviour' of our host. He had actually provided 'a bottle of wine on the table' at the meal. During the 1950s, we considered that no normal person should have dreamed of doing such a thing at home. Consumption of wine was normally limited to visits to expensive restaurants.

My fixed six-year contract of employment was due to expire within a couple of months. By this time, the annual salary which had been agreed six years earlier had fallen some way behind the general market salaries of brewers of my age. I had hoped that I would have been approached officially to review the end of my contract and offered a new one. However, this had not occurred, and I decided that it was time to explore the market and look for another employer. At least I might find out what I was really worth.

St Helens

At that time, brewers' posts were advertised widely in the monthly IBG Journal. Furthermore, the IBG Directory gave full details of the location and all staff in every brewery in the country. I obtained interviews in South Wales and in London. Courage Barclay at London Bridge were advertising for a shift brewer at their adjacent Barclay Perkins site. The Courage's head brewer was dressed immaculately in a city business suit, but appeared to know little in answer to my questions about the pattern or length of working hours, or conditions of his shift brewers. He called in a more junior brewer from who I established that I would be working for longer hours at marginally more pay – and more importantly, with no living accommodation provided, or available anywhere near the brewery. I would have to commute, almost certainly by rail, the cost of which was significant. Also, during part of the shift cycle, I would have to sleep overnight in the brewery. At the end of the interview, I was offered my travelling expenses, which were collected by a clerk wearing an equally immaculate city suit. I was later offered the job by post. Taylor Walkers at Brick Lane also offered me a job with a similar work pattern and salary.

Finally, I saw an advertisement for Greenall Whitley's at St Helens in Lancashire. I had never heard of St Helens, but one morning when I was fast asleep, having just returned from my night shift, I was woken by the telephone next to my bed. The call was from Mr Collis, head brewer at St Helens. He invited me to come up and see him. He suggested eleven o'clock, and I asked him how to get there, and how long he thought it might take. He replied that he thought it would be about two or three hours up the A6 road. He seemed slightly surprised to discover that I had not got a car, but I agreed to find out the train times and let him know. My journey from Liverpool on the branch line to St Helens was an interesting experience. The scenery gradually became less urban and more rural until I reached the pleasant small station of Thatto Heath. I was sitting in the front carriage, with a wide unobstructed view over the shoulder of the driver – a feature of the new short-distance diesel trains of the period. Just beyond the station, we left a grass-lined cutting, which revealed the top of a long incline and a panoramic view down into St Helens. The scene was a startling contrast, reminiscent of Durer engravings of manufacturing towns in Victorian times during the Industrial Revolution. The town was totally dominated by a number of factories with tall chimneys, all belching out a pall of black and yellow smoke. A pale cloud of smog hung over the town.

I was ushered into the head brewer's office by a small fifteen-year-old boy, who again reminded me of urchin characters from Dickens novels. I was greeted by the Head Brewer Eric Collis, a tall distinguished looking gentleman, who I subsequently discovered always wore his white coat and never fastened the buttons. With the air of a hovering seagull, he extended his arm and shook my hand, and offered me a seat. He politely enquired some very basic questions about my present occupation, but it soon became clear that apart from the obvious pleasantries, he had absolutely no idea what to ask me. However, after a very short time, he telephoned 'Freddy' to come up and join us. Freddy Lanfear, the second brewer, was an extremely pleasant and amiable middle-aged man with a walrus moustache. As Freddy entered the door, he was greeted by Mr Collis who stood up and introduced me. Before Freddy closed the door, Mr Collis followed with the totally unexpected words, "Freddy – I think Mr Berry will like it here with us." After a few more pleasantries and references to the job, he then went on to offer me accommodation in a small ten-year-old bungalow in Thatto Heath that had been designed and owned by the brewery architect who was now retiring. When I accepted the job, the brewery would buy the bungalow for me. In fact, the salary was slightly less than the London offers, but nearly fifty percent more than my then current Cape Hill shift salary. Mr Collis then wrote a small note and rang for Sidney, the diminutive urchin who had delivered me. When Sidney arrived, the head brewer gave the memorable instruction to 'Go over the yard and take this note to the company secretary and bring back Mr Berry's expenses. DO NOT LOOSE THEM on the way back.' The contrast between my visits to Courage and Barclays and Taylor Walkers in London and that to St Helens could not possibly have been greater. When I returned to Birmingham, I promptly accepted the Greenall Whitley offer and declined the two London ones.

After accepting the new job, I was asked to visit St Helens again but invited to bring my wife to see the new bungalow. This we duly did, and we were unbelievably delighted. It was a charming detached bungalow on a very secluded quiet road in Thatto Heath. The back garden was overlooked by banks of Rhododendrons. Freddy Lanfear lived a few doors away and had offered for me to call him at any time if we needed any help. We were invited to suggest any alteration to the bungalow that we might require. Shirley commented that the kitchen was rather small, and the estates director promptly agreed to have a new larger one constructed. In the meantime, Shirley had arranged to be transferred from her Bank of England job in Birmingham to a similar one at the Bank in Liverpool.

I continued with my shift-brewing role at Cape Hill until the end of my contract but spent a great deal of leisure time creating and acquiring basic furniture items for our future home in St Helens. Our only joint possessions were wedding presents – a double bed given by my brother-in-law and a cocktail cabinet given by my fellow brewers. We had bought half a dozen very elegant high-quality Gordon Russell dining chairs. We couldn't afford the Gordon Russell table, so I had built an eight-foot long dining table to match. The furniture was to last us for the rest of our lives. I had built also a large 'state of the art' hi-fi system with an amplifier, cabinet containing a record player and FM radio tuner, a separate large speaker enclosure with a twelve-inch Hi-fi dual-cone speaker, and an eight-foot dining table. We had also bought an electric kettle. Our other treasure was Waterford Cut-glass. Shirley's sister Molly's had bought us some a dozen sherry glasses of Waterford glass as a wedding present. Shirley and I set out to acquire over time a full collection of all types of these beautiful treasures. Eventually, any one of these would cost over a hundred pounds each. Finally, we were to acquire a full set of glasses, which cost some thousands of pounds. Ironically, sixty years later, equally elegant sets of genuine cut-glasses were to be found in charity shops for less than a pound each.

When I finally left Cape Hill, almost all of the brewers congratulated me warmly but were surprised and perhaps disappointed. However, when I finally went to see Bert Cox, I explained that my main motive was to find decent accommodation for my wife and me. He was somewhat less than sympathetic, although he 'wished me well' and invited me to return to visit him and the brewery at any time in the future. In fact, I never returned to the brewery, and when I next met him at a Birmingham Brewing School Dinner, he was very definitely less than friendly. Nevertheless, I have always regarded my nine years as a brewer at Cape Hill as some of the most valuable and formative of my brewing career.

There were four other brewers at St Helens. Eric Collis was in his early sixties and had been a pilot in the Royal Flying Corps in France throughout the First World War. Fred Lanfear was in his late forties, had been in the Eighth Army in North Africa and Italy during the Second World War. The third brewer, John Chutes, was in his sixties and had been at Gallipoli in the First World War. His role appeared to consist of keeping brewing records and acting as a reserve shift brewer. I later learned that he was viewed with some reservation by Eric Collis and Fred Lanfear since he was apparently separated from his wife but was living with 'another woman'. The other shift brewer, Reg White, was in his late thirties and had been a prisoner of war throughout the Second World War. Perhaps unsurprisingly, he tended to be rather quiet and reserved. I was the only brewer among the St Helens brewers who had been to university. I was also the only brewer who had not been in either world war, although I had been in the army in Hong Kong. Nevertheless, I was unquestionably the 'baby' of the brewing staff. Reg White never talked about his wartime experiences, but John Chutes recalled life in Gallipoli. Apparently, unlike France and the Western Front opposing trenches were on a steep hillside and extremely close to one another. There was relatively little artillery bombardment, but a great deal of sniping and throwing grenades between trenches. Warfare consisted almost entirely of infantry raids between opposing trenches. So close were the trenches that the occupants could hear their opponents talking, and in between raids even used to throw corned beef cans and other debris at one another.

The maximum output at St Helens was approximately six thousand barrels per week, and they produced a surprising variety of draught and bottled ales and stouts. The St Helens brewery was little more than half of the size of Number Two Brewery at Cape Hill. The working procedures for the shift brewers at St Helens were in total contrast to those at Cape Hill. At Cape Hill Number One Brewery, shift brewers had to walk or even run frantically to give instructions, check plant and vessels, and record the movement, and monitor the progress of at least twenty or thirty brews on every shift. At St Helens, the only one or two brews of the day were moved by foremen or charge hands, and only checked in a relatively leisurely fashion by the brewers when informed. Samples were always brought to the brewer, rather than having to obtain them for himself.

In contrast to living in Birmingham and working at Cape Hill, life in St Helens was leisurely and very satisfying. Shirley enjoyed her work at the Bank of England in Liverpool and made many friends. Living on our own detached bungalow was a joy. I had not lived in a comparable home environment – only in lodgings, since twenty years earlier, before the Second World War. There were only two shifts at St Helens – morning and afternoon. Reg White and I were the only shift brewers. The morning shift from Monday to Friday started at six o'clock and finished officially at two o'clock. In reality, it finished before noon, followed by drinks in the sample cellar and lunch in a tiny dining room big enough only for the shift brewer. The afternoon shift began at two o'clock on Monday and until Friday and finished at about eight or nine o'clock each evening. The afternoon brewer also visited the brewery briefly on Saturday afternoon and Sunday evenings. A 'long weekend' for each brewer occurred every fortnight from Friday two o'clock to Monday at the same time. My only disappointment at St Helens was that there was no brewers' home allowance of beer. Instead, Freddie Lanfear assured me that I should regard the sample cellar as my 'personal club' and was free to bring any friends or guests to it at any time in the evenings and weekends. It was only after a few weeks that I revealed to Freddy Lanfear that my wife was an Olympic Medallist. He immediately told the other brewers, and when I next met the head brewer, he said that none of the brewers had realised how 'special' were their new 'young people'.

Humphrey Griffiths who was the managing director used regularly to join the brewers in the brewery sample cellar at lunchtime. He was married in to the family of Lord Daresbury who was one of the owners of the brewery. He often regaled us with stories of the history of the brewery. One such story concerned a past company secretary who apparently used to become confused between the ownership of the company's revenue and his own pocket money. Humphrey explained that after the 'third' time that this had been revealed, the company really felt that he and they should part company.

A most curious social feature of the town of St Helens was that along with two or three others in Lancashire the population was almost equally divided between Protestants and Roman Catholics. This created issues which permeated even Greenall Whitley's, who sought to demonstrate complete impartiality. One of the results was that the company secretary belonged to one faith, whilst the office manager belonged to the other. They recruited new staff in turn and were able to recognise their faith by the school to which the applicant had been educated. When the duty shift brewer was asked by foremen to authorise overtime, it was inevitably assumed that the candidates would be of the same faith as the foreman of that department. Another local feature was that the bottling plant operators were mainly young single girls and middle-aged married women. The brewery pursued a policy which required girls to leave their employment if and when they got married. They were allowed to return if they wished, if and when they reached middle age. Presumably, this avoided the necessity of granting leave of absence in the event of their becoming pregnant. In the 1950 era, employment legislation was rather limited.

Unlike Cape Hill, where morning shifts began at eight o'clock, I now had to get up at five o'clock every morning on alternate weeks in order to begin the six o'clock mash. Cycling down Croppers Hill in winter in the ice and snow could be a somewhat hazardous exercise. However, both a cooked breakfast and lunch were provided for the morning brewer if required, The Brewers' Dining Room at St Helens differed completely from the luxurious Brewers' Mess at Cape Hill. It was a small room containing a three-foot long table and two chairs. Breakfasts and lunches were brought to the room by a female catering assistant from the Brewery Canteen on the other side of the yard. The morning brewers used the room for breakfast and occasionally for lunch. John Chutes and the morning brewers used to go home for lunch. On one cold winter morning for some reason, Fred Lanfear joined me for breakfast, and we were served with sausage and mash. When it arrived, he took a mouthful of sausage and turned to the dinner lady. His rather disapproving instruction was, "Kindly, take this back to the cook and ask her to put some 'heat' into these sausages." I had some difficulty in keeping a straight face.

In complete contrast to my duties as a brewer at Cape Hill, I was allowed and actively encouraged at St Helens to spend time in the other departments, especially the bottling plant and stores. There was a small sample room in the stores which was visited only occasionally by brewers. I requested that a sample shelf with both daylight and artificial illumination should be installed. I soon discovered that the premium highly regarded bottle beer called 'Champion Pale Ale' began to develop and show a haze after only ten days. This was despite the fact that we were adding an expensive anti-haze enzymic ingredient supplied by an allied trader. I arranged with Horace Cunliffe, the bottling manager, with whom I got on extremely well, to carry out a short bottling run without the ingredient. Samples from the run lasted for over six weeks without displaying any haze. The head brewer was more impressed than disturbed and agreed to refer it to the suppliers and not to add the discredited ingredient. More importantly, he agreed to my request to install a mechanical 'Bottle Tapper' to a crowning machine in order to demonstrate that this inexpensive device significantly reduced the air content of bottles and enhanced their 'shelf life'. As a result of my efforts, the 'shelf life' of 'Champion Pale Ale' was extended to between eight and ten weeks. I also took an interest in the Greenall Whitley bottled stout. In the light of my routine experience back at Cape Hill, I knew that a small quantity of common salt was added to Mitchells and Butlers' stouts. Eric Collis agreed to try this as an experiment. The following year, the brewery submitted the 'Champion Pale Ale' and their 'Oatmeal Stout' to the Annual Brewers' Exhibition in London. We were all disappointed that the pale ale did not win any awards; however, the stout was awarded a third prize. My other major achievement at St Helens was in pest control. During my army service in Hong Kong, I had been selected randomly and sent compulsorily on a two-week civilian pest control course in Kowloon. I was able to apply this rare knowledge to controlling and largely eliminating a huge cockroach infestation that I had encountered and revealed for the first time in the brewery Mash Room. The senior brewers were unaware of the problem because it only became apparent at six o'clock in the morning when steam was applied to the mash tuns. Reg White had never bothered to mention this. On my next visit to London, I obtained a paper on cockroaches from the Natural History Museum. As a result of my new knowledge, I therefore arranged for a number of extravagant applications of the then new pesticide of Gamma BHC to be obtained and applied by the Mash Room foreman. This continued for some weeks. On each occasion, this left the floor beneath the mash tuns covered in a half-inch thick carpet of dead and dying cockroaches of both breeds.

Oliver Griffin was one of our great friends from Birmingham Brewing School. Shirley and I spent our first annual holiday from St Helens at his parents' home in East Suffolk. They owned a pub in a small village, which consisted of a main street with a stream running through a ford halfway along it. Oliver's parents wished to go on holiday, and Shirley and I were invited to run the pub during his parents' absence. I was delighted at the opportunity, not only of a free holiday but more importantly to obtain experience in running a pub. This was something that very few brewers ever did, or could get the opportunity of doing. The pub was a 'Free' pub, which meant that it was not 'tied' to any particular brewery company. This would provide me, as a brewer, with a unique advantage compared with 'tied' pubs, since it was selling a wide range of beers from other companies. I would be able to sample and compare all of these. However, whilst this feature gave great independence to the landlord, we discovered later that it also had a practical social disadvantage. Unlike 'tied' pubs, which received deliveries once or twice a week, 'free' pubs received at least four times as many deliveries. These deliveries could come at any time of the day. This resulted in the publican being unable to leave the premises completely closed and unoccupied at any time throughout the week. Nevertheless, running and managing a pub for two weeks was a unique and invaluable experience, a unique holiday, and absolutely cost free. Perhaps unsurprisingly, unlike most subsequent family holidays, my beer consumption continued at a normal brewer's level.

I had been attending an evening course in management at the local Technical College. Although I was learning the subject, I soon realised that it was not up to the level of my previous certificate obtained at Aston Technical College in Birmingham. After a few months, I abandoned the course. My only other contact with brewers was on occasional visits from Malcolm Donald, the head brewer of Magee Marshalls, who were part of the Greenall Whitley 'empire' in Lancashire. Most curiously, I never met any brewers from Greenall Whitley's at Warrington, which was only nine miles away. Even more surprising was the fact that although the Warrington Brewery was almost the same size as that at St Helens, there was absolutely no similarity between any of the beers of the two breweries. There was rarely, if ever, any communication between any staff of the two breweries. Warrington might just as well have been a completely separate rival firm.

My domestic life in the bungalow in Thatto Heath was idyllic. Shirley was earning a generous salary at the Bank of England in Liverpool, and we had begun to acquire the necessary furnishing and fittings for a very comfortable home. This had been helped by our being able to purchase almost everything at heavily discounted prices, directly from a local high-quality furniture supplier who were contracted to furnish all of Greenall Whitley's pubs. Our only St Helens friends were the Brewery Chief Engineer Bill Marsden and his wife, who were older than Shirley and me and had no children. The rest of our friends were all found through Shirley at the bank, most of who lived in or near Liverpool. The husband of one of Shirley's friend June was Owen Pugh who worked at the Atomic Energy Authority on the Wirral on the other side of the Mersey. He later moved to Dounreay as head of the atomic plant there. He was a physicist and gave me most helpful knowledge about the installation and heat balance of domestic heating. I would benefit very profitable from this in the years to come.

Unfortunately, whilst cycling up Croppers Hill on my way home from the brewery I lost the Rolex watch that I had bought in Hong Kong. This loss may have been influenced by my having indulged too freely in the brewery sample cellar. Apart from occasional weekend visits to see our parents, Shirley and I had only one holiday. We went to Austria via France with our friends June and Owen Pugh and returned via Switzerland, where I bought another Rolex watch at a very favourable price. The watch was a rather better model than my previous one. I bought the watch without a bracelet, which I thought was expensive, and fixed the watch to my thigh with sticking plaster, in order to evade customs duty. I then bought a bracelet in England where for some reason they were sold at a considerably cheaper price than in Geneva. Arthur Leyland was another colleague of Shirley's, and he became a great friend. He had a car, and we often went to nearby Southport with him at weekends. On one occasion, Shirley and I visited a fortune-teller who told us that we would never be rich, but we would never be short of money. Her forecast of our future proved to be true.

On a number of weekends, we were visited in Thato Heath by my dental friends from Birmingham. Mark Griffiths and I were both Hi-Fi enthusiasts, but Mark had considerably more fundamental technical knowledge than I did. I had volunteered to install new sound equipment in the Brewery's Social Club. Mark saw this as an opportunity to test out our theories of acoustics. Mark and I used an early three-speed tape recorder that I had made, and we bought half a dozen balloons. These were used to test the acoustics of the dance hall. We recorded the sudden sound of exploding balloons at the highest speed of the recorder, and then played them back at the lowest speed. From this, we were able to calculate the acoustical absorption of the hall. As a result of our experiments, I asked the brewery to order a suitable Hi-Fi amplifier and four large speakers. After the new equipment was installed, I returned to the hall and tested it. The quality was vastly superior to equipment that it had replaced. Shortly after the new sound equipment had been installed, a Saturday Night Dance was held for employees in the hall. It was well attended, and the hall was well filled. I went along to hear how much the sound had improved. I was unsurprised to find that the sound quality had improved enormously. I was appalled to discover that the volume had deteriorated equally enormously, and the music could hardly be heard. Both

Mark and I should have known that the human body is an incredibly efficient means of sound absorption. The practical effect was that the ambient sound volume was less than half of that from the previous equipment. I was deeply embarrassed, and it was one of the most humiliating technical failures of my life. Mark and I really should have known better.

The garden at the bungalow was quite large. I had no previous experience of gardening but had been told that spent hops from breweries were an ideal fertiliser for flowerbeds. I therefore asked Fred Lanfear if I could obtain some of these from the brewery. Disposal of these hops was always a problem, and breweries usually had to pay for them being taken away. However, at Greenall Whitley, the brewery had a special tipper lorry which was manned by two old employees who were no longer considered to be fit enough to deliver beer. They duly delivered a load of spent hops to the bungalow. Unfortunately, the gate at the front of the bungalow was not quite wide enough to allow the lorry to back into the drive. They apparently had not appreciated this, and they completely demolished both the gatepost and the brick boundary wall. However, they continued backing into the drive and tipped the whole of the lorry contents on to the ground, thereby blocking up entrance to the back door. They were rather apologetic, and the Estates Department later rebuilt the wall. In the meantime, I was left with the problem of disposing a lorry load of spent hops, when I had only required a couple of sacks full. The task discouraged me from gardening for the rest of my life. I subsequently often admitted that I would rather go to prison than become a gardener.

On one of the occasions that I visited my parents in London, my father suggested that I should buy a hat. At the time, bowler hats were extremely fashionable, particularly for office workers in the city. He explained that the most exclusive hatters were Lock & Co in St James. I knew absolutely nothing about bowler hats, and my visit to them was a revealing experience. After asking for my head size, the formally dressed young assistant opened a large cupboard behind the counter, which contained about twenty hats. He opened the cupboard and then proceeded very swiftly to put one after another of these on to my head. To my complete surprise, these were all rigid, the same height, and had a rough, almost dark grey slightly coarse exterior. Eventually, he seemed to be satisfied and asked me to look in a mirror. In an attempt to be knowledgeable, I asked him whether I should have a smoother or slightly higher hat. He somewhat condescendingly explained that Lock & Co. only sold hats with their own characteristic texture. He also respectfully suggested that for a young man such as me, that if I wore a higher hat, I would be slightly 'over-hatted'. It was a phrase I never again heard repeated. I meekly agreed. He then placed what appeared to be an instrument of torture on my head. It consisted of segments of wooden board above which was ring of spiked rods separated by springs. He placed this implement on my head and patted and pushed the segments into place. When he was apparently satisfied, he gave a smart blow to the spikes, which then became fixed in position. He then removed the whole device from my head, picked up the chosen hat, and disappeared through a door behind the counter. Some minutes later, he reappeared with the hat and placed it on my head. To my utter astonishment, the hatband was rigid and distinctly warm but fitted my head perfectly. He then asked for my initials, which were then embossed in to the headband of the hat. When I paid him, he got out a large ledger and explained that Lock & Co. had been hatters for over two hundred years. In their ledger was the sale of hats to Lord Nelson. I walked out of Locks with my bowler hat and rolled umbrella feeling somewhat privileged and superior but also in one sense rather humble.

Towards the end of my second year at Greenall Whitley, I had become progressively more disturbed about national events in the Brewing Trade. An increasing number of breweries of all sizes were being taken over, amalgamated, and closed. The most important result from my point of view was that these brewery companies employed many brewers who had worked loyally for their brewery companies for many years. Head brewers, and in particular, slightly younger brewers who were aspiring to become heads, suddenly and unexpectedly were made redundant. Unfortunately, senior brewers were almost universally only promoted from within their own brewery. Rarely, if ever, were redundant brewers able to continue in the brewing trade, other than as 'Cellar Inspectors'. The most important irony was that despite the high status and certainly highly respected and privileged position of brewers, this was completely unrecognised outside the industry. As I subsequently discovered, the reaction of managers in other industries and businesses was commonly one of mild amusement and condescension. On one occasion some years later when I applied for a job in the Unilever Food 'empire', my interviewer manager patronisingly commented that he couldn't possibly imagine what use an ex-brewer, or anyone else from the Brewing Industry could be to their organisation.

Finally, when Walkers of Warrington, the largest of our competitors, was taken over, and the middle-aged head brewer was summarily made redundant, I decided that it was time for me to move on and out of the brewing trade. I decided to apply for a grant from St Helens' Council to attend Edinburgh University for their one-year course in management studies. This course was completely new and at that early time was only one of two such courses in the United Kingdom. Since I had already been to university for three years, I was ineligible for an education grant. However, I was informed by St Helens' Council that I could apply for a special grant which they were still administering for further education. This was a bequest from a Victorian lady for '…books and bibles for the poor boys and girls of St Helens'. The current value was now a hundred pounds, and a third of which would be awarded to me at the beginning of each term.

It was with great sadness and regret that I tendered my resignation to the head brewer. It would not be an exaggeration to say that he and Freddy Lanfear were uncomprehending and devastated. Eric Collis had recently asked me whether I would like to become head brewer at Chester Northgate, a medium-sized brewery in the Greenall Whitley empire, where the head brewer was about to retire. Both Eric Collis and Freddie Lanfear had been unbelievably friendly, helpful and supportive, throughout my two years at St Helens, and it was not difficult to understand how and why they felt disappointed and 'let down'. Humphrey Griffiths, the managing director, had always been extremely sociably towards me on his frequent visits to the sample cellar at St Helens. He had been particularly impressed after he had met Shirley at the Annual Brewery Dinner Dance and learned that she was an Olympic Medallist. Whilst almost all of the staff was in evening dress, Humphrey attended the dinner in his sports jacket and flannels. He subsequently explained to us in the brewery sample cellar that this was necessary in order to avoid the less senior brewery workers feeling embarrassed if they did not own evening dress. When he learned subsequently that I had tendered my resignation, he was rather less understanding. His parting, somewhat ill informed, comment to me on my final interview with him was that he couldn't see what I could possibly learn about management from '…a gang of Scotch teachers from the Gorbals.'

Shirley and I sent our beloved furniture and fittings away into storage. I carefully kept the architect's scale drawing of the bungalow, and Shirley went back to Croydon to live with her parents and work at the Bank of England in

London. Rhododendrons were prolific in Thatto Heath where the soil was very acid. They grew in profusion in the park that was immediately behind our bungalow. Fred Lanfear kindly visited us before he left and gave us a rhododendron plant as a parting gift. We took this to our later homes and replanted it on each occasion. I caught the only through train from Liverpool to Edinburgh via St Helens just after midnight. After leaving the train the next morning, I reported with my suitcase to the Student Accommodation Office of Edinburgh University. I asked them where I might find suitable lodgings. Twelve years after entering the Brewing Trade, I had ceased to be a brewer. I was very sad to leave the privileged membership of a profession that I had loved for the previous fifteen years. However, that was not to be the last time that I was to be employed by the Brewing Industry. I would spend another thirty-five years closely and profitably associated with it.

Edinburgh

Edinburgh University differed from Birmingham University in almost every respect. Edinburgh University ruefully admitted that it was the 'youngest' of the then five Scottish universities. It had not been founded until 1583, unlike St Andrews, the most senior of Scottish universities, which had been founded in 1410. In contrast, Birmingham University had been established by Queen Victoria's Charter in 1900 and was somewhat scathingly described by its critics as the biggest technical college in Birmingham. The red-bricked buildings at Birmingham were on a large sloping 'green field' site in Edgbaston. The magnificent main building was modelled as a copy of the exterior of the Blue Mosque in Istanbul. Contained in the centre of its courtyard was a splendidly tall red-bricked 'Big Ben' type of clock. The many science faculties and departments occupied their own, usually multi-storied, building. In contrast to Birmingham Brewing School, which was in a Faculty of Science, I was now in an Arts Faculty in Edinburgh, which was located in George Square on the high part of the 'Old Town'. George Square, perhaps unsurprisingly, was secluded, with a beautiful private garden in its centre, which was bounded by iron railings. It was surrounded by splendid four-storey Georgian terraced houses. Leading up to each house or 'Department' was a flight of six or eight stone steps at the top of which was stationed a silk top-hatted man dressed in a magnificent brown swallow-tailed coat over a brass-buttoned waistcoat. On mounting the steps, each student was greeted with a polite salute and salutation and the door was duly opened. The title of these splendid men, as I learned later, was 'Servitors'. The head servitor was known as the 'Bedellus', which apparently was Latin for 'Beadle'.

The department for my post-graduate course enjoyed the somewhat grandiose title of the 'Department of Management and the Organisation of Industry'. I discovered that it was the first course of its kind in the country, and I was one of only ten students, all of whom, with one exception, were under thirty years of age, one was a PhD, and only one was Scottish. Apparently, the only other course that existed, which was claimed to be similar, was at the London School of Economics, but Scottish academics were somewhat dismissive of this. The range of Edinburgh course subjects included economics, statistics, cost accountancy, organisation structure, sociology, marketing, contract law, mercantile law, and a brief introduction to computers. On our first day, we were given a booklist of over a hundred references to all of these subjects. At Birmingham, there had been only one textbook for brewing, the author of which was our Professor Hopkins. At the time, I had raised a few eyebrows by also reading the only other textbook on the subject and that had been authored by Dr Bishop, the head at the rival Herriot Watt Brewing School. In contrast, when we were presented with our booklist on our management course in Edinburgh one of students, apparently, like the rest of us, was somewhat disturbed by the size of the list. He asked Professor Hunt how we could be expected to read so many textbooks. The student received a somewhat humiliating response. Professor Hunt pointed out that we were now in a Faculty of Arts at Edinburgh. We were not there to be 'taught' but 'to be offered the opportunity to learn', and this required selectivity and the development of judgement on the part of the student as to what to read and what to ignore. The last of our subjects was actually Scottish Mercantile Law, which apparently differed significantly from its English equivalent. One of the students somewhat unwisely queried the value of this for the overwhelming proportion English students on the course. Perhaps unsurprisingly, Mr Maxwell, our Scottish tutor, who had written the standard textbook on the subject, provided a very terse response to this question. He pointed out that Scottish Mercantile Law was derived from, and based, on Roman law, whilst the English version was later and less widely established and was not recognised in Scotland. In contrast, marketing was a very new and not well-established subject. The only textbooks available were American. These were expensive; usually about twenty pounds each. Most annoyingly, they illustrated their theories by using examples of American products, many of which were completely unknown in the United Kingdom. However, most of these books were available in the department's library. Fortunately, this enabled me to avoid the excessive cost of purchasing books that I could not possibly afford. However, one subject with which I was unfamiliar was economics. The American textbook was by Samuelson, and it really was comprehensive and definitive. I found myself unable to prevent buying a copy, and it became my economics 'Bible' thereafter.

One of the new subjects to which we were introduced was the very new early development of the use of computers for commercial purposes. Previously, they had been mainly for military and some scientific use. We were shown a film by the then fairly new company of ICL. The company was British, and IBM, its American competitor, were the main manufacturers attempting to apply computers to commercial applications. The film simply showed a few illustrations and scenes of possible business applications. One of the actors in the scenes was John Le Mesurier, who eventually became famous as Sergeant Wilson in 'Dads Army'. However, most importantly, it began and inspired my subsequent career-long interest in computers and computing. At the time, I did not realise how important and how profitable it would become for me. I became very anxious to learn programming, but no books were available at that time.

The eldest of the students on the course was in his late thirties and had recently returned from being a tea planter in Malaya. He was extremely amiable and uniquely owned a two-seater Porsche car. On the one occasion that he gave me a lift, I decided that it was one of the most uncomfortable vehicles that I had been in since my days in army. He was also the only other student who owned a Rolex watch. On one occasion, we were discussing their ability to rewind automatically after only a few hours' activity. He commented that the only people who found it necessary to wind them manually due to lack of activity might be the 'odd tea or rubber planter' in Malaya.

My first lodgings were about a quarter of a mile from George Square in a rather genteel road of large detached houses. The landlady and her husband were extremely friendly and hospitable. I was the only 'lodger' and was allowed to eat meals with the couple. However, I was completely unused to their diet, which I found rather limited and frugal, but more importantly, I could not reconcile myself to their house temperature. After meals in the evening, I was obliged to retire to my small bedroom in which I also studied. Although it was late autumn, there was no heating in the room, and I therefore was obliged to wear my overcoat whilst studying and writing notes on the dressing table. When I finally retired to bed, I had at least, fortunately, been provided with sufficient blankets. After a couple of weeks, I returned to the University Accommodation Office and asked to move. They somewhat unhelpfully commented that Edinburgh residents tended to have much 'cooler houses' than those in the South. However, after some consideration, they offered me a lodging further out to the boundary south of the city. This was a mile from George Square but just about within a reasonable half-hour walking distance of the department. In the spring and summer terms, this was a pleasant walk. In the winter, it was somewhat less so. I was to remain in these lodgings for the rest of my stay in Edinburgh. Most opportunely, it was also cheaper as well as warmer than my previous accommodation.

I shared the accommodation with four other post-graduate students, none of who were on my course. One was a practising medical doctor from Lancashire, whose name somewhat astonishingly was Frank Bradforth. Another was a PhD student studying English. The third was a post-graduate architecture student, and finally, there was one with whom I shared my bedroom, who was studying some sort of sociology. Unlike Birmingham, many of the management students wore city suits. I wore a blue pinstriped double-breasted suit, as also did Frank Bradforth. On one occasion, I jokingly opened my jacket to reveal a 'Utility' label. Frank responded similarly, also showing his 'Utility' label, but adding the comment, "Thanks from a grateful nation – my demob suit from the army." As it was now fifteen years since the end of the Second World War, the Bradforths clearly were not extravagant in buying new clothes. The landlady was a widow with one young teenage son. Extremely fortunately for all of her 'guests', she was the widow of a local butcher. She still owned the shop. We were provided therefore with generous quantities of a primarily meat-based diet at all times. Breakfasts were, perhaps inevitably, usually bacon and eggs. Needless to say, I remained at this accommodation for the rest of my stay in Edinburgh.

Our course lectures were all in individual houses around three of the sides of George Square. Each of the houses was occupied by a different department and professor, with its own servitor on duty at the door. We simply walked from one house to another. Our classes were more like normal university tutorials rather than lectures, and we were freely allowed to interrupt and debate with the tutors the subject content. During the spring and summer terms, we used to take advantage of the private gardens in the middle of George Square. We were able to study and revise for our coming examinations in extremely pleasant and secluded surroundings. Just outside the corner of the top of George Square was a most impressive Civic Hall. It was always closed. However, on one occasion when I passed the front door, it was open. I felt unable not to satisfy my curiosity and entered. To my complete surprise, I was greeted by a lady, who asked me to follow her. I passed a notice that I had not time to read, and she led me into a large room in which there were a number of beds. She invited me to take off my jacket and sit on one of them. I glanced at a notice on the wall and discovered with some alarm that I was in a temporary Blood Donation Clinic. Unable to withdraw with dignity, I somewhat reluctantly and apprehensively gave a pint of blood. For the rest of my life, I never repeated the process.

During the two vacations, I used to return to Croydon where Shirley was living with her parents. The fares were expensive, and I was anxious to try and offset these. During the Christmas vacation, I managed to get a temporary job in Croydon Post Office as an assistant letter sorter. These temporary jobs were necessary in order to handle the Christmas mail. Despite the title of the role, I and the other temporary workers were never required to sort letters. We periodically simply carried full sacks of mail to and from the sorting office. I had expected this to be a hectic or even frantic occupation. In fact, I seemed to spend most of my time on the sorting office restroom drinking tea. Nevertheless, this provided a very welcome, though brief, supplementary income.

Just before the Easter vacation, I had considered the possibility of returning eventually to the brewing industry. I had therefore responded to an advert for a brewery post at Heineken. At that time, they had breweries all over the world but did not have a brewery in England. However, they invited me for an interview in Amsterdam. The interview involved going via London and Harwich and on the cross-channel ferry to Zeebrugge. I duly attended and was interviewed and entertained hospitably. They appeared to be impressed by my CV, and after I returned to England, they offered to employ me. The salary and conditions offered were excellent and considerably better than those of any brewer of similar experience in the UK. They had explained that wherever abroad they employed me, they would allow expenses for my wife and me to visit England, and for any children we might have to be educated at boarding schools there. They generously paid my travelling expenses all the way from Edinburgh to Amsterdam via London and said they would write to me. After my return to Croydon, they offered to employ me. Unfortunately, they had refused to tell me in which country I would be employed, or for how many years. The thought of spending years in some remote tropical country whilst trying to raise a family there was a prospect that I found completely unappealing. I thanked them but declined their generous offer. However, once again I had covered the cost of visiting Croydon in my vacation and also had a most enjoyable excursion. Some years later, whilst on holiday Molly my sister-in-law met a Carlsberg executive. He recalled my interview and said that Heineken had been extremely disappointed by my rejection of their offer to employ me.

My leisure time activities in Edinburgh were severely constrained by the fact that I was earning no income. Although I went on a number of very short outings with fellow students both to the nearby border country and also to Stirling on one or two weekends, these involved little expenditure of money. Very occasionally, we went to a local pub for a modest couple of half pints of beer. However, I had every intention of having a new house one day in the future. I regarded the bungalow at St Helens as ideal, if not idyllic. I therefore began to design a three-bedroom 'Dormer' house. This was a popular and a particularly economical design; the construction of which was described in detail, along with the plans in a popular 'Do it yourself' or 'DIY' magazine. However, I wished to adapt the design to a house based on our late wonderful bungalow. I had previously acquired a copy of the architect's plans. I applied all of my method study and work study skills to the task. First of all, I knew the room shapes and sizes that we liked. I based the dimensions and arrangement of the rooms on those in the bungalow in St Helens. My first task was to determine what was the best layout and spatial relationship between them. This revealed a ground floor layout that could be one of two layouts, each of which was the mirror image of the other. A similar technique was then applied to the upper floor. I decided that the precise room dimensions should all conform to standard carpet sizes, rather than arbitrary ones selected normally by architects. This would enable me then at minimum cost, to have fitted carpets in every room in the house. At the time this would have been considered a luxury. I then calculated the heat balance for the house, which essentially required walls which used insulation blocks rather than conventional 'breeze' building blocks as the inner leaf of the wall. The exterior blocks could then be attractive Cornish granite blocks, which I had admired on Harold Wilson's bungalow in the Scilly Isles. I then calculated the radiator sizes and pipe run layouts for each room and the optimum position of electric power points. Finally, I was faced with the design of the dormer roof. At this point, my technical construction knowledge ran out, as to the sectional dimension and configuration of the roof timbers that would be required. Fortunately, a fellow resident in my lodgings was studying a post-graduate architecture degree. However, he appeared to be somewhat vague about the nature of my problem and failed to find a solution. Nevertheless, I now knew exactly what I wanted as a future new house.

As part of the management course, we were required to produce a research dissertation. During my statistics studies, I had become interested in income distribution. I therefore chose this as my dissertation subject. I relied exclusively on the official government 'Abstract of Annual Statistics'. This comprehensive tome, along with many other things, provided an astonishing range of detail about income distribution in different industrial sectors and different parts of the country. I started analysing this and experimenting with techniques to illustrate and display the data. I discovered eventually by trial and error that if the data was recorded on graph paper, the vertical axis of which was logarithmic, the distribution became a straight line. Changes from year to year and sector to sector could then be illustrated and compared unambiguously. My economics lecturer appeared to be quite impressed but drew my attention to the fact that my curves might resemble those of that were known as Pareto Curves, discovered some hundred years previously by an Italian economist. Fortunately, whilst the principles behind my curves were similar, in practice, they could not be described as 'Pareto Curves'. Happily, my dissertation was accepted at the end of the academic year, and to my astonishment, I was offered a three-year PhD lectureship by Professor Hunt. Needless to say, that did not fit in with my immediate career or domestic plans. I was very grateful for his generous offer but declined it most apologetically.

Before I left Edinburgh, I applied for employment a number of times. On one occasion, it was for a job as a manager of a sweet factory in Southport in Lancashire. I had thought, naively, that my experience in the Brewing Industry and my management qualifications would be attractive elsewhere in the food industry. Unfortunately, I was mistaken and apparently failed to impress them. However, I once again received travelling expenses, which at least took me halfway to London. On another occasion, I applied for a job as a brewer at Greens of Luton. The head brewer appeared to be fairly impressed by my C.V. but suggested that I should apply again after I had left Edinburgh. His second brewer was less enthusiastic and made it clear that if I was appointed, I would be junior to him. However, I once again received my travelling expenses from Edinburgh and continued my journey to London. My final return from Edinburgh to the South was in the car of a fellow student Neville Carrington. He was the only student on the course who held a PhD. He lived at Dorking in Surrey and worked as a chemist for Beechams, the pharmaceutical chemists. Once again, I had managed to avoid my travel costs. However, I had one last, though rather unenthusiastic, attempt to return as a brewer. I applied for a post at Young's Brewery in Wandsworth. I was welcomed and shown around by the head brewer who was charming and appeared to be in his sixties. The brewery was extraordinary. It was considerably smaller than that at St Helens and contained a number of unusual features. The first was a genuine original Newcomen steam engine that was in daily use and must have been built in the early nineteenth century. The other feature was that in the brewery yard was a very large stable full of horses. It had the idiosyncrasy that it was the only building on the site that was equipped with loudspeakers. Through these was played soothing music exclusively for the benefit of the carthorses. After meeting the other brewers, we enjoyed an excellent lunch. However, after lunch the head brewer very kindly and gently and in an almost fatherly fashion told me that he did not think that the vacancy was a suitable job for me. He suggested that I should apply to a large national brewery company such as Watney Mann. He offered me my travelling expenses from Edinburgh, which I felt I could not possibly accept, and hopefully, very graciously declined. In response, he insisted on paying my rail fare from and to Croydon. I felt that I had already covered my final travelling costs back from Edinburgh.

The Doldrums

After leaving Edinburgh, and having no home, Shirley and I moved in to stay with her older sister Molly, who lived on her own in a modern first floor flat in South Croydon. There was plenty of room for the three of us, and Molly worked as a secretary at the Triumph car distributers immediately opposite the flat. Shirley was able to support me by commuting daily to the Bank of England at Threadneedle Street. In contrast, I had nothing to do all day, apart from my weekly visits to the Labour Exchange to 'sign on' and for the rest of the time, to look for employment. Perhaps unsurprisingly, I spent much of my time in the flat searching for job advertisements. However, I also continued to pursue my interest and expand my Edinburgh dissertation on income distribution. Under the circumstances, this was perhaps ironic, but it also enabled me to visit the local library to continue browsing the National Abstract of Statistics and study income distribution. I continued to look at my Edinburgh dissertation, and to expand it, and wrote a paper derived from it for the Incorporated Brewers' Guild Journal. The journal accepted it, although there were no fees for contributions. I also managed to join the newly formed British Institute of Management, popularly known as the BIM, as a student member. They had a formal qualification for membership as a graduate member by sitting a written examination, which included ten or twelve subjects. I managed to be exempted from half a dozen of these because of my Edinburgh qualification. I sat and passed the exams for the remaining subjects and was duly enrolled as a 'graduate member'. Shortly afterwards, I discovered that they were currently inviting members to submit entries for an international prize paper for 'Young Executives'. The paper had the rather altruistic title 'Human Progress through Better Management'. Entries were being submitted internationally by thirty-three countries. Each country was allowed three entries. I decided that with my Edinburgh research and subsequent library studies, I should extend and develop this and submit an entry for the competition. Actually, I had nothing else to do and plenty of time in which to do it. Having done it, I then submitted it. Shortly after I submitted my paper, I received a letter from the BIM few weeks later. They informed me that my paper had been one of three selected to be submitted on behalf of Great Britain in the international management CIOS competition. Three papers from each of the eleven other countries worldwide had already been submitted.

A couple of weeks after I had moved into the South Croydon flat, I saw an advertisement for an assistant work study manager at Watney Mann, at that time one of the very largest brewery groups in the country. I replied to the advertisement and was invited for an interview at Mortlake. There I met Gordon Brace, a very personable, moustached young man in his mid-thirties, who was the group work study manager. He appeared to be impressed by my C.V. but explained that he was really recruiting new work study managers who were to be appointed to each of the breweries in the Watney Mann Group. Although I had some qualifications in work study, he considered that I would need further training before being allocated to one of these posts. However, I realised that I would be almost unique in being the only work study manager with qualifications and previous experience of the brewing trade. All but one of the other managers may have had previous experience as work study officers or managers but none in breweries. To my utter delight and relief, he offered me a job. It was to be the first ever work-study manager at Phipps Northampton Brewery, but I would first require six months training in London at Mortlake, which was the Watney brewery and Whitechapel, which was that of Mann, Crossman, and Paulin. Both of these breweries were of a similar size to those at Cape Hill. The Northampton ones were about the same size of those of Greenall Whitley. I knew that I would obviously be completely familiar and 'at home' with all of these. However, Gordon Brace had explained that he would be unable to pay me the salary of an experienced work study manager until I had successfully concluded my induction training and begun as manager at Northampton. Needless to say, I accepted the job immediately and the salary, which was considerably more than I had been receiving before leaving St Helens. I already had considerable knowledge of work study and its history, which had originated in America at the beginning of the twentieth century. It had been created from two separate sources with different techniques and somewhat conflicting philosophies. These became known as 'Time and Motion Study'. Time Study was originated by Fredrick Taylor in a heavy industrial environment and consisted of using a stopwatch and carrying detailed timing and assessment of manual work and operating practices. The times were then 'normalised' to create 'standard times' and 'incentive' payment and bonus schemes, which were set to match these timings. In contrast, 'Method Study' was created by the Frank and Gillian Gilbreth and involved examining in minute detail complex manufacturing operations and then devising new improved methods. The record of 'Time and Motion Study' was mixed. Whilst it had been extremely successful in its original context, which were simple labouring tasks in heavy industry, its practice was nevertheless subject to severe criticism. In particular, its application in the early 1920s, Time Study had led to redundancies and was therefore strongly resisted and opposed by labour. The incentive schemes were also susceptible to manipulation by employers. After agreeing initially to the incentive 'Time Standards', these would be subsequently 'adjusted' and 'revised' downwards by employers when employees were found to be receiving significantly higher wage payments as a result of their improved performances. I always took the view that setting 'work standard' times without first eliminating inefficient methods was a somewhat pointless exercise. It was first necessary to improve the methods. On a later occasion, I commented on this difference to Gordon Brace, who like the other work study managers was a dedicated time study man. However, he quite rightly pointed out that in order to improve methods, it was first necessary to measure them. I was unable to disagree. I would be given the opportunity to do this.

My first assignment was to Whitechapel, where a new Work Study Department had been set up some six or nine months earlier. The manager was Mike Cattell, an experienced time study man in his early thirties. I always got on with him well, although he had a somewhat cynical opinion about my lack of previous experience. In contrast, he had considerable experience of work measurement and the introduction and operation of incentive schemes in other industries. In his new department, he had two young assistants, both of who had been brewery clerks. His department was in the process of measuring the work and designing incentive payment schemes for various departments in the brewery. The Work Study Department provided me with an ideal opportunity to gain experience in this process.

On the day of my arrival, I was introduced to the head brewer 'Archie' Lucas and the second brewer John Duncan. I also met later Charles Lanfear who was the brother of the second brewer at St Helens. Unlike his brother, Charles appeared not to have reached a particularly high level of seniority. However, both brothers were equally charming and friendly. In total contrast, Archie Lucas had a reputation for authoritarianism, meanness, and hostility to labour. I never encountered this elsewhere in any other brewery but only in stories of head brewers prior to the Second World War. Apparently, Archie Lucas labelled me as a 'Renegade Brewer'. Having shaken my hand, he never had any further contact with me.

The brewery at Whitechapel was more dilapidated and unhygienic than any other brewery I ever entered. My first assignment was to the newly installed kegging plant. This was located in a dank and seriously dilapidated cellar, and the stainless-steel equipment had been newly installed to handle Heineken Lager. Following the experience of my earlier visit to the Heineken Brewery in Holland, I found it difficult to believe that the company could have agreed to the location of this present installation. However, this was my first opportunity to use my new work study instruments and techniques. These consisted of a foolscap-sized light wooden 'millboard', to which, in the top right-hand corner was clipped a specialised stopwatch. The watch was of a 'fly-back' type, which had the unusual property of alternately starting when the activator button was pressed, and returning to zero, and immediately restarting when it was pressed a second time. The board and watch were held in the crook of the left arm and the pencil was in the right hand. The operator therefore had to read and record the time of each 'element' of activity, which was measured in hundredth of a minute, instantaneously just before pressing the button to record the next element. Immediately after doing so, he had to record the activity and time on his 'time sheet'. At the same time, he also had to 'rate' the effectiveness with which the element had been performed. A rating of 100% was regarded as a 'standard' motivated performance and the timings of ratings above and below this level were adjusted subsequently to the value of a notional 'standard' time. Perhaps unsurprisingly, these observing, judging, and recording skills required more than a little time to perfect. I spent the first few hours in my new role observing and timing the brewery operatives filling the kegs manually from the filling heads of the 'racking' machine.

A number of my studies at Whitechapel were on transport. On one occasion, I accompanied a delivery to the then so-called China Town. We arrived on a wet day at a cobbled street on which were parked a number of cars, all of which blocked the entrance to the public house to which the delivery was to be made. The driver and his burly mate climbed out of the cab, seized the nearest mini car, and simply dragged it out of the way of the entrance. I was very impressed. My final transport work study exercise was a delivery to the Hastings Depot. The round journey took three or four hours. I rapidly came to the conclusion that conventional work study measuring and recording techniques with a hundredth of a minute stopwatch were completely inappropriate for such activities, except at the beginning and end of their journeys. Since these only formed a relatively small part of the working day, the important issue was the deployment and routing of the vehicles. These were not work-study issues but were matters of deployment and management.

A later transport delivery incident involved two students who were training to become work study assistants. Their current task was to accompany crews on brewery delivery lorries, which were popularly known as 'drays'. The drays had metal posts with two hooks along the dray platform. Chains were suspended between these hooks when travelling, in order to prevent barrels from falling off the dray. It was standard practice for work study officers never to wear rings or jewellery whilst carrying out studies. One young man failed to do this, and when jumping off the side of a dray during the delivery caught his ringed finger on one of the unchained hooks. His finger and ring remained on the hook. By sheer chance, the delivery was opposite the Whitechapel London Hospital. The draymen retrieved the finger and took him to the hospital. Incredibly, I was told that the finger was reattached, and the student recovered. Had I not been at Whitechapel at the time, I would have found the story almost impossible to believe.

Perhaps unsurprisingly, I was unable to detach myself from my somewhat extensive previous brewing experience. I could not believe the sight of two huge open wooden vessels of a thousand barrels each in one of the brewery cellars. They were both full of what was commonly known as 'breakings'. This was beer that had been returned from pubs as unfit for sale. This spoiled beer was duty-paid, usually sour, and had been rejected by excise officers as eligible for any duty repayment. It was basically a very unsanitary version of vinegar. At Cape Hill, a special plant had been developed and installed, which neutralised the acidity, and sterilised the breakings before blending it in very small quantities back into newly brewed beer. No such plant existed at Whitechapel. The breakings had clearly been at Whitechapel for a very considerable time, and what they intended to do with it was a complete mystery to me. I made the somewhat unkind comment that if they intended to put vinegar into their beer, it would be cheaper to buy it, since that would not have any excise duty attached to it.

A slightly more constructive suggestion that I made was actually implemented. The cold storage room contained four adjacent rows of tanks. Between each pair ran a stainless steel main through which beer was supplied and emptied. The filling and emptying processes were slow and lengthy. Unfortunately, severe delays occurred when tanks in two different rows needed to be emptied or filled at the same time. I pointed out that if short length of stainless-steel main was installed to join the far end of the rows, beer could be run simultaneously from both pairs of tanks around what would then in effect be a 'ring main'. The chief engineer was roughly the same age as me, and I met him a number of times in the brewery lunch canteen. He was always very pleasant, and as usual, as with all brewery engineers, I got on very well with him. I suggested my idea to him. Apparently, my comments were passed on to the brewers, and my solution was implemented. Delays were eliminated. However, I never ever received subsequently any response or feedback. My social experience at Whitechapel was finally extended when I went to find a suitable 'packed' lunch to take with me on a transport study. I visited a local grocer's shop and was unable to find anything suitable. Their main product on offer appeared to be 'salt beef sandwiches', an item of food of which I had never heard, and I found distinctly unappealing. I later discovered that this was an item of Jewish cuisine, which was extremely popular in the local East End of London. I failed to educate my taste and declined to buy one.

After a couple of months at Whitechapel, I was transferred by Gordon Brace to the Watney Brewery at Mortlake for the next phase of my induction training. I was not sorry to leave Whitechapel.

Mortlake

The brewery, site, and general atmosphere at Mortlake could not have been more different from Whitechapel. Gordon Brace and the head work study office were located there as well as the Watney Work Study Department under Bill Ellis. I began work in the cold room cellars of the brewery studying workers transferring beer from one set of tanks to another from the brewery to the kegging plant. I had gained a modest skill in time study and the handling of my stopwatch, pencil, and board. On one occasion, I was approached somewhat surreptitiously by the cold room foreman. He asked me whether I would time and assess his performance, since his fellow workers had begun to suspect that he was being unfairly allowed not to be studied. However, I became particularly interested in the beer recording procedures. I was well aware that the transferring of beer from one tank to another rapidly almost always involved a loss of beer. This was due to the necessity to couple and uncouple the pipes between the tanks. The amount that was lost depended very heavily on the skill and carefulness of the operatives. The beer was being transferred from one department to another, and there were different operatives at each end of the process. They simply telephoned one another and agreed the quantity transferred. In practice, this resulted in no beer loss, since the beer was finally followed by clean water in order to flush out the pipes. The total quantity of beer and water that went into the receiving tank was then precisely the same quantity as had left the original tank. As part of my study, I was required to obtain all records that were associated with the process. Needless to say, I immediately recommended that the procedure should be changed. Operatives should record only the quantity of beer present before the transfer, and the quantity in the receiving department should be recorded without this knowledge. After discussing this with Bill Ellis and Gordon Brace, I designed a completely new recording procedure. After the implementation of my scheme, losses of many thousands of pounds were revealed. I took the analysis one stage further. I designed a card system that enabled real losses to be analysed statistically and controlled precisely. However, it required to be monitored by a member of staff. A foreman from the brewery was duly appointed to control all transfers of beers using my card system. The system was effective and led to very large savings of both beer and money. So great were the savings that Gordon Brace even suggested that they were enough to justify buying a computer in order to process the new more detailed and complex recording procedures.

Unlike Whitechapel, my work at Mortlake was largely under the direction of Gordon Brace rather than Bill Ellis who was the Mortlake work study manager. The Mortlake Work Study Department were in the middle of a very large expensive scheme of keg handling that had been recommended as part of their studies. This scheme was a complex set of powered conveyers installed in order to mechanise the loading of kegs onto beer lorries. The loading of kegs on to drays was a very time-consuming heavy labour-intensive task. The mechanisation would be very beneficial and cost-effective. Unfortunately, the conveyor equipment proved to be ineffective, and despite every effort to make it work efficiently, eventually it had to be scrapped. This was deeply embarrassing both for work study and the engineers involved.

Gordon Brace's deputy was Bill Bridges, who had worked with Gordon for some time previously. He was older than Gordon, rather lugubrious, and presented the most unlikely image of a work study man. I was never able to work out what Bill actually did, but Gordon seemed to have great faith in his opinion, and conferred with him frequently. The other member of the head office was Charles Everett. He was middle-aged, the only other ex-brewer in work study, and had been a middle ranking brewer at Whitechapel. He was absolutely charming and had a wonderful dry sense of humour. Needless to say, he and I got on extremely well, and we had similar viewpoints about the application of work study in the brewing industry. Some years later, Gordon Brace confided in me that he could never understand how Charles and I could go together for lunch at the Ship Hotel beside the river, drink two pints of beer, and then work quite normally for the rest of the day. I explained to Gordon that this was entirely due to the bracing effect of the River Thames air.

After I had been at Mortlake for a couple of weeks, I was called to Gordon Brace's office, where he said there was a call for me on his telephone. It was a call from Switzerland telling me that I had won First Prize in the CIOS World Competition for young executives. Apparently, it was the unanimous choice of all five judges worldwide. The prize was to be awarded in New York in a few weeks' time. The prize money was in Swiss Francs to an equivalent amount of about £800. This was rather more than my last year's salary before leaving St Helens, and it was also tax-free. Needless to say, I was somewhat stunned. Gordon Brace was delighted and immediately took me to see Sanders Watney the Watney managing director.

Sanders Watney was a splendid traditional genial country gentleman, who was the only man I ever met who wore a monocle. He first congratulated me and then insisted that I should go to New York to receive the prize. He also said that Watney Man would pay all of my expenses, including those of my wife, who should accompany me. I could also take a one-week holiday if I wished to stay in America at my own expense. Gordon then explained to Sanders that on my return, I was ready now to go to Northampton as work study manager. I would set up a new department there, for which two assistants would be recruited. I would also have my salary increased to the level of other work study managers. At the end of the meeting, Sanders became very relaxed, and reminisced about when he was my age, and was a young director responsible for purchasing. One year, he had decided that the market price of sugar was rising abnormally. He therefore contracted forward to purchase the next year's sugar at the current price. When the chairman discovered this, Sanders was admonished severely. He was told never again to gamble with the company's money. His job was to purchase current supplies. After we had returned to Gordon's office, I once again felt that my decision to leave St Helens had been a wise one.

A few weeks later, it was Boat Race Day, and Watney employees and guests were allowed to view the finish of the race from the roof of Mortlake Brewery. The event was a splendid piece of hospitality, with plentiful food and refreshments but proved to be more significant than I had expected. Shirley informed me that she was pregnant. When we had got married, we had both decided and agreed not to have any children until we were thirty years old. This had proved to be a wise decision. We were now both thirty years old. Needless to say, I was delighted at the news. I also intended that when we went to Northampton, I would be able to have built for us the 'ideal' house that I had designed. I have no idea as to which team won the boat race, but I definitely felt that both Shirley and I were the real winners.

Shortly after the boat race, I received a rather ironic request from Gordon Brace. In order to become a member of the British Institute of Management, it had been necessary for me to get someone in authority to endorse the fact that I was actually a manager. Gordon had not hesitated to confirm the fact to the BIM. However, he himself was not a member of the BIM. He now wished to become one and needed a member to endorse him. Now, as I was a BIM graduate member, I had no hesitation in doing so. It was a somewhat incestuous sequence of events.

America

When I was due to go to New York, Shirley's doctor had said that it was undesirable for her to fly because she was pregnant. This was obviously for a very good reason, but it was nevertheless a great disappointment to both of us. So I departed from Heathrow alone on a British Airways Overseas Corporation Boeing 707. To my surprise, I travelled first class. I discovered subsequently that this was entirely by accident, and only because the ordinary accommodation had been overbooked, and was full. The flight was my very first airline trip, and I found it to be unbelievably luxurious. The stewardesses, all of who were young and very attractive, wore beautifully tailored suits. Their outfits were designed by Hardy Amis, who at the time was an English fashion designer and a Royal Warrant holder as designer to the Queen. The food and drink, perhaps inevitably, included very generous quantities of caviar and champagne. Unfortunately, I was somewhat greedy with this unfamiliar cuisine, and when I eventually reached my New York hotel bedroom, I was violently sick. I never again repeated the exercise of over-indulgence in rich food. However, it may be possible that occasionally I have consumed over-generous quantities of beer.

Perhaps unsurprisingly, I found New York to be fascinating. The first most noticeable feature was the motor traffic. It was not only intensive but also unbelievably noisy. New York drivers appeared to have their hands permanently attached to their electric horn buttons rather than their steering wheels. This carried on not only during the day but also throughout the night. They also appeared to have some confusion between the use of their accelerators and their brakes. The other curious traffic feature was the deployment of fully armed policemen as part of the control of traffic lights and crossings. Needless to say, I went to the top of the Empire State building and visited many of the popular shopping centres. The other thing that I found strange was the television programs. In contrast to England where there were still only two or three channels, there were literally dozens of channels and stations available to

Americans. I also went to see a Broadway musical. However, the object of my visit was not to be entertained as a viewer or a tourist but to present myself to receive my World Prize. One rather extraordinary, and somewhat disturbing experience, was that one of my suitcases, which were left locked in my hotel bedroom, was forced open and ransacked. Fortunately, nothing of value was stolen, and I subsequently recovered from insurance the cost of replacing the suitcase.

The presentation of my prize, in the form of a cheque in Swiss francs took place in a New York hotel before an assembly of international dignitaries in the commercial and academic world. In particular, I was introduced to Professor Chris Argyris, who was the author of one of the main management psychology textbooks that had been used at Edinburgh University. He also knew and was a friend of Professor Hunt. I also met one of the founders of method study who has worked with the Gilbreths who were its originators at the beginning of the century. I was also introduced to the head of one of the Detroit motor manufacturers. I had decided that whilst in America I would like to visit the capital city of Washington and return via Ottawa. Shirley's very good friends, her Olympian coach Geoffrey Dyson and his wife, now lived there. I had originally intended to go by rail to Washington but found that flying would not only be more convenient but was also a comparable price. The aircraft was a Lockheed Super Constellation and was in complete contrast to my flight from England. It was a shuttle service, and I had a window seat. The air hostesses were middle aged and rather unglamorously dressed in well-worn and slightly shabby suits. When the engines started, I looked out of the window and was amazed to see that the exhaust pipes of the engines were not only red hot but were belching out streams of incandescent flame. This seemed to me to be technology and staff from a bygone era. Unlike my flight from England, where I had not spoken to any other passengers, the gentleman sitting next to me immediately entered a conversation. He asked me where I came from, and then where I intended to stay in Washington. Within minutes, he explained that he had never before met anyone from England and insisted that I should stay with him and his family who lived in the suburbs of the city. Although I was somewhat reluctant, it was impossible to refuse his very generous offer. During the following two days, he and his family took me all over the sights of Washington including the White House, Lincoln Memorial, and the surrounding Virginia New England countryside. They could not have been more kind and welcoming. After taking me back to the airport, I flew to Ottawa.

I spent two very happy days in Ottawa with Geoff and Maureen Dyson. They were extremely hospitable and showed me the parliament buildings and tourist sites. I found that I could return via Quebec, where I could once again break my journey home. I duly visited the city and its sights. I was fascinated by its Roman Catholic Cathedral, which was constructed entirely of wood. I also was astonished to visit the city shopping centre which appeared to be completely underground. Apparently, this was constructed in order to make it accessible throughout the winter, when the outside of the city was completely covered in snow and ice. I also visited the Heights of Abraham where General Wolfe had fought the French and secured Canada for the British. I returned to England on an overnight flight via a change of planes at Gander in Newfoundland. I arrived at Heathrow early the next morning and went straight to Mortlake. Somehow, my 'Grand Tour' detours had been without almost any additional flight costs.

My parents had been delighted to hear of my prize, visit, and prospects of their first grandchild. My father, who was a newspaper advertisement manager on Fleet Street, arranged for my photograph, and an account of my prize and past employment at Greenall Whitley to be published in the St Helens local newspaper. I hoped that this might perhaps soften the brewery's disappointment and disapproval of my resignation. In complete contrast, a detailed article had appeared in the Watney Mann House Magazine describing me, my paper, and the competition. Apparently, Gordon Brace had considered that this would be good publicity both for me and work study. In fact, few people in Watney Mann ever mentioned the subject subsequently.

Northampton

My first visit to Northampton was with Gordon Brace, who took me there by car. 'Phipps Northampton' actually consisted of two separate breweries that had previously been fierce rivals but which were side-by-side at the bottom of the main street. They had been separated only by a brick wall, which was duly demolished when they were both bought by the Watney Mann Group. The main offices faced on to the main street. When we arrived there, I was introduced to Guy Phipps-Walker, who was the managing director to whom I would be directly reporting. He was in his early forties, absolutely charming, and the image of a 'country gentleman'. I was also introduced to the two head brewers, the head accountant, and the personnel manager. I discussed with my future boss that I had plans to have a house built for me, to which he seemed rather surprised but suggested that I could talk to the brewery estates manager. This I did and obtained the details of two of the local builders. I returned to London with Gordon Brace and then contacted Glenn and Sons, one of the local builders who seemed most promising. I had prepared detailed house plans for submission to the local council, and I visited the builders shortly afterwards. I was taken by Mr Glenn Senior to look at various building sites that they owned and chose the one that I considered ideal. I also mentioned to him the difficulty I had encountered in finding the correct cross-sectional dimensions and structures for the roof timbers. He dismissed the problem instantly. He explained that he would install 'Belfast Trusses', on which he claimed that any weight could be carried easily. I had never heard of these, nor ever encountered them in the future. It transpired that they simply consisted of two beams of timber separated by diagonal struts. His prediction was absolutely right. I submitted my plans to the local council and began to seek a mortgage using my existing endowment insurance policy. The mortgage was to be for six thousand pounds and was due to be arranged, at no cost to me, through the Brewery Legal Department. Apparently, they were horrified at the price of the proposed house and suggested that at my age it would be impossible to get so large a loan. I should seek something at a lower cost. In response, I simply applied for a mortgage from the Halifax Building Society, at a half a percent rate lower and was accepted. The Brewery Legal Department and the external solicitors that they employed then decided that perhaps they would be able to arrange and process my mortgage as I had originally requested. I concluded that they would have been faced with the danger of losing the commission that they would otherwise have received on the transaction.

The building of my new house went well, but perhaps unsurprisingly, it would still be unfinished at the time that I was due to move to Northampton. However, Mr Glenn offered to allow me to rent one of a couple of houses which he owned, for the few weeks before my new house was completed. I accepted this and had the furniture which Shirley and I had in store from our bungalow in St Helens moved into this temporary accommodation. Inevitably, we were to be there for about ten weeks. However, I moved in immediately and began setting up the new Work Study Department at Northampton. The other change in my lifestyle was the acquisition of my very first motor car. This was a yellow second-hand Triumph Herald Convertible. I had bought it from the main dealer in Croydon, at which Shirley's sister worked. It also had what I regarded as most important, a tonneau cover, which allowed only the head and shoulders of the driver to be exposed outside an open car. The car was my pride and joy and was the first of another four Triumph Herald Convertibles that I would own during the next twenty years.

When Gordon Brace had taken me to the brewery for the first time, I had met Guy Phipps-Walker, the managing director to whom I was directly to report and was to be my local 'Boss'. He was in his late thirties, extremely charming, and urbane. When I finally took up my new post at Northampton, I was introduced to all of the other managers and learned the names of the other directors. The directors were classic examples of local 'country gentry'. Gerry Paige was the vice chairman and was a wonderful kindly amusing 'country gentleman'. He always had lunch in the canteen and sat wherever there was a seat, knew every manager, and most workers by their first names. Two of the directors had the surname 'Ballion', the younger of who had the unique forename of 'Brabazon' and was popularly known as 'Brabs'. Brabs was an architect and had a wonderful puckish sense of humour. Later, he always agreed my proposals enthusiastically and made sure they were implemented, as did Gerry Paige. I was also introduced to the two head brewers Lesley Milner, who was a typical, somewhat conservative, middle-aged head brewer, and 'Dusty' Miller, who was definitely not. I was always to get on well with both of these heads, but I was always particularly friendly with 'Dusty', who lived a couple of doors away from my new house. He was exceptionally innovative and always willing to listen to and implement any changes that I suggested. His second brewer was Bob Hipwell, who was slightly younger and always appeared to me to be embarrassingly servile. Bob had never been to a brewing school, and whenever he spoke to 'Dusty', he always repeatedly called him 'sir'. It was a form of address only rarely used by junior brewers to their immediate seniors. The Chief Engineer Harold Cockerill was a wonderful character, who had once been Mayor of Northampton, and as always with engineers, I got on extremely well with him. He was always enthusiastically supportive of my future proposals and went out of his way to implement them successfully. I was also introduced to the Finance Director Derek Sladden and the Chief Accountant Leslie Knight, and the personnel manager, Leslie Robson. I was never to get on well with any of them. Shortly after I had moved in to our temporary house in Northampton, Shirley gave birth to our first son. I had telephoned late on Friday afternoon from a local telephone box to the maternity hospital in Croydon into which Shirley had been admitted. I was told by the hospital that there was no need for me to travel there until the following day. In fact, at the time that I phoned, Shirley was actually in labour. When I arrived in Croydon the next day, I was met by Shirley's father who told me I had a son. I was absolutely delighted that I had a son but mortified to find that I was the last member of the family to learn of the news. Shortly afterwards, I brought Shirley and my new son to the temporary house in Northampton. His cot was installed between the two massive Hi-Fi loudspeakers that I had made. We used to listen to the radio and play records using these speakers. After a few weeks, we began to wonder whether our new son was deaf. He failed to respond to any noise that was played. We finally realised the he had simply adapted to tolerate all loud sounds. A few weeks later, we thankfully moved in to our new house, which had finally become ready for occupation.

 I was to have two assistants. The first of these was Eric Billings who had been a brewery clerk but had now been trained in work study. The other assistant was David Brown who had been a work study officer for British Rail. My first task as a work study manager was to survey the two breweries and their departments and then select one for my first actual work study project. The survey revealed what I already knew, that like all processing plants there were few workers, most of who had jobs which were required during twenty-four hours, for seven days a week. The only significant savings were likely to be in reducing materials losses. In contrast, the bottling plant, despatch, and transport departments had large expensive equipment, and were highly labour intensive. For my first 'proper' work study project, I chose the Empty Bottles Return Department, in which were employed sixteen male workers. When Bob Hipwell heard of this, he somewhat scathingly enquired what I hoped to achieve in such a boring part of the brewery. After it had been studied, I recommended the installation of a specially designed short new conveyor, which could separate large from small beer cases, and the introduction of hand pallet trucks. My recommendations were implemented with the support of the bottling manager and enthusiastic support of the chief engineer. The number of workers was reduced from sixteen to nine. As there was a shortage of labour in the two breweries, there were no redundancies. Bob Hipwell never referred to the matter again.

One of my next early projects had been to examine the systems used to record the movement of beer from the breweries to the bottling plant. I repeated my successful exercise that I had carried out at Mortlake. Unfortunately, the accountants had recently introduced their own form-filling paper system and were apparently very proud of their efforts. Their scheme involved numerous pre-printed forms, and I proved that their system was completely useless. Perhaps, somewhat undiplomatically, I revealed this by putting all of their forms on to a wallboard and showing that all of the original data entries were simply copied from one form to another and moved in a great circle. The accountants never forgave me. Perhaps unsurprisingly, all of my subsequent difficulties and opposition at Northampton involved the accountants and personnel manager.

My next project was to study the actual bottling plant and equipment. This was the heart of the bottling department and like all bottling lines consisted of a long-interconnected series of expensive, labour intensive machines. Incoming empty bottles were removed from their wooden crates by a rather superior and sophisticated automatic 'de-crating' machine. This placed the bottles on to a moving track conveyor, which led to the washer and filling machines. The machine was of a fairly advanced design and was attended by operatives who examined all passing bottles for cracks, chips or 'foreign bodies' that might have been left in the bottles. Unfortunately, the machine jammed periodically and temporarily ceased to supply bottles to the washer. This in turn brought the whole bottling plant line to a halt shortly afterwards. The effect of these failures was to reduce the output and performance of the whole plant. I had recently visited a large Watney Mann brewery in Manchester where they were using semi-automatic de-crating machines. These required the operatives to use devices which were a pair of handlebars similar to those on a bicycle but were suspended and counterbalanced. They manoeuvred these into and out of the crates and placed the bottles into the feed of the washing machine. These semi-automatic machines never jammed or halted production on the bottling line.

As a result of my study, I recommended that the Northampton de-crating machine should be scrapped and replaced with two new semi-automatic ones. Somewhat to my surprise, both the bottling manager and the accountants accepted my proposals to 'de-automate' the production line. The accountant director made what I regarded as a somewhat naive remark that it didn't matter removing the old machine as it had been fully depreciated. On that basis, the company might just as well have removed almost all of the equipment in both breweries. However, the new equipment was ordered and installed. Although there was no reduction in the number of operatives, the overall output of the bottling plant and its eleven operatives increased by a highly significant margin of over ten percent.

My next work study project was to extend the use of fork-lift trucks in the beer warehouse. The warehouse was occupied by an extensive and complex layout of beer crate conveyors. These had all been designed recently by 'Brabs' Ballion, the architect director and Harold Cockerill, the chief engineer. I proposed that all of the conveyors should be removed, so that the whole area could be used by forklift trucks. To my utter astonishment, both men agreed enthusiastically. 'Brabs' arranged for walls to be modified and doorways widened, and Harold arranged for the removal and disposal of the redundant conveyors. Needless to say, the work force would be reduced, and the new forklift operators would receive higher pay. In contrast, the accountants and the personnel manager were not only unenthusiastic but surreptitiously hostile to the proposals.

Both the accountants and the personnel manager had a long history of attempting to resist and restrain all potential wage increases. In particular, they were hostile towards unions, who they seemed to regard as opponents and enemies. In contrast, I got on extremely well with all union representatives and shop stewards. Needless to say, they welcomed all of the wage increases that I was making possible. Unsurprisingly, the accountants were always involved in any proposal that involved new capital or operating expenditure. A classic example was the necessity to replace a number of fermenting vessels in the Phipps brewery. These were rectangular, very old timber, leaked frequently, and were all sorts of shapes and sizes. Leslie Milner, the head brewer, had obtained a quotation for brand new modern stainless-steel replacements, all of the same size. The accountants had strongly opposed this proposal. Instead, they supported an alternative, more difficult proposal of lining the existing old wooden vessels with stainless steel. This was not only slightly dearer but clearly absurd. Their justification was that the lining of the vessels could be categorised as repairs, rather than capital expenditure, and thus somehow avoiding tax. Perhaps unsurprisingly, the accountants as usual got their own way.

Before Shirley and I had moved into our new house, I had asked for a number of minor changes to be made to the quotation. I knew that wall plaster took a number of weeks to dry out properly. I therefore asked for the walls not to be painted. The foundation level of the house had been raised in order to get sufficient gradient into the main drainage system. From recent technical literature, I knew that by using a new method of connecting to the drains, the increased height was unnecessary. The builder was extremely dubious but allowed me to take full responsibility for the change. I had also asked for central heating pipes under the floor to be installed, since I intended to install all of the rest of the heating myself. I also asked for the local gas board to provide a gas supply, although I had no immediate intention of using gas. When the gas board installed the supply to the house, they did not physically connect the meter but left it lying in the garage. A few weeks later, the gas man came to read the meter. I went into the garage, picked it up and offered it to him. He was as amused as I was. As a result of all of my 'adjustments' to the Bill of Quantities, I reduced the cost by some hundreds of pounds. Most commonly, final costs were always higher than the original quotation due to additional 'extras' that became added to the bill. The elderly owner of the building firm described the changes as 'very vexatious'. It was a Victorian term that I never heard before or later. Another unique Northampton form of address was 'my duck'. It was a friendly term used by and for both males and females. During the next two years, I installed a complete central heating system in our new house. I bought the gas boiler, radiators, and all fittings through the brewery at 'Trade' prices. I received much help and advice from the chief engineer, who had become a great friend and supporter.

I carried out a number of studies on distribution and transport. In order to do these, the traditional work study procedure was to record times of passing points on delivery journeys, by using a hundredth of a minute stopwatch. I regarded this technique as absurd. Instead, I obtained and issued one-inch Ordnance Survey maps covering all journeys. I told my assistants to record the grid-reference of passing points and time of day from their wristwatches. I then wished to calculate grid distances when they returned. The only problem with this was the subsequent calculations, which were tedious and time consuming. However, the accounts department had recently installed one of the very earliest of IBM computers. I considered that all of the calculations could be done by using this machine. Unbelievably, if viewed from the twenty-first century, business computers were incapable of calculating square-roots. In order to carry out this function, it was necessary to hire an adaptor from IBM. Nevertheless, and somewhat surprisingly, the accountants agreed to this additional expense. Fortunately, I was soon to be able to use this facility for another somewhat unusual project.

The Northampton breweries owned a local distribution depot in Birmingham. The premises were in Watery Lane, a back street, were cramped, and a new location was required. By coincidence, it was near to where I had worked so many years before, at Dares Brewery, which used to obtain supplies from Watery Lane. I visited the depot and suggested some immediate palliative improvements. Crates of wine and spirit bottles were stacked in cases, one on top of another. This limited the number and variety of types and brands which could be accessed easily. I suggested the installation of metal prefabricated shelving, so that a wider variety of items could be accessed easily. I also suggested that the entrance of the small yard alongside the depot could be widened to allow brewery delivery lorries to enter. Currently, only small vans were able to be used, or lorries had to park beside the pavement. This was clearly absurd. The manager was very cooperative and surreptitiously widened a small side door in stages over a few weeks, in order to avoid the council planning procedures.

The Birmingham depot had an extremely wide area of delivery. It stretched from South Wales to Derbyshire in the north. I obtained a list of all of the delivery locations and recorded their Ordnance Survey grid references. I fed these into the computer to calculate the distances from the depot and 'centre of gravity' of them all. To my utter astonishment, the answer was within a radius of about two miles from the existing present location. I recalculated the data using the estimated weights of products delivered to each customer. Perhaps unsurprisingly, the result was almost the same. I concluded that the original owners in Watery Lane had been remarkably astute 'Brummies'.

Another of my transport studies was to look at deliveries to public houses. I spent a number of days sitting in the front seat of lorries. On a number of occasions, the driver was the Transport Union shop steward Dave Bruley. He was always regarded with dislike and contempt by the transport, despatch, and account managers. He was a rather large humorous Northampton local, with whom I got on extremely well and found him to be very cooperative. It was traditional for delivery crews to be given a pint of beer each at every public house to which they delivered. Perhaps somewhat surprisingly, I was also offered this on most of the occasions. Needless to say, having been a brewer in the past, I accepted politely, somewhat to the surprise and amusement of the crews. Only on one occasion did a publican refuse to offer me a drink, on learning that I was a 'Time and Motion Study' man. He said that in the 1930s his sister had been made redundant by a 'Time Study Man'.

During my studies, I was surprised to observe an astonishing variety of lack of access at delivery locations. As a result, I subsequently asked the despatch and transport managers and the shop steward to allow a written survey to be carried out by crews of all delivery facilities. To my utter astonishment, neither of the managers had ever ridden with a crew or had been present at a delivery, and they were completely unfamiliar with all premises. The results of the survey were somewhat revealing. Amongst the descriptions was 'chesting', which apparently involved the necessity of crews to carry kegs on their chests whilst descending what in some cases were 'crumbly stairs'. The full kegs weighed approximately ninety pounds. Both the managers and I were equally embarrassed by these and other revelations.

Subjects in which I became particularly interested in the brewing trade were sales forecasting, stock control, and production planning. They were subjects that all brewers were involved in at some level, and of which they used their own versions in one way or another. I had developed a method of first establishing moving averages of a small number of weeks of past records of sales. I then adjusted these for 'moving feasts' such as Easter and other similar bank holidays for the following year. The figures were then turned into 'Base Indices' for the forecasting of each week of future demand. The final step was to run them backwards over the production 'lead time' in order to determine the necessary production levels. 'Dusty' Miller had put in proposals for installing additional cold storage tanks in a new room for bottled beer. This was a very expensive project costing many tens of thousands of pounds. I ran my 'moving average' model over the past sales. I concluded that if he brought forward his 'lead times', there was no necessity for the proposed new facilities. I expected him to resist my assertion strongly. To my astonishment, he accepted my advice and was delighted with my production planning method, which he then intended to use in future. Bob Hipwell, the second brewer, appeared to be less enthusiastic.

By this time, I had settled in very comfortably to my dream house. Shirley and I were looking forward to living in Northampton for the rest of our lives. My daughter and second son had been born. When we were first married, Shirley and I had agreed to have three children. I had wanted three or four, and Shirley had wanted two or three. Our programme was now complete. We had made great friends with neighbours of a similar age, John and Sarah Hunt, who had three sons also of a similar age to our own family. We had many joint outings with them, and they were always to remain our closest friends. On one occasion, at my request, we all went to nearby Naseby, which was the location of the final turning point of the English Civil War. The actual site turned out to be a deserted open turnip field in the middle of nowhere. I was embarrassed. However, on a later occasion we also went to Bosworth, which was the site of the final battle of the earlier Tudor Civil War. Fortunately, this was a beautiful interesting site, occupied by a wonderful heritage centre. Somewhat embarrassingly, fifty years later serious doubts have been raised as to whether it was the actual site. It seems more likely that another flat empty turnip field nearby the bottom of the hill was the real location.

Shirley and I and the family had a couple of summer seaside holidays in Broadstairs in Kent. We somehow managed to cram ourselves and three children into our Triumph Herald convertible. We had found a boarding house that catered exclusively for parents with young children. Mealtimes for dozens of small children could easily be Bedlam, but fortunately, the proprietors fed young children all together. Parents were then fed later in the evening. The town and beach were delightful, and somehow the weather always seemed favourable. There was a small funfair on the beach, and a Punch and Judy Show. There were also excellent tool and antique shops. We used to visit Margate and Ramsgate regularly. In Ramsgate, there was a large funfair, and in our last visit, I discovered that my young elder son was very competent with an air rifle. It was a skill that I imagined he might have inherited from me. I also discovered the Rovex factory on the way to nearby Margate. I was able to buy model railway components there at ridiculously cheap prices. There was also a second-hand photographic shop in Broadstairs from which I bought many rare historic railway photographs. We also used to visit our parents in Croydon and Orpington on the way there and back. They were halcyon days.

In my second year, the Northampton chairman instigated a most successful exercise for a weekend seminar at the company-owned motorway hotel at Oxford. All senior managers were to spend a long weekend together, and management consultants were to run a strategy course at which the consultants would give lectures and assess the managers. Managers were required to examine all aspects of the present structure and operation of the Northampton Company and to recommend any future changes that they considered to be necessary. It proved to be an extremely successful exercise. It also provided a unique opportunity for managers to get to know their colleagues and operational problems. An unexpected, unplanned, and unscripted demonstration also occurred. A young couple who were staying at the hotel happened to be stunt artistes in the film industry. After a sociable evening during which we had met these fellow guests in the bar, they bid us goodnight. They had regaled us with stories of their film exploits, and the male artiste offered to give us a parting demonstration of their skill. He stood facing backwards at the top of the long flight of stairs leading down to the foyer. He bid us goodnight and then slowly leaned backwards and fell the whole length of the stairs to the foyer at the bottom. It was a fitting end to the weekend.

I had recently become interested in what was at the time a new technique of 'Critical Path Analysis'. This technique allowed projects to be planned and analysed in order to identify the best sequence of events to occur. Delays could then be avoided or minimised, and the project controlled. I asked Guy Phipps-Walker, the managing director, if I could be allowed to go on a weekend course on the subject. The course was to be held at the Grand Hotel in Brighton. His response took me by surprise. He said that certainly I should attend. He would be delighted to accompany me, since he had not been to the Grand Hotel for many years. He also suggested that we should travel in my Triumph Herald, since it was a convertible, and the weather was likely to be fine. We attended the course two weeks later. The weather was still fine. Guy Phipps-Walker was a very personable companion, and the whole weekend turned out to be highly successful. I would go on to use the technique of critical path analysis many times in the future.

A few weeks later, I was asked by Gordon Brace to visit the three breweries that the Watney Mann Group owned in Norwich. The run through the East Midlands and East Anglia during the summer in my triumph Herald Convertible was a delight. The breweries were fascinating. Bullard Brewery backed immediately on to the River Yare. The chairman's office both overlooked it and hung slightly over the river. When Gordon Brace had visited him, the chairman was wearing his usual thick woollen pullover and contentedly fishing out of his window. I met the chairman briefly, although he was not fishing at the time, and was introduced to the head brewer. The head brewer was equally charming and interesting. He had lost his right arm during the Second World War and greeted me by shaking me with his left hand. He introduced me to his second brewer, who was equally personable, had also been in the Second World War, and who took me around the brewery. Both brewers were deeply concerned about the possibility of the closure of their brewery, since the two other breweries in Norwich were also owned by the Watney Mann Group. The site beside the river was particularly valuable. A short time later, the brewery was closed; the head brewer was made redundant, and the second brewer was made manager of a tiny depot in Ely. I subsequently visited him there. I found it deeply embarrassing and disturbing. He clearly had very little to occupy his time, and he invited me for lunch at his new home. It was a delightful small bungalow overlooking the fens. He explained to me that one of his and his wife's favourite occupations was sitting in the back garden looking at and admiring the 'wonderful cloudscapes over the fens'. I felt great relief that I was no longer a brewer or had risen to the not insubstantial rank of second brewer in a large brewery. Perversely, in my retirement many years later, I too would derive great pleasure from looking at cloudscapes.

I also visited one of the Norwich depots which were supplied from Northampton. It was situated outside the small town of March in Cambridgeshire. The manager, a Mr Major, was similar in manner to popular caricatures of army majors. I was introduced to him in his office, which was a picture of neatness, tidiness, and serenity. It was in total contrast to the despatch manager's office at Northampton. At Northampton, visits to the manager would be interrupted every few minutes by the ringing of the telephone phone and would then involve him in operational conversations. It was almost impossible to conduct a long conversation with the manager. In the March office, I was with Mr Major for over half an hour, during which time his telephone never rang once. The depot was supplied from Northampton, and Mr Major had recently designed and installed an extensive and complicated roller track system for handling beer cases. It was similar to the ones that I had recently successfully asked to be removed from the breweries at Northampton, since they were costly and inefficient. Unfortunately, the installation of these conveyors at March meant that beer had to be sent in lorries from Northampton using a two-man crew. If the conveyors had not been installed, deliveries could have been palletised and delivered with a one-man crew. Needless to say, when I returned to Northampton, I produced a written work study report to my managing director. I suggested that at very little cost, the conveyors at the March Depot could be replaced by a forklift truck. This could easily handle all of the operational needs of the small depot. Perhaps unsurprisingly, my managing director informed me that neither the depot nor the Norwich brewery that owned it had accepted my recommendations.

My final project as a work study manager was the use of pallets and forklift trucks in the despatch area of the beer storage warehouse. Space was limited, but it involved preparing and stacking lorry loads on pallets the afternoon before they were to be loaded and despatched on to vehicles on the following morning. This not only reduced the labour for the vehicle crews and warehouse workers but also enabled vehicles to be loaded and despatched much more quickly. The despatch manager, with whom I got on very well, had once told me that the crews were 'bone idle' in a morning. He said that at eight o'clock they were still to be found eating breakfast in a local cafe. What that revealed to me was that he had obviously never observed the crews at six o'clock loading seven tons of beer on to the back of their vehicles before leaving for their deliveries.

On the afternoon before the first day that my new system was due to start, I had checked everything on the night before the first deliveries. Unfortunately, I only arrived at seven o'clock the next morning, rather than six o'clock when loading normally began. When I arrived, chaos reigned. Somehow, the wrong beer crates had been put on the wrong pallets on the wrong loading bays.

Departure of all of the other vehicles was delayed, and there was a queue waiting to be loaded and to depart. On all subsequent occasions, the system worked well. Shortly before Christmas, the chairman arranged a luncheon for all managers, which unfortunately I was unable to attend. Soon afterwards, Gordon Brace, the work study head visited me. He said that all of the managers on that occasion had launched extremely strong complaints about the incursion of work study. In particular, they claimed that my activities were undermining their authority. Inevitably, this deputation was led by the accountants. Gordon said that regrettably, he had agreed that he would replace me by Don Barraclough, who was my deputy. I had been joined a year previously by Don from his post in London. He was the same age as me, and he had specifically asked to work with me. He was an experienced work study officer, and he and I became great friends. He was the ideal replacement. Gordon then went on to explain that there were no other work study manager posts currently available. However, he had arranged through an old friend of his to offer me a one-year appointment as a research fellow at Cranfield College of Aeronautics. The appointment was in the 'Materials Handling Research Unit'. Needless to say, I was bitterly disappointed at having to leave the breweries; I was nevertheless extremely grateful and relieved by the offer. I immediately accepted and was told that my salary, pension, working, and travelling expenses with Watney Mann would continue to be covered as usual.

Cranfield

Cranfield is about twenty miles south of Northampton. Via the newly constructed M1, it could be reached in half an hour. The college was on a large site in a delightful country area and consisted of a number of permanent single and double storey buildings alongside which was an airfield. The 'Materials Handling Research Unit' was located in a small detached two-storey building. On the upper floor was a small office occupied by the two only researchers. The other office was occupied by Professor Briggs. He welcomed me on my arrival but explained that the working office was too small for three people and that I would be housed nearby. The two other researchers to whom I was introduced were Emile Kay, a Polish mathematician, and Arthur Robins. I was never really to discover the backgrounds of these two new colleagues. I was taken by the professor to the location of my new office. It was a large aeroplane hangar in the middle of which were a number of rather noisy machine tools – lathes, milling, and drilling machines. There were two or three technicians working on these machines. Along one side of the hangar was a raised pre-fabricated platform on which were a number of closed rooms. I was taken up the iron steps to one of these. Inside was revealed an office chair, a cupboard, and in the middle of the floor a pile of Dexion steel-angle parts, rather like a large Meccano set. I was invited to assemble them, since this was to be my desk. I was somewhat surprised at this hospitality but wondered whether it might be intended to be an initiative or aptitude test. However, I went down to the floor of the hangar and introduced myself to the technicians who neither knew nor were particularly interested in who or what I was. Nevertheless, they kindly allowed me to borrow a couple of adjustable spanners with which to assemble my desk.

After assembling my desk and returning the tools, I went back to reintroduce myself to my two new colleagues. I discovered that they were working on the operation and distribution of transport containers. I explained that I was to research warehouse layout and materials handling. Arthur Robins was warmly friendly, whilst Emile Kay was coldly formal and distant. Unlike Arthur, he was an extremely nervous chain smoker of cigarettes. Their small office always reeked of cigarette smoke. I explained that my first task was to find out how much previous research and investigation had been done on warehouse layout. Arthur told me where the college library was and helpfully suggested that I should visit the Industry Reference Library in Melton Mowbray. He also gave me a list of companies throughout England who I might like to visit. Finally, he gave me a list of various colleagues in other departments who I might find it useful to meet.

Following my discussions with my colleagues, I determined my introductory plans for my research. Therefore, I thought it was time to report my initial progress to Professor Briggs. I visited him in his office, and after beginning to explain my findings, he interrupted abruptly. He told me, rather impatiently, that he didn't expect me to come and visit him every few weeks to tell him what I was doing; he expected me to get on with my research. However, he said that he may wish to see me again after a few months and would let me know. I was completely taken by surprise at his response. I also wondered what on earth he did with his time if he rarely met his academic staff.

After a few weeks of research, both in the college library and a visit to Melton Mowbray, I came to an astonishing conclusion. There was absolutely no academic research either on warehouse layout or materials handling. However, I had already decided that what was required was a mathematical model, similar to those that I had encountered previously in my engineering studies at Birmingham University. I soon began to create such a formula. At that time, electronic calculators had not been invented, but the nearest similar devices were expensive electric calculators. Fortunately, I had the opportunity to use the department's new electric calculator, which could actually multiply and divide as well as adding up. In my previous work on forecasting formulae and base indices, I had used one of the large rather clumsy mechanical hand-operated adding machines. The problem that I was seeking to solve was to determine the most efficient combination of height, width, and depth of stacks of products that should be stored in a warehouse of any given size. This was essentially a mathematical problem. I had found Emile Kay to be particularly unhelpful and dismissive of my suggestion and appeal for advice. In contrast, it was outside Arthur's area of expertise and knowledge. However, I had spoken to a college mathematician, a German who had advised me that I needed to use 'partial differential calculus'. I had always had difficulty in understanding the normal 'differential calculus', so this appeared to be a challenge. Fortunately, I managed to grapple successfully with this apparently rarely used technique. Eventually, I developed an equation that seemed to justify my efforts to solve and apply the calculus. I returned to seek the advice of the mathematician. His response was surprising. He said that there was no point in trying to create and solve complex mathematical equations, since they could often be solved more easily by using a computer model. It was one of the most valuable pieces of advice that I was ever given. What turned out to be the most important feature of the college was that it possessed a computer. This was a very early British electronic valve machine called a Ferranti Pegasus. The mathematician explained that all I had to do was write a computer program to simulate the problem. I apologetically explained to him that I didn't know how to write computer programs. He then helpfully pointed out to me that as a member of staff I was allowed to attend any college lectures on any occasions that I chose. He suggested that I should attend the lectures on computer programming. I duly did this, and as a result, a completely new career opened up to me.

I wrote my first program in the computer's extremely low-level language, which was 'Pegasus Auto code'. The Pegasus, which was British though very rare, was amazingly primitive. All input and output from the computer was by means of punched paper tape. The tape had to have the necessary limited program codes punched in to it by hand. The tape then had to be wound by hand into a small manageable coil by the programmer who had written the program. The computer was in an air-conditioned room and was enclosed in a steel casing the size of a couple of bath shower cubicles. It contained hundreds of thermionic wireless valves, which generated considerable heat. It carried out all processing overnight. The computer had to be turned off every morning to replace valves that had 'blown' during the night. The output from a single program produced enough paper tape to fill one of the very large plastic dustbins that were provided specifically for this purpose. If a program that had been written contained an erroneous 'loop', the output of paper tape from the machine would continue indefinitely. On one occasion, I accidently included such a loop. After the paper tape output had filled three dustbins and was continuing to fill a fourth, the operating technician turned the computer off. I was deeply embarrassed. More importantly, I had gained my first experience of computer programming. This was an extremely rare opportunity, and this was to prove to be invaluable to me in the future.

However, my efforts were successful, and my model allowed me to write a scientific paper, which was published in the appropriate Engineering Journal. I also continued to visit a number of factories to confirm my findings. The companies included Tate and Lyle in Liverpool, Burton Tailors in Leeds, Boots in Nottingham, and Girling Brakes in Cheltenham. I was delighted to see in the Girling factory an example of a form of storage that my computer model had predicted as being most efficient. However, I had imagined that such a layout could not possibly exist. It involved the storage of items that were extremely long and thin. The inherent problem with my solution was how to lift and place the items in the optimum position. Girling had overcome this by bundling very long heavy brass rods together. To my astonishment, they then lifted the bundle in to the optimum position by using a large overhead electro-magnet. I was baffled by how they could pick up brass rods magnetically. They then explained that they inserted one thick steel rod into the centre of each bundle.

One of the departments at Cranfield had produced and was displaying a huge three-dimensional model of the countryside on the other side of the M1 Motorway. In its centre was a tiny little-known village called Milton Keynes. The department was carrying out a survey for a proposed new development there. Little did I appreciate that it was to become a large modern and hugely successful 'Garden City'. One of the benefits for staff at Cranfield was free membership of the Gliding Club at weekends. I would have loved to take advantage of this. However, with a wife and three children, the prospect of absenting me from my family for two one-hour journeys and another two or three hours participating in the flying was clearly unreasonable.

Gordon Brace had been visiting me regularly at Cranfield and had explained that although there were no work study management appointments vacant, he hoped to find me a new post. On one occasion, I suggested to him that following the earlier offer of academic research at Edinburgh University, I might try to pursue an academic career. I added that I wished to escape from the sort of petty politics that I had encountered at the Northampton Brewery. Gordon's response was derisive. He said that politics within academia was far more virulent and widespread compared with business or industry. His comments were prophetic. However, after I had been at Cranfield for nine months, Gordon brought welcome news. He said that I was to go to the Group Headquarters in London for an interview with the Watney Mann financial director. I was to be offered a post in the newly formed Group Computer Department that was located in London. I duly attended the interview and the objective was explained to me. The company had decided to centralise in South London all of the computer financial processing for the group. The centre already employed many people with computer expertise, but none of them had any experience in brewing or the beer industry. There were also many people who knew all about the brewing industry but none who knew about both. He offered me the opportunity to join the new computer department for a period of the next two years. Perhaps unsurprisingly, I accepted his offer. My only concern was that the post would require me to live in London. I had become extremely happy to continue to live in my 'dream home' and bring up a family in Northampton. It had been my intention to stay there indefinitely and never to move or return to London. However, I could see little possibility of finding local employment comparable to my present position. Shirley was delighted and of course relieved by my news, so I therefore set about planning our move.

My first step in planning was to obtain a train timetable for the southern region in the London area. I examined the timetable carefully to identify all of the locations that could be reached within half an hour from Mortlake, Whitechapel, and Stockwell. Stockwell was the current location of the new Group Computer Department. I had also decided that any house to which we moved must be within a twenty-minute walk to the nearest railway station. My survey revealed locations in Kingston, Epsom, Sutton, Croydon, and Beckenham. I sent letters to all of the estate agents in these areas. After visiting houses in all of these locations, I finally selected a house in a particularly secluded part of East Croydon. It was occupied by a British Army Brigadier and his wife. He was due to leave his home because he had been posted to Germany. He accepted my offer, and I began to make the necessary financial arrangements. Two weeks later, I received an extremely polite apologetic letter from him saying that his posting had been cancelled. He promised to give me the first offer if he was posted out in the future. Actually, he was as good as his word, and I did in fact receive a letter from him eighteen months later. However, I needed a new potential home now. I had hoped to build another copy of my Northampton home design. I actually found a builder in Epsom who offered to do this. However, the prospect of being in a temporary home for at least nine months until the house was completed was totally unacceptable.

I finally found a house near to Sutton. The location was called Willow Grove, and the detached houses were located in a beautiful, wooded, secluded private estate on the lower slopes of the North Downs. Each of the houses in Willow Grove had unique front elevations and large secluded gardens at the rear. The Grove was within half a mile of a brand-new primary school. The houses were not only exclusive but perhaps unsurprisingly, rather expensive. I had looked at two or three of these houses and finally found the cheapest of which had been on the market for over a year. It was £9,000. My house in Northampton had been valued at £8,500. I immediately made an offer for the full price of the proposed new home. I did not receive a reply from the agent for over a week. He then informed me that the house had been taken off the market. I discovered later that the agent had bought the house, sold off part of the land, and then put the house on sale again. Needless to say, I was furious. I told him never ever to contact me ever again. Shortly afterwards, I received notification from the Estate Agent Department of Bentall's at Kingston of details of a house in Willow Grove. I arranged to meet the agent at the house. We arrived there separately at the same time. There was a large furniture van at the house, which I assumed was for the last owners who were leaving. However, it was for the new owners who were arriving. After returning to Northampton, I informed Bentall's that I no longer required their services. Two weeks later, I received a telephone call at Cranfield from a junior of the agency that had withdrawn the house that I had offered to buy. I had met him previously. He was extremely apologetic but told me that another house in Willow Grove was about to come on to the market. He was quite sure that I would like to be the first person to see it. Somewhat reluctantly, I agreed. Two days later, I met him in his office, and he took me to Willow Grove. We approached the house, and before we even entered it, I decided that I must buy it. Following my previous inspections of other houses in the road, I knew exactly what I was looking for, and what the interior would look like. The location and appearance of this house was perfect. It was my new 'dream home'. Although it was a thousand pounds more expensive than the price of the previous house that I had seen, I made an offer immediately and set about raising the extra money. Fortunately, with my current salary, and the opportunity to obtain a larger mortgage, I raised the money without difficulty, and my offer was accepted. Even more fortunately, Watney Mann had agreed to provide moving expenses and a 'Bridging Loan', which corresponded to the valuation of my house in Northampton. The valuation had been carried by the Brewery's Estates Valuer. It was considerably more than the house had cost me.

Shirley had been unable to accompany me on my house viewing visits. Understandably, she was very disappointed that we had not managed to buy the house in Croydon. It was located near to all of her family. However, I took her to see the Willow Grove house. She was incredulous and delighted. I had always regarded moving house as fraught with marital difficulties and even grounds for divorce. I was determined that this would be our last move and that I would only finally leave this house 'feet first'. Fifty years later, I shall probably prove this resolve to have been right.

Perhaps needless to say, Gordon Brace and the other managers were somewhat taken aback by my choice of new home. The Watney Mann estates manager commented that as a young man I would have been far wiser to have put aside the equivalent extra cost of the new home and saved it in the bank, where it would earn interest. The money could then be used sometime in the future. For example, it could be used to pay for such maintenance costs as replacing the electrical wiring or installing a new bathroom or kitchen in the house. I began to wonder what planet professional people who gave such advice were on.

Computing

The new Watney Mann Group Computer Department's offices were at that time in a modern multi-storey office block near Victoria Station. I was to continue to report to Gordon Brace, but I would receive day-to-day instruction from the company secretary. The department consisted of about twenty programmers and systems analysts. The computer programming language was the newly introduced 'COBOL'. I was to learn the language and would be sent on the necessary IBM courses at their nearby training establishment in St Johns Wood. In the meantime, I was installed in a tiny office on the fourth floor. The office was not much bigger than my bathroom at home but contained a desk and chair. For the first few weeks, I was provided with a series of IBM computer self-teaching educational books from which to learn all about the new computer and its programming. After a few weeks of this education and visits to courses at St Johns Wood, I was finally deemed to be fit for release to the wider wonder world of computing. I was then sent to Stockwell where the new Group Computer Centre had been established. The computer department had recently vacated the valuable premises at Victoria.

COBOL was an American business language, of a type that was known as a 'High Level' language. The 'coding' of COBOL used English words and abbreviations rather than mathematical symbols and variables. I personally found it very cumbersome and inflexible compared with my previous limited computer programming experience. For example, it appeared to be extremely difficult or impossible to do any calculations other than simple adding, subtracting, multiplying, and dividing. Nevertheless, I did learn the language and was allowed to work with other programmers.

After I had been at Stockwell for a couple of months, it was announced that the department would be moving once more, this time to new premises at Brighton. Somewhat astonishingly, COBOL was to be replaced by a brand-new IBM language called PL/1. Much to my delight, I was immediately sent on courses to learn the new language. PL/1 proved to be my dream language. It was incredibly comprehensive and flexible and allowed all future commercial programs to include as many mathematical functions and features that could possibly be required. By this time, I had become reasonably competent as a programmer, and Gordon Brace visited me once again. He explained that what was required was a computer system that would provide production and stock control for the Watney Mann Group. In the light of my previous work and experience in sales forecasting, production planning, and stock control, I was to lead a team of two programmers to design and produce a new system. Needless to say, I was delighted. Shortly afterwards, the computer department moved to a brand-new building in Brighton. There was little road traffic in the 1960s, and the southern motorways were yet to be built. Nevertheless, I was able to reach the computer offices in less than an hour by car through the quiet countryside between Sutton and Gatwick. My travelling expenses were to be paid for by the company.

Programs were all written by hand in pencil on pre-printed 'coding sheets'. Shortly after entering the brewing industry at Dares, I had sat down and completely revised my writing style. I had been rather contemptuous about the handwriting of Billy Glew, the head brewer. I thought it to be distinctly infantile. I had therefore created for myself a style based on classical script writing. I then continued to use it, or attempt to use it for the rest of my life. The time had now come to revise my printing style. I attempted to copy carefully the recently introduced British Standard Specification engineering characters. The reasons for this change were entirely practical. Programs were written during the day on pre-printed 'coding sheets' that were sent to the Data Preparation Department each evening. The coding was then punched onto eighty-column punched-cards by female operators. The programs were run overnight, and the resulting output was printed out the next morning. If even a single hand-printed character on the coding sheet was incorrect or difficult to read, the program 'failed'. Twenty-four hours had then been wasted.

The group computer was an IBM 360, which was the leading commercial computer of the period. The representative for IBM was Roy Hurst, a young thirty-year-old who, like all IBM representatives, was always charming and immaculately dressed. However, I found him particularly supportive to all of my ideas. In particular, he introduced me to the new concept of remote processing and the use of the BASIC language. The system allowed a remote central computer to be accessed via a normal telephone line. Whilst the system was unsuitable for commercial processing, it was ideal for scientific development and analytical applications. I was to use the language to my great advantage for the rest of my commercial life.

My two young programmers were excellent, both were experienced, and we all got on well together. One of the programmers was a bluff, bearded, young Yorkshireman who had a mathematics degree, and fully understood the forecasting and analysis techniques that I was trying to introduce. The other was a local young man who was a fellow convertible car enthusiast and who ran an Austin Sprite. I christened the production and stock control computer system that we were designing as 'PLANIT, and the project was progressing well.

Back at Willow Grove, I was making great progress in property improvement. I had discovered that the electrical wiring throughout the house was time expired. It had been wired in what at the time of building had been an expensive and superior method. Rubber-covered wires were protected by lightweight steel conduit, popularly known in the trade as 'tin-tab'. Unfortunately, after forty years, the enclosed rubber had perished, thereby leaving potentially lethal bare wires. The only solution was to completely rewire the house. Echoes of the estates manager's comments had come back to haunt me. However, the newly introduced system of Ring Mains had become the modern standard. I was fully familiar with this and proceeded to install it. Fortunately, the upper flooring boards were not tongue-and-groove softwood, as in most houses, but were rather superior plain hardwood boards. These were much easier to lift and replace. Similarly, cable could be dropped easily down the outside cavity walls of the house. I completely rewired the house in the most generous possible manner. After I had finished the rewiring, I increased the heat insulation of the roof and employed a contractor to fill all of the outside cavity walls with insulating material. Finally, I arranged for the two outside brick chimneystacks to be demolished and sealed. The two contractors were both steeplejacks and employed a technique which would have been completely unthinkable a decade later. One of the men climbed a ladder up to the top of the stack and then demolished the chimney pots. He then put one leg down inside the stack, and began chiselling off the bricks one at a time, and throwing them down to his mate. Eventually, his leg came down to roof level, and he installed roof tiles over the empty gap. Half a century later, contractors would have found it necessary to erect scaffolding just to replace a single broken roof tile. I had calculated the heat loss of the house and as a result of my changes concluded that I would recover all of the costs within five years. Needless to say, I obtained all of the materials and fittings at a generous discount through the brewery.

After a few of months at Brighton, I was visited by Gordon Brace once again. He explained that the group had employed management consultants to examine the organisation structure of the group and recommend any desirable organisational changes or innovations. They had recommended the setting up and employment of Group Functional Executives who would be responsible for the overseeing of all operations throughout the group. Responsible for all brewing functions throughout the group would be a group production executive. Under him would be four functional executives one of which was group production planning executive. I was to be interviewed for this post. Gordon warned me severely not to ask any 'difficult' questions at the interview. I was just to accept it, since I was already considered to be the preferred candidate. If I was appointed, I would also be able to continue to be in charge of my 'PLANIT' computer application. The salary was to be more than a thousand pounds than that of a work study manager, and I was to be entitled to a company car.

I was interviewed at the Watney offices at Mortlake by John Pretty who was the young group production director, and the older Bill Hoyles, who was in his late forties and had already been appointed as group production executive. The interview was fairly uneventful, and I was told shortly afterwards that I was to be offered the job. Unsurprisingly, I accepted the offer and realised that at the age of thirty-five I would now be earning far more than I could possibly have earned as a brewer or work study manager. I would certainly be earning more than any of my contemporaries. Needless to say, Shirley was delighted.

Executive Life

The new group executives were located on the first floor of Riverside House, a small two-storey block separate from both Mortlake Brewery and the offices. I shared an office with the Group Quality Control Executive, and the group keg executive. I had an excellent and charming production planning and control assistant. He was Alistair Healey, a brewer who had been at Birmingham Brewing School the year after I had left. The group quality control executive was Bob Hipwell who had been 'Dusty' Miller's second brewer at Northampton. He had never been to brewing school and subsequently, somewhat surprisingly, proved to have little or no knowledge of either biochemistry or microbiology. The keg management executive was Gordon Dobby, an ex-naval officer who became a great colleague friend and neighbour. Bill Hoyles, the group production executive, was in the room beside our office, beyond which were two female secretaries. He had been the manager of Watney's largest bottling plant at Edmonton in North London, but I never managed to establish whether he had ever been a brewer. He certainly had never been to a brewing school. He also had an assistant executive, Tony Button, in an adjacent small office. The whole setup was remarkably exclusive and rather superior. In contrast, the group marketing, market research and financial executives were all located at the group head offices in Victoria along with most other normal administrative departments.

On our first day together, Bill Hoyles called for a meeting in the small conference room adjacent to our office. We were all been formally introduced, and Bill Hoyles outlined his policy and our expected responsibilities. Shortly afterwards, we each had separate meetings with him, and we discussed our next immediate tasks. At my meeting, it became obvious that I would be responsible for visiting all of the production and depot facilities throughout the group. These were located all over the British Isles from Brighton in the South to Truro in the West, Southern Ireland, East Anglia, the Midlands, Manchester, and Scotland. I estimated that this would involve about twenty thousand miles of travel each year. My contacts at all of these locations would be the heads of production or management of depots. I explained to my new manager that my first proposal was to visit all of the group's locations and produce a survey of their capacities and production requirements for the future. Bill Hoyles agreed and approved of my plan. Like the other executives, I was to be entitled to a company car. He explained that I would be offered one of a number of fairly large saloon cars. At that time, the fitting of seatbelts to vehicles was not a statutory requirement. Despite this, I had fitted five sets of seatbelts to my Triumph Herald for myself and my family. The three on the back seat were specifically for small children. Apparently, the Watney Group did not provide any seatbelts to any of their vehicles. However, managers were allowed to buy their own seatbelts and to pay for them to be fitted. They also had to pay to have them removed when the car was returned. I explained this to him and also said that I would rather not drive around the country in a large family saloon but would prefer my own car. Better still, I wondered whether it might be possible for me to have a Triumph Vitesse saloon, which being a relatively small two-litre car would be even more suitable for long distances. Perhaps, unsurprisingly, Bill Hoyles was aghast and warned me not to upset the system 'for the rest of us'. As an alternative, which I accepted, he offered to allow me to be paid a mileage allowance for use of my own car. My first interview with Bill Hoyles had not been an unqualified success. Some years later, to my annoyance, I discovered that elsewhere in the group a brewer who had been at the brewing school after I had left had been provided with a Triumph Vitesse as his company car.

My first visit was to Ushers Brewery at Trowbridge. I had been there once before from Northampton. It was a large very traditional well-run brewery with very traditional brewers. The head brewer welcomed me cautiously and left me with the second brewer who was to accompany me on my inspection tour. He was a very amiable friendly local Wiltshire man. Having offered to show me the Mash Room, he was surprised that instead I wished to be shown the 'liquor' or cold-water supply tanks at the top of the building. I explained that I wanted to assess the plant from the very beginning of the brewing process to the very end. I then recorded the capacity of all of the vessels and equipment throughout the brewery. Finally, I calculated the maximum potential capacity of the whole brewery to be nine thousand barrels per week. The head brewer was somewhat taken aback by my assertion and asked 'how on earth did I expect the brewery to produce that output, when their present maximum output was only seven thousand barrels?' I explained briefly how I thought this could be done, and he somewhat reluctantly agreed that it might be possible. Some years later, my calculations proved to be a slight underestimate.

The brewers' office was a large room with three desks and with two steps alongside one wall leading up to a door. Apparently, behind this door, which opened inwards into the office, facing outwards was a lavatory toilet. On one embarrassing occasion, the door had swung open to reveal the brewer seated on the toilet whilst reading the morning newspaper.

I was taken to lunch in the Senior Staff Dining Room. One of the directors was present along with a brewery foreman who had been invited as a 'special guest'. The 'guest' might have been invited because he was also a shop steward, possibly to expose him to any controversial changes that I might be recommending. In any event, he was a very polite Wiltshire man and clearly on his best behaviour. In contrast, one of the directors who was present was an ex-Spitfire pilot from the Second World War. He repeatedly harangued and belittled the foreman and his politics. It was not only inexcusably but deeply embarrassing.

My next visit was to Murphy's Brewery in Cork where not only their stout was brewed but so also was Watney Red Barrel Keg. They also had a small experimental continuous brewing plant. Cork City was delightful; the brewery was large, and I was welcomed very warmly by the head brewer. After leading me immediately to the sample cellar, I was then taken to lunch. I saw only part of the brewery during the afternoon before being taken to my hotel, from which I was later invited to dinner. I continued my tour of the brewery early the next morning and was taken around by the brewery foreman, with whom I entered the fermenting room just after nine o'clock. The fermenting room was entirely traditional with very large round wooden vats, all of which contained warm partially fermented Murphy's Stout. The foreman respectfully asked me whether I would care to sample a vat. I had little option but to be polite and agree. I expected a small sample glass to be offered. Instead, he plunged a large pint glass into one of the vats and offered it to me fully filled. I was unsure whether he was merely being polite or challenging my capacity to drink draught stout. Unlike Irish drinkers, stout drinking in England was considered by most beer drinkers to be something of an oddity. However, I happened to like stout and decided to rise to the challenge. I drank the whole pint, warmly complemented the stout and the foreman, and politely declined the offer of a second 'sample'. I felt that my visit as an 'English Outsider' had been justified.

Every Monday morning, Bill Hoyles held a meeting with his group executives. The meetings rarely lasted less than two hours, during which time Bill Hoyles would discuss in excruciating detail every item that was of interest to him. He would delve persistently into every minute aspect of the items reported to him. Whilst he seemed obsessed with detail, he seemed rarely to be able to demonstrate any strategic thinking. On one classic occasion during a period when Britain had been exposed to extreme winter gales and storms, one of the delegates arrived half an hour late at the meeting. He explained that the road had been blocked by a fallen tree. Hoyles acknowledged this but immediately followed his response by the question 'What sort of tree was it?' Those of us at the meeting subsequently often used the phrase derisively when people asked absurd questions. The adequacy of his lack of technical understanding was displayed on one occasion when he reported his analysis of beer losses for every brewery in the group. He had simply added up the percentage losses for every brewery and displayed what he amazingly believed was a 'Group Average'. It was a mistake that any ten-year-old schoolchild would have recognised as basic ignorance. When the result was questioned, he simply replied that he thought his figure was helpful anyway. Bill Hoyles' working hours differed from the general normal practice of 'nine to five'. He rarely arrived before 9.30 but would always call for an informal meeting with beer drinking at approximately half past five. This often continued until seven or even eight o'clock. After some weeks of this routine, I finally pointed out to Hoyles that I had a wife and three small children, who I would like to see, other than at weekends. Instead, I would be perfectly happy to come to meetings at seven or eight o'clock in the morning if necessary. Perhaps unsurprisingly, my suggestion was not well received.

Back at home, I had always felt that the houses in the Grove were rather gloomy, partly due to the heavy painted panelled doors. I therefore replaced all of them with polished hardwood doors, which were completely glazed with small panels. The doors were expensive and came unpolished and unglazed. This therefore involved a lot of meticulous work on my part polishing the door panel frames and fitting the obscured glass, but I always thought it well worth the effort. More importantly, I had decided that the house was too small for a family with three children, as there were only four bedrooms. I decided that each child should have their own bedroom, and one bedroom would remain spare and for visitors. The houses in the Grove were all designed on an 'L' shaped layout in plan. Shirley's maiden aunt had just died and left her a thousand pounds. I therefore redesigned the house layout, and after I had drawn and submitted plans and obtained planning permission, we employed a local builder to carry out the work. I filled in the 'L' to make the house rectangular in plan. In this extension was a new bedroom, en-suite bathroom, downstairs playroom, a toilet and washroom, and a large additional useable roof space. I did all of the electrical installation, central heating, and plumbing myself.

One day, I received an unexpected phone call from the head office at Victoria from Roy Gander, who introduced himself as group market research executive. He explained that he had heard about my exploits and concluded that I was someone 'who knew what he was talking about', and that he would like to meet me at Mortlake. He had been appointed to the group from his previous career as a lecturer at Birmingham University. He duly arrived, wearing a tweed suit, large brown brogues, and a trilby hat. It was obvious that he differed somewhat from the style of almost all other group executives. He explained somewhat unsurprisingly that he was particularly interested in sales forecasting and the recently introduced technique of the Box-Jenkins method of exponential smoothing. He also knew of my use of Base Indices for production forecasting. He was about to go to Lancaster University where there was a one-week course on forecasting and wondered whether I would care to join him. Shortly afterwards, I obtained permission to go on the course. Needless to say, in a short time, he and I became great friends, although always in our executive environment.

I visited the Northampton breweries twice. On the first occasion, I was welcomed warmly by 'Dusty' Miller who later took me out to an excellent lunch. Later, I visited the bottling plant, which was not under his control, where I was shown a newly installed can-filling machine. This was unique and had been designed to fill seven-pint cans known as 'Party Sevens'. Unfortunately, it appeared to be wasting large quantities of beer, which slopped over the cans and ran down to the gutter. I discussed this with Clifford Jury, the bottling manager and Ken Homans, both of who I had always found very helpful. They both sheepishly admitted that they had made every effort to reduce the loss but had repeatedly been told that nothing could be done to remedy the problem. When I returned to Mortlake, I reported my findings to Bill Hoyles. He completely rejected my account and claimed that it was an exaggeration. Apparently, because of his expertise as an ex-bottling manager, he had been instrumental in the design and installation of the plant. On my second visit to Northampton, I arrived at six o'clock in the morning with a very large polythene sheet. Ken Homans and I carefully arranged it so that it covered all of the floor and the drain below the canning machine. After an hour's running of the machine, the sheet was completely flooded. We measured the volume of beer that the sheet had collected and calculated that the machine was wasting gallons of beer per hour. When I returned to Mortlake, Hoyles appeared to be somewhat ungrateful for my news. I was asked to make another trip to the Trowbridge Brewery with Bill Hoyles. He said that we should travel from Mortlake in his car. During the two-hour journey, Hoyles talked about nothing except breweries, brewing, bottling, bottling stores, and the brewing trade. After a few uneventful hours at the brewery, we set off to return. The original conversation continued. Halfway back, Hoyles explained that as it was Friday he was going to visit one of his relatives who lived at Berkhampstead, and he would drop me at the railway station there. This was about twenty miles north of London and about thirty-five miles away from my home. He duly dropped me at the station at which I had to wait half an hour for the train. I then had to cross London on the rush-hour underground and buy a ticket back to Mortlake to collect my car in which to return home. I finally arrived home after a two and half hour journey. I decided that it was beneath my dignity to claim travel expenses for the rail fares.

    I had visited most of the breweries and depots in the country, but I also made a trip to Scotland. All breweries produced 'live' liquid yeast as a by-product of the beer fermenting process. Most of this was usually pressed and then destroyed or sold at a modest price for further processing to produce marmite. I had learned from my great friend Oliver Griffin that scotch whisky distillers were buying yeast and were not always satisfied with the quality. Oliver offered to introduce me to some local distillers to see whether they would be interested in being supplied from the Watney Group. I flew to Inverness from Heathrow after work on a Friday afternoon. I was met at Inverness by Oliver who said we had been invited to dinner nearby. When arrived there, it was clearly a baronial mansion, and all of the guests, both gentlemen and ladies, were in full formal highland dress. In contrast, I was in a standard dark grey city suit. The dinner was excellent, if not superb, and after the traditional withdrawal of the ladies, it was followed by the arrival and circulation of the port. At this point, I explained to my fellow guest, who was sitting next to me, that I was feeling extremely uncomfortable. I had not been to the toilet since leaving Heathrow some four or five hours earlier and wondered where I could go now. He explained politely that in many Scottish Baronial Houses, there were no toilet facilities inside the house that were available to guests. Instead, gentlemen were expected to use the flowerbeds at the front of the house. I simply had to walk through the front room in which the ladies were withdrawn, completely ignore them, and then walk out of the front door. He further suggested that on some occasions it was not uncommon to find oneself joining half a dozen other male guests similarly spraying the roses. Oliver and I eventually returned to his home on the other side of Inverness. His house was halfway up a hillside overlooking Loch Ness, with a wonderful panoramic view of the Loch.

The following day, Oliver took me to visit three distilleries, two on Speyside, and one north of Inverness. The head distillers were all extremely hospitable and after a brief tour of their distilleries always hospitably offered us 'refreshment'. This always turned out to be a sample of their product, and on one occasion, this was supplied in a chipped white enamel mug. The last of the three distillers offered to take a sample of yeast later and give it a trial. My visit had been justified. Unfortunately, subsequently when the trial sample was sent from London by express passenger train, it proved to be unsuitable. Well, at least I had been enterprising and had tried.

Although I visited all of the main breweries, I was not allowed to visit the bottling plants in London, the largest most important of which was at Isleworth. The plant at Isleworth, which was just down the road from Mortlake, was claimed to be one of the largest and most modern in Europe. In reality, it had a reputation for being extremely inefficient, with frequent breakdowns and failures. Bill Hoyles had previously been bottling manager of Edmonton in North London and had been heavily involved in the design and installation of the new plant at Isleworth. He stated to me that he would continue to be responsible for Isleworth and specifically excluded me from visiting the plant. However, on my visits to Tamplin's Brewery at Brighton, I did visit their bottling plant. I was trying to establish a satisfactory method of analysing and controlling bottling plant performance. It was a complex problem to which no one had ever found a satisfactory solution. Bottling plant lines were essentially a series of the sequential processes of washing, filling, crowning, labelling, pasteurising, and crating. Any one of these processes could fail temporarily during the day, thereby bringing eventually the whole line to a halt. There was a small buffer of bottles on the track between each pair of machines. Unfortunately whenever any of these buffers became full or empty, it was impossible to know whether the failure was due to the machine in front or behind in the bottling sequence. No one had ever been able to produce a proper analysis or to solve this problem. However, I decided that the problem could be solved by means of computer simulation. The first requirement was to install simple electronic detectors on each machine and record their speed on a central computer data recorder. Somewhat to my surprise, Bill Hoyles agreed to my proposal. I commissioned a local electronics firm to specify and install the detectors, and Roy Hurst agreed to provide an IBM data tape data recorder and a simulation analysis program.

My bottling analysis system worked well, and performance was improved. John Pretty, the executive director, heard about it and apparently was impressed. As a result, he arranged for me to visit Carlsberg at Copenhagen, where apparently they had been attempting to develop a similar system. I duly spent four pleasant days there but discovered that their system did not really address the problem that I had just solved. In contrast, Bill Hoyles had rejected outright any suggestion that my analysis system could or should be applied at Isleworth. He asserted unequivocally that technically, it would be entirely unsuitable and inappropriate.

Just before Christmas, I visited the Tiptree Depot, which was located in a rather desolate part of the Essex Marshes. The day was brightly sunny but bitterly cold. In the journey in my car, I had become very hot and was actually perspiring when I arrived. However, I had no overcoat, and when I eventually returned home, I developed a very severe cold and fever and was obliged to go to bed. I attempted to get my local GP to visit me, but apparently, he was overwhelmed by the number of visits that he currently had to make. However, he offered to send me a prescription. Shirley duly collected the tablets, and by the end of the week, I began to recover. When I visited my GP a week later, he laughingly told me that I had suffered pneumonia. However, it hadn't mattered because he had prescribed the same penicillin that he would have provided me if he had visited me. Somehow, I was unable to share his merry amusement.

Keg beers had only recently been introduced nationally, and the leading brand sold by the group was Watney Red Barrel Keg. There were three or four competitive brands of which the original was Flower's Keg. Ray Gander had arranged a consumer testing exercise for Working Men's Clubs. Two or three members from each of half a dozen clubs were invited to spend an evening 'testing' keg beers. None of the kegs was labelled or identifiable to the participants. They could drink as much beer as they wished, for as long as they liked. However, they were required to drink only from the first keg that they selected and not to sample any of the others. Unsurprisingly, the participants were enthusiastic and somewhat doggedly determined to consume generous quantities of their chosen beer. They were then invited to return the following evening in order continue their 'testing'. The outcome was somewhat unexpected. None of the Red Barrel drinkers returned for the following test, whilst all of the other participants did. In response to his subsequent enquiries, Ray Gander discovered that all of the Watney participants had suffered excruciating hangovers. I discussed this subsequently with Doctor Bishop, who said he had known about the problem for a long time. He explained that the antidote was a large dose of vitamin B12. He had suggested some time ago that this should be added to the Red Barrel beer. His suggestion had been ignored. As a result of this revelation, I immediately purchased a large supply of Vitamin B12, a stock of which I maintained for the rest of my life.

The other masterstroke of marketing had been inspired by the group marketing executive. He was in his late thirties, an Oxford rowing blue and had also rowed at Henley. He introduced a massive publicity campaign of associating Red Barrel with the 'Red Revolution'. Although Russian Communism was widespread in Europe at the time, it seemed to me to be an entirely inappropriate theme. The red slogan and association were extended to all of the Watney pubs. The exteriors of many entirely traditional and architecturally well-designed pub frontages were painted completely 'Post Office' red. In my opinion, and that of many other people, it ruined the classic attraction of the pubs, and they looked absolutely ghastly. In fact, Red Barrel Keg had a fairly wide reputation for its poor palate and quality. A few years later, it ceased to be produced or marketed.

Gordon Dobby was the group keg management executive, and a large part of his job was the ordering and purchasing of new five-gallon aluminium kegs. This involved huge amounts of expenditure, which seemed to be continuing to grow. Forecasting was simply based on looking at past purchases and repeating them. Although I was not normally involved in this procedure, Bill Hoyles asked me to look at forecasting the keg requirements of Mann's Brewery at Whitechapel for their coming Christmas trade demand. Hoyles considered that the quantity of new kegs that they had ordered was excessive. On investigation, I discovered that publicans were not required to record their return of empty kegs to the brewery. The brewery simply took stock estimates of how many empty kegs were in stock at the brewery at the end of each week and whether there were enough kegs for the following week's expected demand. I realised that this system was almost useless, since they had no record of how many kegs were to be expected back in the coming week. I therefore created a simulation model on the computer and from its analysis was able to calculate the likely return of kegs in each week. As a result of my study, John Duncan, the head brewer, at Whitechapel became furious at the rejection of his excessive demand for new kegs. Even more embarrassing was the discovery of a widespread highly profitable flourishing industry among East End Publicans. They were selling empty kegs to local scrap merchants for the valuable price of the aluminium. This could have been avoided if a simple system of recording the return of empty kegs from pubs had been adopted. My revelations did not prove to be popular with the Whitechapel head brewer. However, a great deal of theft and wasted money was prevented for the future.

Early in the New Year, a takeover bid of the large brewery of Taylor Walkers in East London was launched by the Watney Group. Whilst this was under way the Grand Metropolitan Group launched not only a rival takeover but at the same time a takeover of the Watney Group. Shortly afterwards, I was asked to see Bill Hoyles. He explained politely that as a result of the takeover activities, the Watney Group had decided to reduce the number of group senior executive staff. I was therefore to be made redundant. I would be given three months' notice, a maximum redundancy payment, and retain my pension. Hoyles explained that he personally would be responsible for production planning and my assistant Alistair Healey would now be reporting directly to him. My PLANIT production planning and control system had been progressing well, and I had written an article in the Brewers' Journal describing it. However, the two programmers who were working on the system would be returned to their previous duties in order to reduce costs. As a generous gesture, the company would not be claiming copyright of the system, and I would be allowed to continue developing it on my own if I wished. Just how I would be able to develop a PL/1 system without an IBM 360 computer at my disposal was rather difficult to imagine. Apart from being totally devastated by my dismissal, I realised that Bill Hoyles had conveniently not only got rid of what he regarded as a thorn in his flesh but also got back control of his favourite areas of the business. I learned shortly afterwards that Roy Gander also had been made redundant. No doubt, he too had been regarded as a thorn in the flesh by the group marketing executive.

Hoyles' final masterstroke was that it would no longer be necessary for me to share an office with the other group executives, and that I would be moved to an office 'over the road'. The office 'over the road' turned out to be a large Victorian three-storey building in which I would occupy a room on the ground floor. I soon discovered that I was to be the only occupant of the building. However, I had one great advantage in that thanks to Roy Hurst – I still had access to the telephone line on which I could continue writing and running programs remotely on the IBM computer. I had already started to write programs for a system of Quantity Surveying for the building of domestic houses. Some weeks earlier, I had considered all of the applications which might require expensive printed documents. I concluded that the top of the list was Bills of Quantities produced by Building Surveyors. I had already been involved in the design and building of my own house in Northampton and extensive alterations to my present house in Willow Grove. I had read in great detail two volumes of a definitive book by Medlicott on house-building construction and innumerable research papers from the Government Building Research Centre at Bracknell. I had also become very proficient in the use of the 'BASIC' programming language. I was confident that I had all of the technical knowledge and resources necessary for the task.

I left Mortlake finally, after completing my three months' notice. Bob Hipwell was subsequently made redundant and obtained a job as the only brewer of a tiny brewery in Rutland. Alistair Healey went on to become the head brewer of the large Greene King Brewery in Bury St Edmunds, and I never discovered where Gordon Dobby went. Sanders Watney retired; John Pretty left the board of directors and bought a small bakery in the Isle of Wight. Bill Hoyles was eventually made a director, before receiving early retirement. The brewery was finally bought by Budweiser, an American company. I visited it twenty-five years later, just before it was eventually closed and demolished. I was intrigued to see the claim that all of their beer was 'matured over oak' in the traditional American style. During my tour of the brewery, I observed that the 'maturing' simply involved an eight-foot-long steel tube of oak sawdust through which the beer passed at high speed only once, on its way from one process to the next.

The Wilderness

I was now once again out of paid employment. Unlike the previous occasions, I not only had a wife but also three young children. However, the children were all at the local school, and Shirley therefore immediately got a job as a secretary at the nearby technical college. I had applied unsuccessfully for a couple of managerial jobs, but my previous employment and salary appeared to be something of a handicap. As an alternative, I had considered the possible prospect of buying a pub and becoming a publican. I could probably raise enough money from the sale of our house, but the prospect of bringing up small children in a pub environment was very unappealing. However, I did visit half a dozen pubs in various parts of the country. All were outside the London area. Two were isolated in the middle of nowhere. One was in the middle of the Newbury Downs in Wiltshire, and the other was in Monmouthshire beyond the Wye Valley. They were either devoid of custom, or relied on weekend and holiday-time restaurant trade. It was somewhat soul-destroying, and eventually, only one pub seemed to offer any real prospect of future development. This was the Angel Hotel in Coleford in Gloucestershire on the edge of the Forest of Dean. I arranged to visit it and stay overnight. It was a large 'free' pub, and the owner manager not only seemed rather undynamic but seemed to have only a limited number of customers. I discovered that the seven bedrooms, one of which I was to occupy overnight, were unused because of new fire regulations. I visited the local senior fire officer the following day, and he explained the alterations that were necessary. They were modest and not likely to be terribly expensive. Another potential advantage was that there was a large unused stable block at the rear of the pub, presumably a relic of its days as a coaching inn. I considered that this could be turned into a small brewery. This would have been the precursor of what many years later were to be known as 'Micro Breweries'. However, my main reservation was that although the pub was in the Forest of Dean and near to the beautiful Wye Valley, it was thirty miles from the nearest large town or city. The landlord had told me that my children would all get into the Gloucester Grammar School, and there was also a boarding school if I preferred. I found the thought of bringing up children in such a rural and remote environment and only seeing them in the evenings and weekends during the busiest times of pub trade was not a desirable future.

In order to continue my computer programming, I needed to acquire a terminal of my own with which I could access the IBM online computer service. I required an IBM so called 'Golf Ball' typewriter, a magnetic card reader, and a modem. These were all available on monthly hire from IBM. However, these facilities were expensive, but I only had funds to be able to pay for them for a few months out of my redundancy money. The Golf Ball terminal was a very high-quality device. It was large, heavy, and operated at only fifteen characters per second. The modem was encased in a large steel box that was two feet square and about nine inches deep. Like the typewriter, it operated at fifteen characters per second. Normal twenty-first century modems would operate at a thousand times that speed and occupy less than the size of five pence piece.

A neighbour of mine was John Kemp who was a pilot for the then British Airways Corporations. He flew worldwide and as a result got regular leave, which he spent at home. He was as great a 'DIY' enthusiast as I was. Importantly, he owned a small cement mixer, which he was happy to lend to me. We both re-laid our front drives and rear terraces with crazy paving made out of broken flagstones. At that time, these were readily obtainable from the local council at a very cheap price. We also carried out many other home improvements. I progressed well with my Bill of Quantities program, and through one of his friends, John Kemp introduced me to Noel Crockford. Noel owned a Quantity Surveying practice in nearby Esher, and he agreed to try out my new system. Apparently, he was impressed with it and agreed to use. As an integral part of my system, I had designed a comprehensive data base of quantity surveying technical terminology. After a short time, Noel decided that the most valuable part of my system was the high quality of the electronically printed output. He therefore bought a Golf Ball terminal and made use of my data base. His use of the system over the next few years provided a small, though very welcome income. However, I could not have chosen a worse time to try and use my system to build a business which depended on the building trade. Shortly after I had begun, house building went into recession. The few builders who had shown a welcome interest in my system either ran out of money or went out of business.

One slight ironic crumb of comfort was from Peter Price who had built my house extension. He gave me the plans of a house he had already built, and I produced a Bill of Quantities for it. He was very impressed but claimed that I had completely underestimated the quantity of concrete of the garage floor. I checked this and found that my calculations were correct. He thought hard about it and then ruefully remembered that he had ordered a bulk delivery of concrete and had to dispose of some of it because he had overestimated his requirements. I felt that my system was vindicated.

Shortly afterwards, I saw an advertisement in a local paper for a data processing manager in a company in nearby Mitcham. Although I did not think that there was much likelihood of me being eligible, I applied, and somewhat to my surprise, I was invited to an interview. The company was SGB, a national scaffolding company. The computer manager was Don Kerr, whose surname I later learned was always to be pronounced as 'Car'. He was in his early forties, extremely smart, personable and dynamic, and to my further surprise welcomed me extremely warmly. He explained that he was seeking a new systems and programming manager for his department of twenty-five systems analysts and programmers. He was apparently very interested in my C.V., and after a further discussion, to my complete amazement, he offered me the job. The salary was considerably less than I had been earning as an executive, but I was in no position to negotiate. However, I asked him if I could continue selling my Quantity Surveying System, and he quite happily agreed. We agreed that I should start my new employment in a few days' time at the beginning of the next month. Unsurprisingly, I was delighted, as was Shirley when I returned home with the good news.

Real Management

At last, I was to be a real manager with a real department. The Computer Department at SGB consisted of three departments, which were the Operating Department, Data Preparation Department, and the Systems and Programming Department, which was by far the largest. My department was split into development teams each of which had one systems analyst and two or three programmers. There was also a maintenance team, which was responsible for all systems that had been developed previously. Somewhat oddly, one of the development teams was led by my predecessor, who apparently had found my job too demanding and had reverted to being a systems analyst. Whilst I might have expected this to present future problems for me, but in fact, it never did.

My first task was to introduce myself to my new department. I explained to them that my previous computer background had been exclusively IBM. I had first programmed in COBOL but had then been obliged to change to PL/1 and the DOS Operating System. In contrast, the SGB Company used an ICL Computer using COBOL and the George3 Operating System. I stated that I intended to familiarise myself as quickly as possible with my new computer environment. The contemporary government had recently set up Regional Industry Training Boards, which were paid for by means of a five-percent Industrial Training Levy, which was imposed on all employers. This proved to be particularly fortuitous for me, as I immediately registered myself to attend a number of ICL training courses. Don Kerr happily supported my conversion training. He commented that no one had bothered much in the past, and he had never had a manager who had wanted to know the technical details or theory of Systems Analysis or the Operating System.

Employment, staff turnover, and promotion and had always been problems in what at the time was called the Data Processing Profession. Systems analysts rarely received any specific training for the job and were almost exclusively experienced programmers who were simply promoted to lead a team. The market for programmers was very volatile, and salaries were rising continuously and rapidly. In consequence, turnover, retention, and the necessary recruitment of programmers was a major task. My solution was to ensure that the maximum amount of information of the job market was recognised and acknowledged. A number of weekly journals contained numerous adverts for programmers and analysts. I therefore created an index of the market rates for analysts and programmers and made sure that all of the staff was aware of it. I also made it clear that I did not consider that good experienced programmers necessarily became good systems analysts. Another anomaly was that whilst there were always at least three or four new systems being developed, programmers and analysts always wanted to be part of the newest developing systems. In contrast, existing systems were all maintained by one small group of very experienced programmers. Nobody really wanted to join such a group, since they all regarded maintenance as boring. The most senior of the Maintenance Team was not an analyst and therefore did not receive the maximum Data Processing salary. All salaries were reviewed twice a year, and the personnel manager was particularly helpful in advertising for and interviewing potential new staff. I laid down a new remuneration policy that all salaries would be kept in line with market rates. All new staff would be required to spend three to six months in maintenance in order to familiarise them with the existing systems. This would also be a requirement for existing programmers, who on completion of new systems would be given a small increase in salary. The whole point of my policy was to recognise that maintenance of all existing and old systems required far more skill and knowledge than the creation of new ones. The senior maintenance programmer would receive the same salary as systems analysts. The whole point of my policy was not to increase costs but to lower them by reducing the continuous excessive staff turnover, which was extremely time wasting and expensive.

Staff turnover was endemic among computer programmers, and the personnel manager and his director were both supportive of my policy. They also accepted my suggestion that recruitment of new programmers should be offered to existing company staff. In fact, junior programmers currently received higher salaries than many of those long-serving staff in other departments. My selection procedure for new programmers was to require them to take the ICL Programmer test. Unlike the IBM test, which was very general, and with which I was very familiar, it consisted of only ten questions, which in my opinion were actually better suited to low level programming than to COBOL. However, I was in an

ICL installation, and I felt that I should respect ICL standards. As a result of my decision, roughly half of the new applicants failed the test and were therefore not employed. Only ICL knew the answers to their test, and all papers had to be sent to them for marking. It was clearly an impartial method of selection, but to be fair, I thought that all of my department including myself should take the test. We therefore all sat down on one Friday afternoon and took the test, the papers which I then sent off to ICL. The results were very satisfying. I allowed all of the results to be known only to the candidates but told them of my score. I then allowed all of the candidates to try and answer the paper together and discover by general agreement what were the right answers, I had managed to get nine out of ten answers right but was baffled by the last question. I then found out that, like me, none of the candidates had managed to get that question right. I took the problem home for the weekend and just about managed to solve it. On Monday morning, I found that one or two others had also done so. However, we all agreed that it was not a problem that anyone could solve in a short time and shouldn't really be part of the paper.

Three existing members of staff from other departments applied to become programmers, and all three passed the ICL Test. Two of them became excellent programmers. One was a married female Polish clerk who had previously been a schoolteacher. The other was an operator from the Operating Department, who became an outstandingly bright machine language programmer. I made sure that all programmers attended at least one training course every year.

SGB consisted of a number of subsidiary companies and depots located all over the country from the South of England to the North of Scotland. All of the systems and work done by the Computer Department were charged out to these subsidiary companies at what were competitive rates, One of the problems for the department was estimating, costing, and charging for the actual work done, The final problem was finally providing full documentation for the systems when they were finally completed and implemented. The staff was always reluctant to produce documentation subsequently, because they were usually anxious to get on with the next new project. Don Kerr's solution to this problem was to tell the clients that if they required full documentation, they would be charged additionally for the work involved. It was a somewhat outrageous suggestion, but it seemed to have been accepted by most clients. In contrast, my own solution to the problem lay in the programming. All high-level programming languages allowed their data names and variable names to be invented by the programmers.

In practice, this meant that even simple names such as 'total' could be abbreviated at the whim of the programmer to 'tot', 'ttl', 'tl' or even named 'Fred'. I regarded this sort of indiscipline as absurd, since it made programs more difficult to read, check, or correct. A further problem was that when systems or programs were amended or updated, a completely different set of names and abbreviations might be used. Therefore, I created a standard dictionary of abbreviations and data names. All programmers and analysts were obliged to use these and to enter any new names that they had created. The other innovation was to put all file specifications and program comments as remarks, embedded in the front of the programs. 'Remarks' were a freeform facility that allowed any piece of explanatory text to be written and included as part of the program. These remarks in no way affected the execution, efficiency, or processing by the computer. The result of these two innovation meant that for all intents and purposes the documentation was incorporated in the computer program and should always be up to date. Therefore, there was no need to create or charge anything extra for documentation of systems and programs, since it was already within the systems.

The only other innovation that I made was in office layout. In my second year, the country was suffering for the 'Winter of Discontent' during which all electricity power was cut off during the afternoon. The main programming office was large and open plan. However, during the restrictions, I rearranged the layout so that all desks were crowded together beside the large windows on one side of the office. Although this was somewhat uncomfortable, it enabled work to continue for twenty analysts and programmers for an extra hour in the darkening winter afternoons.

Finally, after nearly two years, I began to look around the industry to see what my future prospects were likely to be. I was not short of money, but I was still earning less than my salary at Watney Mann. The only step up was to become a computer manager, and if I stayed with SGB that would be unlikely for at least another couple of years. The other important factor seemed to be that I had never encountered or heard of a computer manager much over the age of fifty. It seemed to me to be fairly certain that I could never continue employment in the Computer Industry to the age of retirement at sixty-five. The next best option seemed to be a job as a management consultant. I applied therefore for a couple of jobs, before attending an interview with Crouch Crosby who were one of the leading Audit and Management Consultant firms in London. They were located near to Kingsway in the centre of London. I was offered a salary close to my Watney executive job, and I accepted gratefully. I returned to Mitcham and tendered my resignation to Don Kerr. After attending the traditional Friday lunch at a local pub with all of the computer staff, we returned to the office. Don asked me to come into his office, and I once again explained my reasons for leaving and how much I regretted having to do so. He was furious and appeared to find my departure as treacherous, a personal affront, and unforgiveable. Instead of requiring me to work my one-month notice, he said I would be paid to the end of the month. I must also clear my desk now and leave by four o'clock. With great sadness, I bid goodbye to my twenty-five staff and ended my life as a systems and programming manager. The last two years had been some of the happiest of my career.

Nadir

My first day at Crouch Crosby began when I reported at 9.30 to their offices on the first floor of a shared Victorian office block near Kingsway and the Law Courts. There was no lift, and the offices had a rather old-fashioned feel to them. They were thickly carpeted, and 9.30 was the normal starting time. I was asked to see George Wilson who was the managing director. He was very friendly, charming, and had a 'Hail fellow, well met' sort of personality, that reminded me of 'Dusty' Miller at Northampton Brewery. He welcomed me and after a brief resume of my background said that he was glad that I had finally 'come in out of the cold'. He explained to me the routine procedures of the consultancy. To my surprise, he said that no one was entitled to the exclusive or permanent use of any desk, including his own. However, everyone was entitled to a total of any two drawers that they could find empty in any desk. Only one of the drawers could be locked, but a spare key had to be left with the secretary. Consultants were required to leave a label inside their drawers with their name. When working in the office, anyone could use any vacant desk, including his. First of all, he took me around the offices to find a spare drawer. He opened one, looked at the label, and then explained that the consultant had been sent to the Middle East and would not be back for some time. He cleared the drawer, gave the contents to his secretary, and offered it to me as my first drawer. He then passed me to Charles Baker, the chief consultant, who I had met previously at my interview. Charles was equally urbane and friendly and proved to have a pleasant dry sense of humour. He gave me a large typewritten manual, which he explained contained the standard procedures for all consultants. I was then told to find a vacant desk and read the manual.

The Standard Procedures Manual was extremely comprehensive and readable. I was quite impressed. It explained everything, especially the full recording of the time spent by each consultant. All time had to be booked against a particular project or client and was charged to their account. Any other time spent in the office and not chargeable had to be booked as 'Client Development'. One of the small side rooms was described as the library and contained a number of domestic-style bookcases. It was intended as a reference room for all matters of management and management consultancy. My subsequent examination of the contents revealed that they were almost all 'popular' contemporary books, with little classical or genuine academic management theory or practice. I was finally told that my first assignment was to an ongoing project with an Industry Training Board Headquarters in Wembley. The project was to introduce job evaluation to all of the staff of the Catering Industry Training Board. This involved interviewing all of the staff and producing job descriptions for their roles. The consultant who had been carrying out this project had been moved at short notice to another project. I met him briefly, and before leaving, he left me a set of case notes. Job evaluation was an interesting subject, which had been explored very fully during my time at Edinburgh University. Whilst the concept was good in theory, it had serious weaknesses in practice, and these had led finally to its fairly general disuse. The problem was that it was perfectly possible to rank the relative importance of all jobs within an organisation. However, it was extremely difficult, if not impossible also to value them comparatively in terms of market salaries. The classic example of this emerged in the case of the canteen cook or chef. His salary was lower than the salaries of many of his comparable employees. However, the market salaries of cooks and chefs were considerably higher than would be indicated by his job evaluation comparison. There was no solution to this problem, apart from ignoring job evaluation. It soon became clear to me that none of the consultants at Crouch Cross had any previous knowledge or experience of the subject. Their only knowledge came from the one rather superficial account of the subject in one of the chapters of a paperback book in their library. Considering that their services were being charged at very expensive Management Consultancy Rates, this seemed to me to be somewhat misleading. At the completion of the investigation, I returned to the head office where the chief management consultant held a meeting with all of the consultants who had been involved in the project. We were to consider the final report, which had been written by the senior consultant who had been responsible for managing the project. All reports were printed on a traditional typewriter by the managing director's female secretary. The technique was unbelievably primitive. Each draft of the report was written by hand by the consultants and typed manually by typists. The draft was then amended and corrected by the consultants and completely re-typed. I queried why consultants were not allowed to use typewriters. It was explained to me that consultants' fees were too valuable to waste consultancy time on typing. Typing was a job for typists. Clearly, Crouch Cross had never even heard of Word Processing.

After three weeks, the assignment at the Industry Training Board was finished and the final draft report was submitted to the chief consultant. All of the consultants who had been involved in the project were called to his office to review the report. During the meeting, it became obvious that one of the anomalies that I had mentally predicted had occurred. Unsurprisingly, after considering a number of remedies, there was no obvious solution. Charles Baker, the chief consultant, then stated the alternatives. We could adjust all of the other figures, which would mean that they would be wrong, or we could ignore the issue. He then explained that, "In either case we must not admit it, we must simply just lie." It was an apparently not unprecedented serious suggestion. It was a suggestion that I had never heard before, nor ever would hear again during the sixty years of my working life. This event helped to prepare me from my subsequent experiences as a Crouch Cross consultant.

I discovered that almost all of the other management consultants were qualified chartered accountants and had experience as auditors. They regularly recruited significant numbers of extremely intelligent graduates, often with First Class Honours Degrees from Oxford and Cambridge. These new entrants then became chartered accountancy trainees and eventually became auditors. None of them ever had any management experience, other than within accountancy. An exception to this occurred shortly after I had joined Crouch Cross. They had recruited a newly graduated young man from South Wales. He was to become a programmer. His previous experience was at university, where he had learned BASIC programming for his exams. He had been recruited specifically to be sent to Switzerland. Bernie Cornfeld was a prominent businessman and international financier who sold investments in US mutual funds and who was tried and eventually acquitted for mismanagement of the Investors Overseas Service (IOS). Crouch Cross were currently investigating his business affairs and required programmers to look at his computer systems, the programs of which were written in COBOL. The new recruit had never ever encountered COBOL, so he was given a manual from the Crouch Cross library. He was given a fortnight in which to learn the language before being sent to Switzerland. Charles Baker discussed the matter with the managing director. The problem was whether to charge his consultancy fees as a programmer or senior programmer. Their joint decision was almost instantaneous. His fees should be charged as a senior programmer. I was absolutely appalled. In order to train a new COBOL programmer at SGB, it was necessary first to send them on a two-week course with ICL. Although they could then begin to write commercial programs, they were required to spend up to six months in an experienced team before they could be considered to be a fully experienced programmer. To become a senior programmer, they required at least eighteen months of experience, preferably in more than one system. The thought of letting loose a programmer whose only knowledge had been gleaned from a popular paperback book was completely beyond my comprehension. To sell him as a 'Senior Programmer' bordered on blatant fraud.

Shortly afterwards, I was sent on what proved to be my largest assignment. Crouch Cross were auditors to a transport company called Silver Roadways who were owned by Tate and Lyle. Crouch Crosby were their auditors and had become concerned about Stock Controls at their depots. I was sent to visit one at Bristol, one at Swansea, and one in Glasgow. The depots also serviced and sold spares for commercial vehicles belonging to other firms. The accountants had costed their own computer system, divided it by the number of invoices produced, and concluded that every sales invoice was costing approximately two pounds. Whilst they regarded this as acceptable for repairs and parts costing hundreds of pounds, it was unacceptable for small transactions. Sales invoices for these were therefore to be produced by hand and not by the computer system. This was clearly an absurd decision, because like most accountants they failed to be aware of or understand the concept of Marginal Costing. It was an elementary fact that every additional document produced by a computer system cost only the price of a piece of paper and not the notional cost of including all of the other costs including the managers', staff, and cleaners' salaries. I asked to see the hand-produced invoices and to see how they were processed. The chief accountant opened a very large six-foot square lateral filing system, which was completely filled with paper sales invoices. These had all been processed clerically by hand. The sales invoices did not correspond to those of the computer system but could have been entered easily at the point of sale in the depot. The clerical cost of processing these separately from the computer was a complete waste of time and money. Another consequence of the accountancy policies was that depot managers had to pursue customers' debts and to refuse to supply them if these were overdue. Whilst this might have been a useful strategy with small customers, it was an absurdity with large ones. The depot manager at Swansea had conscientiously followed his company accountancy rules and threatened Swansea Council with legal action in the event of further late payment. Swansea Council was one of his largest and most valuable customers, and one that he was least likely to influence, and most easy to lose. Another masterpiece of ignorance was in stock control. Depot managers had been told that for financial reasons stock had to be kept at the lowest possible levels. However, national inflation at the time was at an all-time high, and in some cases running into double figures. When annual Stock Taking was carried out, the most profitable depots were those with the highest revalued stock.

When I returned to London, I produced my daft report to Charles Baker. He seemed to be less than pleased with it. He said that Silver Roadways were one of Crouch Cross's most important and valuable auditing clients. He had no wish to pursue the matters that I had identified and did not expect them to be included in my report. I felt that I needed to lie down in a darkened room whilst I invented a benign anodyne report. After almost ten years of writing accurate work study and other business reports and articles, it was a new experience for me to be required to write fiction. It was the second time that I had encountered the apparent fact that honesty was not the best policy when working with accountants and auditors.

My next assignment was to a small import company whose offices were behind Oxford Street. They had installed a mini-computer for accountancy purposes. Mini-computers were a recent innovation at the time but were more suitable for companies who could not justify the cost of a larger mainframe computer. They involved very little, if any, programming or computer knowledge but relied largely on pre-written program packages supplied by the manufacturers. This particular installation was run by the office manager who now enjoyed the title of computer manager. He clearly knew nothing about computers, but the machine only processed a daily workload of about two dozen transactions each day. There was very little I could contribute to the situation, but I looked first at the input documents. The details of import shipments were copied on to input forms, which were then used to enter the data into the computer. The items on the input data forms were in a completely random order, which bore no relation to the sequence required by the computer. It would have been almost impossible to find a more inefficient piece of systems design. Any of my analysts at SGB would have been severely criticised if he had produced such rubbish. However, since the operators had so few document to process each day, the benefits of redesigning the form were very small. The situation simply illustrated that my presence as a very expensive consultant was a complete waste of time and money.

I was next given an assignment to Sea Containers Ltd., who occupied a rather superior modern office block in Hanover Square behind Regent Street. Apparently, Crouch Cross had been contracted to introduce a new computer system into Sea Containers, since the company had no previous computer experience. The consultant in charge was a young man in his very early thirties. He was very friendly and keen and appeared to have been a programmer. Clearly, like almost all programmers, he had no knowledge of systems analysis or design. The first steps in creating any new system were for the systems analyst to produce a systems specification, file specifications, and program specifications. Until all of these specifications had been completed, the programmers could not be involved. The so-called computer consultant from Crouch Cross had been producing program specifications for newly trained programmers at Sea Containers. This was in order to give them experience in programming in anticipation of the new system that he was supposed to be introducing. He had completely failed to produce either systems specifications or file specifications. Without these, it was an absurd waste of time to start writing programs. However, he was in charge of the project, and he gave me a sample specification and then asked me to write more program specifications for him. I was at a complete loss to understand how anyone could continue to write program specifications without first having produced systems and file specifications. However, I took home the details of his request and contacted John Muxlow. John had been my senior analyst and was now my successor as systems and programming manager at SGB. I had great confidence in his systems and programming experience. He was as baffled and horrified as I was at the request, or practical possibility of writing program specifications under such absurd conditions. I thanked him gratefully and reported back to Charles Baker, the chief consultant, the following morning. His response was immediate. He said that I clearly did not fit in as a computer consultant at Crouch Cross, and therefore, very reluctantly I would be given one month's notice. Since I would then only have been at Crouch Cross for five months, I would not be entitled to any redundancy payment.

On the advice of Charles Baker, I had very foolishly allowed my Watney Mann pension to be transferred to be reinvested by Crouch Cross. I had very naively assumed that as leading chartered accountants they would be able to invest it more profitably for my future benefit than Watney Mann. This no doubt proved to be the case, entirely to the advantage of Crouch Crosby. However, when I finally received my pension twenty-five years later, it was precisely the same face value without any interest or adjustment. Its real value and benefit to me had depreciated considerably.

Convalescence

I was yet again out of work. I was still receiving a small amount of income from my Quantity Surveying package, but there was no prospect of it providing a realistic income. However, I was now nearly forty years of age, and I had already considered how I could reach retirement in twenty-five years' time rather than much sooner. The safest possible course seemed to me to be to enter full-time education as a lecturer in some academic institution. As it was now late summer, recruitment for the coming academic year should be beginning soon. Such proved to be the case, and I applied for a post as a management lecturer at the local technical college. I received an invitation to attend an interview and arrived along with half a dozen other candidates. One of these who was roughly the same age as myself had a PhD. My interview appeared to go quite well, and I was told to wait until after all of the other candidates had been interviewed. When all of the interviews had been completed, the head of department came out and thanked us for attending. However, he explained that the committee had been unable to select any of the candidates for the appointment. Nevertheless, the college would be re-advertising the post, and he suggested that I and the PhD candidate might care to reapply. After the head had gone, the PhD candidate and I looked at one another in disbelief and contempt. If the committee was unable to make up their minds on this occasion, why should we reapply? Similarly, who on earth would want to work with them or for them?

My next interview was with Kingston Polytechnic. The post was in the Data Processing Group. The interview was completely different from that at the technical college. The department consisted of six lecturers, a technician, and a secretary, all of who had worked in the Computer Industry. I was interviewed by the head of group, Fred Thomas and his deputy, Chris Palmer. They were extremely friendly and courteous and apparently impressed by my previous posts. However, Fred Thomas was somewhat concerned by my previous salaries. I had deliberately understated these, but they were still barely in line with lecturers' starting salaries. Nevertheless, Fred reminded me that lecturers' salaries had incremental annual increases and that I would soon be up once again to my previous salary level. With that closing advice, he then said that I would be offered the job, and I would receive it in writing within the next few days. I was delighted, grateful, and incredibly relieved. I was now forty-one years old, and unlike almost all of my contemporaries from my brewing days, I was likely to be able to reach full retirement at sixty-five. When I received my official Contract of Employment, I could hardly wait to begin the autumn term a few weeks later.

My first day began at Penrhyn Road in Kingston, which was the main centre of the Polytechnic. There were a dozen new lecturers, and we were invited to join in a welcoming glass of sherry with Bernard Lawley, who was the principal. Bernard Lawley was a charming and most unassuming character in his early sixties, and he mingled with the new entrants in a very informal manner. He asked me what department I was joining, and I replied that it was the Data Processing Department. He immediately and politely corrected me. He explained that data processing was not a department but merely a specialist group. However, he said that he was pleased that I had joined the group and wished me success in my future teaching. With that somewhat embarrassing beginning, I then returned to the office and rooms of the group to meet my future colleagues. The group consisted of Fred Thomas, the head, and his deputy, Chris Palmer, four other lecturers, a secretary, and a technician. Three of the lecturers were married women in their mid-thirties, only one of who had a small child. Their male colleague was Mat Nicholson who was in his early sixties. The secretary and technician were in their late twenties. The group all seemed to get on very well together, and I never encountered any rivalry or animosity between any of them. All of the lecturers had been in the data processing or computer industry before coming into education. Outside experience of business or industry was extremely rare or completely absent amongst almost all departments of the Polytechnic. Most lecturers had been in education all of their working lives.

Immediately after my reception and introduction to my future colleagues, Fred Thomas explained my future role and offered me what proved to be invaluable advice. He said that I should regard my first year as an investment. My teaching workload as a lecturer was for up to eighteen 'contact hours' per week of face-to-face lecturing to students for more thirty weeks of the academic year. This amounted to a total of about five to six hundred hours of lecturing per year. It would be necessary to prepare all of my one-hour lectures in advance. However, a major course was a six-week course in systems analysis which was run to the National Computing Centre's syllabus. All of the lecture notes, documentation, overhead projector transparencies, and exercises for the course were provided by the NCC. This was a huge advantage, although it would still be necessary to provide my own supplementary lecturing notes. The other part of my teaching load was to be a three-hour per week evening class on systems analysis and design. This was to be run for the second year of the Higher National Certificate in the Computer Science Department. As part of my induction into teaching, I, along with all new lecturers, would attend a three-hour teaching class each week for my first term.

As an ex-work study manager, my first step was to study the work required by my new role. My first task was to find the most efficient method of producing and deploying lecture notes and overhead-projector transparencies. By sheer good luck, I discovered that the group office had obtained a mechanical typewriter, which used a very large typeface. It produced print, which was about thirty-point or one centimetre high. I never saw another such machine anywhere else at any time. For many years to come, it would be impossible to produce such scripts without the use of a computer. I then had to design a standard format for my lecture notes, which recorded details of each course and session on which I had delivered them. The format deliberately restricted me to one sentence line per lecturing comment or topic and never more than four pages per lecture. In the right-hand column, I recorded the course number, week number, and sheet number of the lecture. I could then refer to these details and assemble any set of one-hour lectures in a matter of a few minutes and be able at the same time to know on which sessions I might previously have used them. The ultimate challenge to my system came when on one occasion I was given only ten minutes to prepare and present a lecture for a class normally taught by Mat Nicholson, who had phoned in at the last minute to say he was ill. I managed to find out what the course and subject were and the particular topic that had been expected. I assembled very quickly a four-page set of notes for my fifty-minute lecture. I had never seen the course before, and the lecture took place in the largest lecture theatre in the Polytechnic. It housed approximately a hundred students in steeply tiered seats and rows. I presented the lecture confidently and successfully and subsequently felt that it was my finest hour, and that it endorsed fully the efficacy of my work study lecturing system. My colleagues were somewhat surprised by the event.

One of my commitments was a weekly three-hour evening lecture to part-time students. I gave my first lecture and found that despite giving the students a couple of exercises, three hours seemed a rather long time. The following day, I commented on this to a colleague. When she heard of my discomfort and possible fatigue, she was appalled but highly amused. She said that I should have realised that evening classes always had a half-hour break in the middle of the evening, and that after a hard day's work, they never got more than two hours of lecturing. The event was probably my least 'finest hour'.

Many of the courses and lectures by the Data Processing Group were held in hotels and other centres offsite. These were all for adult bodies such as the civil service, regional and national electricity, and gas boards. These were usually two to six-week residential courses and were held in hotels or other centres. These courses were all arranged and promoted due to the efforts of Fred Thomas and produced a considerable amount of income, which more than covered our salaries and other expenses. Many of these courses were at the splendid Star and Garter Hotel at the top of Richmond Hill overlooking the Thames below. The other frequent location was the nineteenth century Horsley Towers on the way to Guildford. This was a magnificent somewhat eccentric site, and its extensive grounds had once been the home of Ada Lovelace. She had worked closely with Thomas Babbage who invented the world's first digital computer, and she was commonly regarded as the world's first programmer. The site was now used as an education centre for the then National Electricity Board, and the courses were all residential. In the case of the systems analysis courses, these were for six weeks and were attended by a total of about twenty delegates from electricity boards from all parts of the country.

One of my first lectures at the Star and Garter was with a class of two-dozen delegates from a regional gas board. They were staying at the hotel, and I arrived one morning to discover that a very disturbing incident had occurred during the night. In the early hours of the morning, one of the young female delegates had run naked and screaming hysterically into the corridor. Delegates in adjoining rooms had rushed out to discover the reason for the disturbance, and one of them had gallantly thrown a blanket over the distressed female. Unable to find some miscreant attacker, the young woman tearfully explained that the ceiling of her bedroom had fallen in on her. The next morning, the hotel manager regretfully apologised and explained that the problem was due to Second World War bomb damage. The explanation was interesting but less dramatic than some of the delegates might have imagined.

My attendance at the New Tutors' Induction Course ended at the end of the autumn term. I felt entirely happy with my new profession, and in the last week of term, lecturing and teaching more or less finished. I had found the course very interesting but had not learned a great deal that I didn't already know. However, one piece of advice that we received from the tutor was how to move from one lecture room to another if accompanied by our students. It was just possible that on some rare occasions, we might find that the room which we were due to occupy was already occupied by another class. In such an event, the most important rule of all was that under no circumstances were we to use 'any initiative'. Such a mistake could mean that if we attempted to occupy another empty room that also might be required by another group who might then make the same mistake. Total chaos could then ensue. We were highly amused, but the advice was well judged, no doubt reflected past experience. In fact, I was to encounter the problem only once in the future.

On the very last Friday of term, staff attended a Christmas lunch, followed by a staff dance in the afternoon. However, on the Friday morning, members of staff tended to migrate and visit colleagues in other departments. In order to be sociable, many carried bottles of wine or Scotch whisky as gesture of seasonal good will. By lunchtime, many lecturers were exceptionally full of good will. On one such occasion, a fellow lecturer still had an evening class to attend. During his own lecture unfortunately, he fell asleep. His students were amused and politely left the classroom to return to their homes, possibly for their own pre-Christmas celebrations. I was very happy and contented by my first term in adult education and looked forward to a secure future. I was not to be disappointed in that ambition. I returned home to enjoy my first ever four-week long Christmas vacation.

The spring term went equally well. I found that I could handle the work easily and that my fellow lecturers were extremely friendly and supportive. The four-week Easter vacation was as welcome as that at Christmas, although without any festive celebration. In the summer term, it was necessary to prepare examination papers for all students. These had to be submitted for scrutiny before printing and had to be accompanied by a marking scheme. The marking scheme identified the main items of the questions and allocated marks to each. I applied my work study and systems analysis skills to this task and in all future years simply repeated variations of the topics in a two to three-year cycle. This also had the advantage of offering students the opportunity to look at old examination papers in order to test their knowledge. My last lecture of the year was devoted to revision. In this, I explained to students how they should take examinations. The first step was 'not' to start by writing anything, other than their name. The second step was to read right through the whole paper. The third step was to identify which questions they were going to answer. The fourth step was that before answering each question, they should try and think of what were the essential 'bullet points', which might be in the marking scheme for that question. When all that was clear, they should then begin writing. My advice appeared to be well received and produced satisfactory results. I rarely had more than one or two students of any class who failed my examinations. The only examinations on the outside courses were the National Computer Council Examinations at the end the special six-week courses on systems analysis. These were followed by an oral examination conducted by outside examiners. Although my fellow lecturers and I were not involved in these oral examinations, we always had one member of staff present as an independent witness. However, prior to these interviews, we always gave a coaching session and mock interviews for the benefit of all of the students.

After the end of my first year of teaching as a lecturer, I was then able to enjoy the summer vacation. This, incredibly, consisted of twelve weeks during which lecturers were required to apply themselves to research and preparation for the next academic year. They were not required to attend the Polytechnic. Shirley and I took our three small children to a holiday hotel in Broadstairs, which catered almost exclusively for parents with small children. The weather was wonderful, and the resort was ideal, with extensive sands on which the children could play safely. There was a small funfair on the beach and even a Punch and Judy show. Needless to say, when we returned home, I was able to pursue my own private activities of developing and extending my computer-based Quantity Surveying package. By this time, I had managed to sell the service on a regular basis to a firm of quantity surveyors in nearby Esher. The practice belonged to Noel Crockford who was a charming forty-year-old who, unusually, had served his national service in the Royal Navy. He and I and our families became great friends. His use of my package provided a welcome small income to offset my costs of paying IBM for the use of their time-sharing computer and accessories.

My income was now more than adequate and would automatically increase each year for at least the next ten years. I looked forward to the prospect of a secure and happy future right up to retirement in twenty-four years' time. The job required less effort and almost no stress compared with anything that I had experienced in my twenty years of previous employment.

Management Education

Towards the middle of my second year, the group was informed of a radical change in the organisation of the Polytechnic. A brand-new centre was to be set up at New Maldon. The centre, which was about two miles away, consisted of a newly built three-storey office block on the main High Street. Our group would now be part of what was to be a Regional Management Centre. Although it would be a part of the main Polytechnic, it would be independent and available only to delegates from outside businesses and employers, rather than to academic students. However, the staff would continue to be a normal part of the Polytechnic staff and would carry on with their previous teaching commitments within the Polytechnic.

Regional Management Centres, Industry Training Boards, the National Freight Corporation, and the Open University were all new highly successful initiatives by the current government. Unfortunately, only the Open University survived the ruthless ideological extermination, which was imposed by the following government. The centre at New Maldon was an ideal working environment. All of the offices and rooms were newly furnished; there was a lift and a carpark in the basement. There were two other groups from the Polytechnic located there, one on accountancy, and the other in business. There were also offices occupied by the National Freight Corporation and a small Publicity Department from the Polytechnic. Each of the groups was allocated separate small clusters of offices. I shared an office for two occupants with Linda Burkett, one of my fellow lecturers in the Data Processing Group. The office was comfortable and well furnished with new furniture. It had a single large double-glazed picture window, which overlooked the main street immediately below. The windows were of a very new modern novel design, with one operating handle along their left-hand vertical edge. The handle could be rotated into four positions. In the down position, the window was locked. In the left-hand position, the window could be opened like a normal window hinged on the right-hand opposite side. In the upper position, the window could be opened and was hinged on the lower side and used for ventilation. In the right-hand position, the window fell into the street below. After a couple of embarrassing incidents by colleagues who had fully tested their own windows, the architects solved the problem immediately. They pasted warning notices on all windows prohibiting users from attempting to open the windows under any circumstances.

The purpose of Regional Management Centres was to provide specialist training for management in industry and commerce. We were to provide short courses, usually of one-week duration to classes, typically of twenty experienced managers. In the case of our group, we were to continue running the outside courses on the premises of the Star and Garter Hotel and Horsley Towers. I immediately began to design new one-week courses on 'Computers for Management' and contacted the Publicity Department. The department consisted of a manager, a secretary, and the occasional services of a commercial artist. I designed suitable logos for the courses and discovered that the department had for their publicity a monthly circulation list of over two thousand businesses. My courses were marketed under the collective title of 'Computers for Managers' and were full daytime courses of one week. They covered sales forecasting, production planning, stock control, and statistical analysis. I used to cover about half of the time and my fellow lecturers covered the rest. I also continued with my routine 'servicing' lectures to other parts of the Polytechnic. The 'Computers for Managers' courses used to be attended by about fifteen or twenty managers and were very successful. They also covered their costs and provided a profitable income to the centre. After moving to New Maldon, we had ceased to run outside courses at the Star and Garter but continued to run them at Horsley Towers.

Apparently, courses for the certified accountant's qualification had been running at Fairfield College in Croydon. Fred Thomas asked me to take over a weekly three-hour lecture in data processing there. I was not enthusiastic about lecturing to potential accountants, but apparently neither was anyone else. However, the syllabus for the lecture contents of the course were provided by the accountants' professional body and it led to a professional examination at the end of the year. In fact, I found my year of teaching on the course to be remarkably easy and appeared to be well received by the students. However, despite a number of requests by me, I was never able to obtain a marking scheme or discover how many students passed the exam. This meant that I was completely unable to evaluate how effective my teaching had been. I suspected strongly that the reason for the secrecy was that the purpose of the examination was to limit the number of successful entrants to the profession. Nevertheless, I was asked to continue teaching during the following year.

The three-hour evening course on data processing that I had previously been lecturing on at Penrhyn Road was moved to New Maldon. After my lecture one evening, a student asked if he could see me in my office. He showed me a small keyboard that he had bought. In fact, the keyboard was the newly invented American microcomputer called a Tandy Model 1. It contained a Z80 microprocessor and 8 kilobytes of memory. He explained that the memory could be expanded up to 64 kilobytes and data storage was on a small portable conventional-type tape recorder. It could also be bought with a small screen or used with an adaptor connected to a standard television set. He then demonstrated a small program that he had written in BASIC language. I was flabbergasted. It opened a completely unprecedented new world of data processing and computing. I had become a skilled programmer in BASIC. I had already written my Bills of Quantity programs and system in that language but on an expensive slow IBM time-sharing telephone terminal. Here was the potential opportunity of a lifetime. I thanked him, asked him where these machines could be bought, and then went home to find out everything I could about these wonderful new innovations. I soon discovered a number of Tandy dealers, the cheapest of which appeared to be available on the other side of Finchley in North London. I duly drove there but had no wish to buy either the small tape recorder, small screen, or printer. If adaptors could be supplied, I wished to use my high-quality Panasonic recorder and a fairly large spare television set that I had at home. The price of the computer was over two hundred pounds; the only question was whether the television adaptor would work with my television set. The dealer was not prepared to guarantee this and appeared to be becoming impatient with my indecision. I somewhat uncertainly made the most important decision that I had made for many years and bought the keyboard and adapter. Mercifully, my technical judgement had been correct. I had my first very own computer. After I took the keyboard home, I immediately attempted to transfer some of the BASIC programs of my Quantity Surveying Package on to my new machine. To my delight, they worked well. They also worked with my IBM Golf Ball typewriter.

In our second year at New Maldon, Chris Palmer came to me to say that he had received a telephone call from a trade union asking if the centre could provide consultancy for the possible introduction of a computer system. Chris had asked Fred Thomas if the centre would be interested but apparently had been told no, but there was no objection to him offering his services personally and privately. Chris asked me if I would be interested in joining him. Needless to say, I accepted, and we visited the ACTT Union, whose offices were located in the very attractive Soho Square in Central London. The Associated Cinematographic, Television, and Allied Technicians Union were an extremely well managed organisation, and Chris and I were welcomed warmly. Somewhat embarrassingly, I was not a member of any trade union, but fortunately, Chris was a member of the teaching union. We were asked to look at ACTT's membership subscriptions operations, which currently were all carried out clerically and manually. They wanted to discover how this could be computerised. After a number of visits, Chris and I decided that it would be possible to produce a system using the recently introduced microcomputers. However, although we would be happy to do the systems design, we did not wish to undertake the programming. Chris therefore managed to find a freelance programmer who was already creating such systems. Chris and I therefore specified the system and file design, and the programmer provided the coding. We had decided to use an American Data Base system, the name of which with hindsight carried the unfortunate acronym of 'AIDS'. The programming progressed very well, until we reached the final stage of testing. The data base system failed completely when more than two thousand records were entered. This was a catastrophe, and for once, I had no idea how to get around the problem. However, the programmer consultant was even more worried but miraculously managed to rewrite the system in BASIC using his own conventional methods of file organisation. It was the most serious problem I had ever encountered in my years of computer consultancy, and happily, I never encountered any similar crisis in the future. However, the system was a complete success, and as a result, we were recommended to our next assignment, which was with Equity, the Actors' Union.

Shortly after Chris Palmer and I had started our consultancy activities, I had registered a business name. I decided that 'Central Business Associates' could abbreviated to a memorable 'CBA' and that I would processes all consultancy activities, costs, and fees through CBA. Value Added Tax had only recently been introduced, and at the time, there was no lower limit on the value of turnover that was required. However, I was required to submit a summary of monthly revenue and payments every three months. To my great satisfaction, as a registered business rather than a Limited Liability Company, I was not obliged to hire either an accountant or auditors. I was not required to keep conventional accounts or an annual report or a balance sheet. I was only required to keep a record of purchases, sales, and expenses. I had now decided that if ever I could achieve an income from CBA that was higher than my annual salary, I would leave the Polytechnic. At that time, my salary was £5,000 per annum, with annual increments. However, there was also a guaranteed retirement pension.

The office block at New Maldon was shared with the headquarters of the National Freight Corporation. We were asked to run one-week courses for them at their centres in various parts of the country. Chris and I did these at centres in Exeter, Leicester, Nottingham, and Manchester. Our arrangement was for Chris to do one half of the week and I to do the other. In our absence, we would take over each other's lectures back at the Polytechnic. The courses proved interesting, and whilst teaching on the course in Manchester, we were housed in a hotel near the centre of the city. During the night, we were constantly awakened by other bedroom doors along the corridor being opened and closed. We soon discovered that we were in the centre of the 'Red Light' District and that the rooms were being occupied by short-time clients. We asked the National Freight Corporation to move us to another hotel. It was in nearby Whaley Bridge and was a great improvement.

The elderly lecturer Mat Nicholson had retired before we moved to New Maldon, and Fred Thomas retired in the following year. After eighteen months, all of the female lecturers had left. Chris Palmer, who was a principal lecturer and I as a senior lecturer were the only surviving members of the once flourishing nine-person Data Processing Group that I had joined only a short time before. A new custom-built education block of buildings had been built at Horsley Towers, and we continued to run the six-week residential NCC courses there in considerable comfort. Chris and I continued to run the courses there with some very limited help from some other members of the Regional Management Centre. We used to run the courses on a half-day basis where one of us would do the morning lectures, and the other would do the afternoon, and any evenings that were required. We were also allowed to stay overnight if we wished. I received a call one day from a lecturer in Jersey. He asked if he could have details of my computers for managers' courses. I was somewhat surprised but agreed readily, and asked him which of them, and when he might wish to attend. He immediately corrected me and explained that he did not wish to attend, but he would like me to run them as weekend courses in Jersey. I was astonished and delighted. Within a very short time, I began to run the courses, which were very successful and well received. Needless to say, I thoroughly enjoyed my weekends in Jersey.

I was never a 'petrol head' motoring enthusiast, although I was a dedicated Triumph Herald owner. At Watney Mann, I had bought a new Triumph Herald Convertible each year and passed the previous year's model to Shirley. However, when the children were growing up, I had needed to buy a saloon. Somewhat inevitably, my choice was a Triumph 2000. Maintaining such cars in the 1950s and '60s was a continuing task. British cars of this period required constant maintenance, replacement, and repair. Of necessity, I had become expert at replacing exhaust systems, usually with custom-built stainless-steel components, dynamos, and rusting body components. However, on one occasion, I had seen a three-litre Daimler Saloon in a second-hand car seller's window. This luxury car had what to me was an astonishing price of just over a thousand pounds. The car, like all Daimler/Jaguars, was actually a Jaguar saloon with a Daimler radiator. Unfortunately, the one in the showroom was pink, but I soon tracked down one which was in British Racing Green at a similar price. I was now 'hooked' on Daimler/Jaguar Saloons, and I bought my first one of many that were to follow over the next twenty years. At the end of the second year at New Maldon, we were told that Chris and I and the remaining lecturers there were to be relocated at Gypsy Hill, which was a vacant college site on Kingston Hill.

Gypsy Hill

The site at Gypsy Hill was extremely pleasant and was located in woodland in a very expensive residential area on the outskirts of Kingston. It was a large site, which had previously been occupied by an art college from Gypsy Hill in London. Chris and I were to be located in a separate building and to continue running and lecturing on our normal courses. We carried on with our previous teaching and outside commitments. One of my commitments was at Canbury Park in which teaching took place in the original buildings of the Hawker Aeroplane Company. The British Aerospace Company was located a mile away near to Ham Common. All of the courses at Canbury Park were for the Aerospace Industry, and the three degree courses on which I was required to lecture were for mechanical, electrical, and aircraft engineering students. Chris and I continued to run the courses at Horsley Towers and our servicing for other departments.

Our system at ACTT was implemented successfully, and all of the union staff was well pleased with it. The head of the ACTT thanked us and took Chris and me out to lunch. He told us that he had recommended Chris and my consultancy to the TUC at their headquarters in Central London. He said that they required a survey to be carried out in order to determine their future needs for data processing and computers. He also had recommended us to Equity the Actors' Union. We were very gratified and flattered by his recommendation, and we duly carried out a survey at the TUC Headquarters in Central London. Our survey lasted a week during which we visited every department. We found all of the staff to be very helpful and keen to have any improvements. We produced our report, which was very well received, but the union did not implement our main recommendation until some considerable time later. We suggested that networked microcomputers should be installed in all main departments in order to increase the speed of communications. At the time, they considered that the cost would be too high.

Shortly after we moved to Gypsy Hill, I was asked by a young fellow lecturer in the School of Personnel if I would be interested in lecturing on short courses that were running at the Fire Service Staff College near Leatherhead. Apparently, he did not feel comfortable with the somewhat rigid discipline or culture there. Having been a gunnery instructor in the army, I had absolutely no reservations about such problems. I was delighted to accept and went to visit the centre. It was the beginning of some of the happiest ten years of activities of my working career. The college was at Wotton in a magnificent mansion in beautiful wooded grounds at the foot of Leith Hill, the highest in Surrey. It had originally been the home of the seventeenth century diarist, John Evelyn. I was introduced there to the deputy commandant, a most dynamic and friendly ex-pilot of the Second World War. He explained that the college required someone to give half-day lectures on computers and data processing. I was delighted to offer my services and would bring with me a computer and printer. I would be grateful if they could provide a large television set for visual display. He readily agreed, and I began to visit Wotton a couple of half-days per month for the next few years. All of the attending fire officers on the courses were highly experienced fire fighters, and the courses were part of their promotion to more senior ranks. I found all of them to be very formally disciplined but incredibly receptive, enthusiastic, and sociable. I came to regard many of them as personal friends.

After we had been at Gypsy Hill for a year, and the demand for data processing seemed to have a limited future in the Polytechnic, I became increasingly conscious of my lack of a university degree. Therefore, I applied to be sent to Lancaster University for a masters' degree in management learning. My request was turned down by the Education Committee on the grounds that Chris Palmer and I were the only data processing lecturers in the Polytechnic, and I could not be spared. The head of the School of Law, who I had never met before, told me that he thought the decision by the committee was completely unfair, but his opinion had been ignored. Sometime later that year, Chris and I were moved to Coombe Martin, a large house on a separate site about half a mile from the main Gypsy Hill campus. He and I and our secretary were now isolated completely from the rest of the Polytechnic. We continued to run the Systems Analysis Courses, but shortly afterwards, events overtook us again. Bernard Lawley, the principal, retired and was replaced by Henry Smith, a professor from Southampton University. Unlike his predecessor, he was a 'dyed in the wool' academic whose ambition appeared to be to get rid of all non-academic courses in order to raise the academic status of the Polytechnic.

The Polytechnic computer was located at Penrhyn Road and was an ICL 1500 mainframe and was somewhat smaller than the one that I had worked with at SGB. There was no manager, but the head of the department was a female supervisor who had previous past experience of ICL mainframes. It had been decided by the new principal that this should now become a new department and run by a new head. Invitations for the post had been advertised. In the light of my previous experience as a manager of twenty-five analysts and programmers in a much larger installation, I decided to apply for the post. I was shortlisted along with two other applicants. One of these was a young academic doctor from Southampton University, from where the new principal had recently come. This applicant apparently had no previous experience of running a computer department, although he might have used the services of one. Perhaps unsurprisingly, he was chosen and appointed to the post. To my surprise, the principal asked to see me a few days later. He almost apologetically explained to me that he was sure that I would understand that the new head of the Computer Services Department was clearly more highly qualified academically than I was. I thanked him and withdrew politely. I realised once again that I was living in a different world.

After a few months, Chris and I were told that we would no longer be associated with the academic staff but would be reporting to the new Computer Services Department. The new head came to see us for the first time and appeared to be both condescending and ignorant about business computing and management. Unfortunately, his deputy who had previously been a young lecturer in the economics department appeared to be equally ignorant and arrogant. Chris and I were then told that we would be required to sign new contracts of employment. Apparently, this was because none of our courses were regarded as being sufficiently academic. In our new contracts, we were required to ensure that we obtained external fees for our courses to the value of at least twenty thousand pounds per year. Chris immediately went to see his union representative, and I equally promptly joined the union. A deputation of union representatives visited Professor Smith who apparently went very pale during their discussion. Shortly afterwards, his proposal was withdrawn.

After my failed application to go to Lancaster, I obtained permission to apply for a masters or doctoral degree on a part-time basis at the Polytechnic. I had chosen to invent a new subject, which would be called binary statistics. It was based on the principle that all living creatures need to make decisions as to whether something is true or false and whether to accept it or reject it. This, in my opinion, could not possibly depend on or be related to conventional statistical theory. All of computer theory and science depends on Boolean Algebra, the application of which depends only on whether events are true or false. In the case of computers, it is whether components are on or off. Nothing can be nearly on or nearly off, or nearly true, or nearly not true. I had written programs to test and develop my theory, and they were working well. However, they were only suitable for using as a simple or crude replacement for basic probability theory. What I lacked was the ability to use binary statistics for correlation. I then made an invaluable accidental discovery. By sheer chance, I came across a small paperback book in the Kingston technical bookshop. It was entitled 'Taxi-cab Geometry'. It was by an obscure American academic who had used the example of the grid-type street layout of New York as the basis for his theory. The layout of almost the whole of New York is a right-angled grid pattern in which all streets run between East and West, and all avenues run North and South. All streets and avenues are at right angles to one another. The effect of this is that any diagonal journey from one part of the city to another can be achieved only by turning right-angle corners. The surprising result is that it does not matter which route is chosen, all routes, however different, are precisely the same distance. I realised that this was composed entirely of binary choices and decisions. It was the very 'break-through' that I was looking for in my research. I took all of my work to a number of lecturers in the Polytechnic School of Mathematics. To my relief, they were very interested and extremely supportive. I then went on with my research and produced a program to use the technique before submitting my application to become registered for a masters' degree. It was approved. However, events were due to overtake me.

Following the recent change of government, we had been at Gypsy Hill for a couple of years. The new government directed that all Industry Training Boards and all regional management centres had to close. Chris and I were told that we would have to join either the School of Computing Science, or the School of Business. We both went for interviews with the heads of both schools. My first interview was with the pleasant young head of the School of Computer Science. During the interview, he revealed that his ambition for the school was for it to concentrate exclusively on theoretical computing rather than practical applications. He said that ideally he would even like to concentrate theory on imaginary computers. I was appalled; however, Chris decided to go to the School of Computer Science. The head of the Business School had a somewhat unfortunate reputation for being irascible and difficult to work with or under. Somewhat surprisingly, I had on my rare encounters with him found him very friendly. My interview with him went extremely well. He read my C.V. and said that he would be delighted for me to join the school. However, despite the fact that I had been to two universities and was a graduate member of the British Institute of Management, he did not consider that my academic qualifications were as high as he would like them to be. He was aware of the approval of my master's research but said that if I joined the school, it would be necessary for me to get an MSc in management. He strongly recommended that I should go to Henley Management College. It was one of the most valuable pieces of advice I was ever given.

My short courses for managers were still running successfully; one of which was on the use of the very recently introduced Spreadsheet packages. The original one had been usable only on the Mackintosh Computers, which later became known as Apples. However, I was using the Tandy version, which was at least as good. After one of the courses, a managing director of a company who had attended asked me whether I would run a weekend course for his fellow directors and senior managers for his company in Slough. I agreed and duly ran the course in a local hotel there that his company used. All of his directors and about twenty delegates attended, and afterward, he thanked me profusely. He said that until now his fellow directors had always spent days and even weeks laboriously preparing and endlessly revising the company's next year annual budget. In future, the company would buy a microcomputer and spreadsheet and would then be able to prepare and evaluate their budgets easily in a very much shorter time.

Chris and my work at ACTT had been successful, and we were well on with our services at the Actors' Union Equity. I had now migrated from Tandy computers to Future Computers, which were a new English firm in Croydon who were manufacturing excellent desktop computers. These had both floppy disc and hard disk drives. They were expensive at well over a thousand pound each, and initially, I had bought four of them. I had decided that these were ideal for the Equity application and hired three of them to Equity in order introduce and develop our proposed system. Equity had well over twenty thousand members worldwide, and their annual subscriptions were run on an old Olivetti electronic teletype system. This machine was operated by one member of staff from clerical records processed manually by four or five other clerical staff. I proposed to design and produce a networked computer system that would enable all data processing to be done by the existing clerks. The programming language and system that I proposed was being written in a new database language called FoxPro. This was a superior version of a language called DBASE2. I had recruited four programmers, all of who were experienced ex-programmers in COBOL They were all married women in their twenties and thirties who were living at home and bringing up small children. They had learned FoxPro easily and soon became very skilful. I specified the file structures and programs and provided them with Tandy Model One Computers, which by this time were perfectly suitable for writing FOXPRO Programs. However, I also needed a systems analyst.

Whilst at Gypsy Hill I had continued teaching systems analysis at Penrhyn Road to a second year class in the Computer Science Certificate for the last nine years. The students were nearly all in their late teens or early twenties. However, on my final year, a thirty-three-year-old female student joined the course. She was very bright and confident, and arrived late on my first lecture. She attempted to creep in quietly through a door at the back of the tiered lecture theatre. As part of my normal routine, I immediately asked her to come to sit in a space on the front row. It was part of my standard practice of discouraging lateness to my lectures. She appeared to be completely undeterred and during my lecture confidently asked a number of entirely pertinent questions. She also attempted unsuccessfully to question some of my answers. Shortly afterwards, I discovered that she was working in a new microcomputer shop in Kingston selling Macintosh Microcomputers. Towards the end of the final term, she asked to see me at Gypsy Hill. She had been sent to me by her tutor Mike Arnold, who was one of my friends and colleagues at Penrhyn Road. He had told her that I was the only person in the Polytechnic who could possibly help her. She explained that she wished to enter the data processing and microcomputer profession and needed advice on how best to do that. There was little if any future for her as a poorly paid shop assistant in Kingston. I advised her that she should attend the next six-week course in data processing, and after passing the NCC Examination, she would be in a position to enter the professional side of the industry. I had absolutely no sales incentive, because the course was already well subscribed to and in fact nearly full. She agreed, entered the next course that Chris and I were running, and obtained the NCC Certificate. Her name was Clara Shaw, and I discovered that she had an extraordinary background. Although she spoke flawless English, she was German. She had been born near Cologne shortly after the end of the Second World War, and at the age of nineteen had married an English Captain in the Royal Artillery. He had then left the army and joined the Diplomatic Corps and was sent as a consul in the foreign office first to Bulgaria, and then to South Africa. Her husband had now been posted to Washington, where she did not wish to join him, and she was now getting divorced. She had a four-year-old daughter who would continue to stay with her.

At Equity, we were proceeding very successfully and profitably. We had created a data base for the twenty-five thousand equity members and installed four Future Microcomputers and a network so that any member of the clerical or other staff could access all records instantly. This was in complete contrast to the original system, where any queries or entries had to be input by a single dedicated machine operator. After a couple of months of our work, I was asked to see the union secretary. Apparently, their annual accounts were being audited by one of the Auditing Accountant firms in the city. The 'Consultant' had advised that our proposed subscription system was unsuitable and recommended that a mini-computer should be bought instead. Needless to say, of course his 'Consultants' would oversee the installation of the system. Mini-computers were by that time were completely outdated, expensive, and basically obsolete equipment. More importantly, for Equity a mini-computer would not enable any of the staff to examine conscription records other than by making a request to the Accounts Department. This was the fundamental weakness of their previous system. In contrast, we had already installed three powerful PCs of the latest future design and networked them together. This enabled all of the Equity Staff who required access to any individual Subscription Record to be able to do so immediately at any time. The staff that was already using the new system was very satisfied and supportive and acknowledged that the new system was significantly superior to their previous system. The reversion to an obsolete mini-computer would be a giant and totally unnecessary step backwards.

The so-called 'Consultant' had apparently suggested that the producers of our system were 'amateurs' who were neither qualified nor professionals. He asked to see the C.V.s of all of the contractors involved. Unsurprisingly, his criticism was totally unfounded, unprofessional, and completely malicious.

However, I readily agreed to provide the C.V.s of all of the members of my team. These included Chris Palmer and me, both of whom had lengthy management experience, qualifications, and teaching in data processing and computers. My three programmers all had at least five years of professional employment each as COBOL programmers, and one of them had a First-Class Honours Degree in mathematics. In return, I asked to be provided with his C.V. and those of his staff. Unsurprisingly, he categorically refused to provide this. The unpleasant politics and unreasonable influence of auditing accountants that I had experienced at Crouch Cross had reared its ugly head once again. These so-called 'Management Consultants' of a leading auditing firm had neither management qualifications nor experience, nor computer qualifications or knowledge. They were simply accountants who 'knew the price of everything and the value of nothing'. They had displayed the same spectacular ignorance, lack of any genuine management experience, and monumental stupidity that I had encountered previously at Crouch Cross. Very sadly, and completely unfairly, our contract with Equity was terminated. However, much more importantly, I was now due to go to Henley the Management College and would be able to spend very little time on consultancy.

I had attended the interview with the Dean at Henley the Management College, and I had been accepted for the next course. The Dean was very friendly but was concerned by my age. I was now fifty years old, and I would be the oldest member of the course by at least ten years. He explained that most students were in their twenties or early thirties. He also commented that many of the younger ones had graduated fairly recently, and some were Oxford and Cambridge graduates. I would be the eldest member on the course by at least ten years. I was slightly surprised by this information but had no reservations about my ability to participate and obtain the masters' degree. The course was split into three ten-week sessions separated by two 'in-service' projects. These involved carrying out working studies into outside organisations. Reports then had to be produced that would form part of student's final examinations and working projects. Despite his reservations, I was accepted for the next course. I tidied up my commitments for private lectures, and in particular to the fire service at Wotton, and looked forward to my release to Henley.

Henley

The site of the college at Henley was idyllic. It was a magnificent group of buildings on the Northern bank of a long sweeping bend of the Thames. The college was always known as 'Henley the Management College'. The emphasis was unquestionably on the word 'the', and in all of my subsequent experience, I considered that it was entirely justified. I went to Henley in my Daimler Jaguar, because Shirley had never driven it and left her with her Triumph Herald. I took with me a Tandy Model Three computer that I had acquired back at Gypsy Hill, since no one there seemed to be interested in it. It would prove to be a valuable aid to my studies. In fact, I was the only student at Henley with or ever had a personal computer. The resources and facilities were extraordinary and almost certainly unique. The main college building was separated from the river by large lawns, which swept down to the riverbank. It was surrounded by accommodation outbuildings, a library, workrooms, a swimming pool, and two boathouses on the river's edge. The most astonishing operational feature of all was that all of the buildings were open and available to students twenty-four hours a day, seven days a week. Students could walk into the library, boathouses, or any of the administrative offices at all times. They could take out boats and row up and down the river whenever they chose. It was a life of ultimate privilege.

The academic syllabus was not dissimilar to the one twenty years earlier, and I had no difficulty in learning from and participating in it. However, one topic that was completely new and different to me was highly significant. Research had been carried out at the college some years earlier into the behavioural psychology of managers and management. One of the tutors at the time was Meredith Belbin, and as a result of his and his colleagues' research, he produced a book on 'Management Teams and why they succeed or Fail'. This had all been based on his and their observations and analysis of management behaviour. The work was based and backed up by very extensive psychometric testing of the managers concerned. Henley had continued to be pioneers in this work, and our course was subjected to a great deal of psychology teaching. All of the members of the present course were subject to a full half-day of psychological testing and examination. The original research had identified eight possible psychological profiles that could be applied to members of management teams. Their observation and theories that were derived from them enabled the success or failure of such teams to become completely predictable. The research was an extraordinary breakthrough, and it was to prove to be invaluable and life changing to me. The results of half-day psychometric testing that had been carried out on me was a revelation and almost completely explained my past history and future behaviour.

The tutors and classes were all superb, and there were also sessions with outside speakers from industry and commerce. I had no difficulty in completing the first semester. Despite my difference in age, I had no problems with making close friends with many of the other students. There were a number group of projects, which were devoted to 'Management Games'. In these teams of five or six students were given management projects, the object of which was to produce a profit from the imaginary 'company'. This was exactly the procedure on which Meredith Belbin and his then fellow tutors had created their theory of Management Performance and effectiveness. Like the original research, we were all observed by tutors during our performances. However, by this time we all knew the results of our own psychological testing. We were able to apply this knowledge to our individual contributions and performances. To me, this was a fascinating development and one from which I was to continue to explore and benefit in the future. It was perhaps a turning point in my academic career.

At the end of the First Semester, there was then a six-week break during which students were required to carry out an 'In Service' project and produce a report. I immediately contacted the deputy commandant at Wotton. He said that there were no obvious opportunities for a project at Wotton but offered to contact the chief fire officer of Surrey Fire Brigade on my behalf. The headquarters of the brigade were located in a splendid mansion called St David's at Redhill in a large wooded estate at the foot of the Surrey Downs. I arranged an appointment to visit the chief fire officer. Based on my recommendation from Wotton, the chief welcomed me and suggested a suitable project. This was to examine the progress and future of a new training building that was under construction and was to be used also for running courses for outside commercial and business organisations. I accepted his kind offer and was introduced to Roger Ticknor who was one of his senior officers. It was an ideal choice, and Roger was to become a life-long friend.

One day, I arrived at St David's and parked my beloved high-compression Triumph Herald Convertible on a wooded road running through the woods alongside the main building. I had parked on the other side of the road next to a deep depression. This apparently was known as the 'Ravine' and was filled with wrecked and crashed cars and other vehicles. These were used to provide training for fire fighters in how best to cut their way in to and rescue victims from their crashed vehicles. When I stepped out of my car, I saw Roger Ticknor coming from the opposite direction, leading a party of visitors for a tour of the grounds. As he approached, I could hear him explaining to his party that the Ravine contained old worn out scrapped vehicles that were used for training. To my surprise and dismay, he completely ignored me. He continued his narrative to the visitors by pointing at my car and explained that – here was another vehicle, which was due to be scrapped and added to the 'Ravine'. He impassively continued to ignore me and led his party past me. It was a classic example of fire fighter humour, which I was to encounter and enjoy many times in the future.

My project went well, and I identified a potential major problem. Although the plans included bedroom accommodation, there were to be no 'en-suite' facilities in these rooms. Instead, residents would have to walk down the corridor to share a bathroom and toilet facilities with other guests. I pointed this out to Roger, who explained that originally the centre had been intended for fire service personnel and recruits. The tradition and convention had always been that such attendees slept in common dormitories. This had been regarded as good policy in order to promote comradeship and fellowship. Unfortunately, I could not envisage this as being a factor that would be attractive to normal outside businesses and their delegates. However, I presented my report to the chief fire officer, and he was appreciative and positive about my findings. He explained that the service was in the midst of savage government funding cuts. Any attempt to change, criticise or change the layout plans could be used by the government as an excuse to cancel the project. I could only sympathise and thank him for the opportunity he had given me to carry out my study. I returned to Henley, where my study was approved, and began my next semester.

Shortly afterwards, I decided, regardless of Roger Ticknor's comments, that the time had come to dispose of my last Triumph Herald Convertible. This had been heavily modified with a high-compression engine head, four carburettors, and a stainless steel exhaust system. Production of new Heralds had ceased some time earlier, spares were becoming increasingly difficult to obtain, and new convertibles had been out of fashion for some time. However, Peugeot had recently introduced a brand-new Cabriolet, and British Leyland had competed by producing a Mini Clubman. I went to showrooms to see both of these contenders and was amazed by the marketing expertise of the British Leyland Dealer. When I asked him to compare the features of his and his competitor's Cabriolet and his own company's clubman, he thought carefully for a moment. He then issued the immortal advice that they were 'much the same, but really it depended on my personal preferences and which I should buy'. Subsequently, it never surprised me why British Leyland were so unsuccessful. Perhaps inevitably, I bought a Peugeot Cabriolet.

Shirley and I went on holiday to the Isle of Man in our new car. It was a beautiful summer, and on the way to the overnight ferry at Liverpool, we called in at St Helens. Our delightful bungalow in Thatto Heath was unchanged, but in the town, there was absolutely no trace of the brewery. The very large site in the centre of the town, which had been occupied by the brewery, was completely unrecognisable. It was now a shopping mall. We left St Helens rather sadly and went on to the ferry and the Isle of Man. We stayed in Douglas for two weeks, the weather was glorious, and we enjoyed ourselves thoroughly. The preliminary two weeks to the Isle of Man Motorcycle Racing were in progress, many aspects of which were quite terrifying. On one occasion, we watched a long downhill stretch of the course from immediately behind the safety of a very thick stonewall. Motorcycles and their riders hurtled past the wall at a distance of much less than a foot. It was the only time in my life that I was ever within inches of objects travelling at over a hundred miles an hour. If they had been cars or aeroplanes, I would probably never have recovered. My other unique experience was buying a burger from a small stall on the fishing-boat quayside at Peel. The burger turned out to contain a freshly cooked famous Manx Kipper. It was unbelievably delicious. We returned home the following week, and I prepared return to Henley, slightly before the end of the Polytechnic summer vacation.

The next semester proceeded well and continued to explore and explain group psychology and behaviour, as well as the usual subjects of economics, statistics, and many case studies. At the end of the semester, it was summer, and we were not required to produce a second project. However, we were offered the opportunity of going on a two-week Outward-Bound Course in Wales.

Approximately, half of the students took up this option, although none of them were female. Needless to say, I found the opportunity irresistible, particularly because of the location of the centre. This was at Aberdovey, which was near to where I had been a gunnery instructor. I arrived at the centre later than most of the other students, and I was greeted by one of the staff. He explained that there were only limited parking facilities at the centre, and he would take me to a carpark on the other side of the town. This he duly did, and we returned to the centre where he asked me to put all of my valuables, money, and keys in the safe that was provided for security reasons. It was only when I joined the rest of my Henley student colleagues that I discovered that none of us had a penny between us. It was clearly a planned part of the training.

During our two weeks at Aberdovey, members of the course were awarded points for a wide range of activities, which ranged from simple individual tasks to group projects in which marks were awarded for individual sub-tasks. We went abseiling, sailing on the River Dovey, crossed the nearby tributary of the Dovey by constructing a raft and finally climbed over Plynlimon, the nearby highest mountain. When we came down from the mountain, we were picked up in a bus from the centre. When we reached Barmouth Bridge, the instructor asked who would like to complete the task of running a mile over water in order to get the extra points needed by the group. I and only two other participants volunteered. We duly ran halfway across the mile-long bridge and then returned to the bus. On the way, back the instructor asked why it was that as a fifty-year-old participant was able to carry out all these activities when all but two of the others were apparently exhausted. I explained to him that it was probably because I had led a very pure life, devoid of alcohol, women, and gambling. The only true part of my statement referred to gambling.

When the final semester occurred, we were given a lecture and exercise in how to present a lecture. The visiting lecturer was a wonderful Welshman who had been in the RAF during the Second World War. Despite the fact that I had been earning a modest living lecturing for the last ten years, I learned a great deal from him. Each of the students had to give a brief lecture, which unsurprisingly I had no difficulty in doing. At the end of my presentation, the tutor, in a wonderful Welsh accent, admonished me. "'Raymond Bradforth', if you do not stop waving your arms, I will cut them off." It was a fault that I had developed in pointing to blackboards and screens to illustrate points in my lectures. I was very grateful for his advice and met him a number of times later. I discovered that he had been a friend of Sir Geraint Evans who was a famous Welsh tenor. Sir Geraint had used his services and explained to him that 'no professional can afford not to have coaching and advice'. It was a lesson well learned.

Students were required to produce a management report and proposals for a new venture. We could choose any topic, and somewhat inevitably, I chose the launching of a small imaginary management consultancy. Since I had already formed my own such enterprise, I simply analysed all the costs and benefits and put them into a spreadsheet on my personal computer. I presented these results to a panel of judges who included the principal of the college and two or three outsiders from commerce and industry. One of these was the principal's son-in-law who was a bank manager. I made my presentation, and it was approved of and applauded by the panel. However, I then asked to be allowed to show some further results that I had produced. I had used my computer to run random numbers through my figures. Each of these made very small adjustments to all of the critical category of figures, including forecast profit. This immediately demonstrated that even small miss-estimates of costs and revenue could seriously either overestimate or underestimate the overall results. I explained therefore that such forecasts and proposals should always be evaluated subject to such margins of error. I pointed out that such demonstrations required a simple computer program. I was somewhat surprised at the response of the judges. The bank manager son-in-law of the principal was incandescent. He said that his bank had long experience in evaluating proposals from clients. Any such complication such as the one I was proposing was completely unnecessary and unacceptable. I was awarded an MBA, and at the end of the course, we had our final farewell dinner. I was asked to give a response toast on behalf of the students. At least half of the students were from overseas, and in some cases ethnic minorities. I began my speech by explaining that I came from a very small rare ethic minority, and that I was aware that this could be a severe handicap. I was half Yorkshire and half Welsh. This appeared to provide some amusement, and rest of the speech appeared also to go quite well. I now had a Masters' Degree and was well satisfied with my life during the last eighteen months. I had become addicted to Henley 'The' Management College. The graduation ceremony was at Brunel University in London. The Management College was affiliated to Brunel at the time. There were less than a hundred graduates from Henley, and the ceremony was a fairly low-key modest event.

Marketing

After the vacation, I returned to Gypsy Hill to discover that there had been a massive change in the organisation. The Polytechnic was to become a university, and the departments were to be reorganised. All of the teaching staff was to be part of new schools or departments, which would better reflect the academic status of the new university. The head of the Business School who had recommended that I should to go to Henley had retired, and David Smiles had been appointed as a professor of a Faculty of Business Accountancy and Law. He had been the deputy head of the School of Business. He explained that there was no data processing or computer discipline within the new faculty. All lecturers, for who there was not a suitable group to join, would become part of the School of Marketing. Unsurprisingly, I was appalled. Marketing was a subject, among all the subjects of management, data processing, and computing of which I had least knowledge and no experience. I protested strongly but was told that there were no other options for me. Bitterly resentfully, I was to begin nine years of teaching marketing. David Smiles would continue to be my nemesis throughout that time.

I had absolutely no intention of putting any more effort in my marketing lectures than could possibly be avoided. I had been allocated almost all of my teaching for the School of Engineering. This had now moved from Canbury Park in Kingston to Roehampton Vale, which was about a mile and a half away. The previous lecturer had been a female who was a genuine marketing lecturer. Her lectures had been so badly presented and received by her students that the school had asked for a change of lecturer. Despite this unfortunate precedent, I did not anticipate any similar difficulties. I was to give approximately forty hours of lecturing a year to about a hundred and fifty students, to some of whom I would lecture twice a week. This represented a total of about a hundred and twenty hours, plus examination setting and marking. I was determined not to spend more than ten minutes preparing any lecture. I recalled my experience in the very earliest days of British Marketing when I was at Edinburgh University. American marketing books were extremely expensive, and much of the content was based on marketing American products that were unknown in the United Kingdom. In response to this potential problem, I went to the University Bookshop in Kingston. Once again, I discovered that there was a predominance of expensive American books at over twenty pounds but managed to find one English paperback that was only five pounds. It was the cheapest marketing book in the store.

My technique for lecture preparation was to copy the old-fashioned polytechnic lecturers' trick of running new courses without previous knowledge or experience. They would select a single textbook and produce lecture notes from each chapter. At the beginning of the course, brief lecture notes were prepared for the first two lectures. The first lecture was then delivered with the lecturer confident of the knowledge in the next chapter to come. On each subsequent week, the lecture notes for the following week were prepared. The lecturer was then always able to keep one week ahead of the students. The other tactic was to fend off any student questions to which the lecturer did not know the answer. The lecturer simply explained that the topic would be covered later in the course. The lecturer would then look up the answer in the book for future response. I discovered that these strategies worked faultlessly, and I fulfilled my intention of never spending more than ten minutes preparing any marketing lecture. The book I selected was very well written and ideal for my purpose. Some years later, I met the author at a conference in Lancaster University, and in his presentations, he proved to be as reliable and authentic as his book. I had made a very fortunate choice.

My new students were all final year honours degree students in mechanical, electrical, and aeronautical engineering. There were about a hundred and fifty of them, only five of which were female. They were all very responsive, and I thoroughly enjoyed teaching them. The only potential problem that arose was because some of the classes had too many students to fit into any lecture theatre at the new Roehampton Centre. These classes were then split into two and were run consecutively. The fatal traps that any lecturer had to avoid in that situation were repetition and loss. It was sometimes difficult to remember whether I had made a comment or reference earlier to the present group or the previous one. If I got this wrong and was told by students that I had already told them something before, it was distinctly embarrassing. A feature of the course was that in addition to the end-of-year examination, I had to provide a case study. Fortunately, I discovered that instead of having to invent these there was an external library from which they could be purchased. I obtained the catalogue of these studies and purchased one each year. Fortunately, the university paid for these. I then had to set examinations and mark them. The work study technique that I had developed was to mark one question at a time for all candidates and throw them into piles of papers with similar marks. This enabled me to see how consistent was my marking and whether I needed to adjust any papers.

In the eight years and many hundreds of hours of my marketing lectures, I only had one difficult experience. At the end of a lecture to aeronautical engineering students, I was approached very respectfully by one of the students. He was being sponsored by the British Aerospace Company that was located at the time near Ham on the other side of Kingston. He wondered whether I could answer a question in order to help him with an assignment he had been given. What was the best way to sell his company's new Jet Fighter aircraft to Germany? It was not exactly a matter that I had ever considered before. However, with a masterly effort at self-control, I managed to think swiftly and clearly. I suggested that the first step was to contact the German Embassy in Trafalgar Square. I assured him that they would be able to provide details of potential customers and buyers, and help him to contact them, and how best to approach them. He appeared to find my suggestion very helpful and to my surprise and relief thanked me very respectfully.

At the end of each year, I pursued a policy that was unique amongst my fellow lecturers. I provided a Lecturer Evaluation Questionnaire. It was one that I copied and extended from one that I had encountered on courses run by ICL the computer manufacturer over fifteen years earlier. It provided a mark score from zero to ten as a result. There was also a section for comments. At the end of each academic year, I required all of my students to complete the assessment. The results were almost always consistent. Out of a hundred and fifty responses, half a dozen usually gave me an almost zero rating, with comments that I was the worst lecturer they had ever heard. Another dozen would give me the highest possible rating, with comments that I was the best lecturer in the university. The remainder ranged between these extremes. My average overall score of all of the responses was always well into the sixties or seventies. I was satisfied that I was not short-changing the students. I never heard of any other lecturer offering the same or similar survey opportunities for their performance assessment.

My old brewing friend Brian Lee, who lived in nearby Cheam, was now working as a Hop Merchant. He invited me to talk to his staff at their head office near London Bridge about the possible introduction of a computer system for processing their activities. The meeting was very successful, and I agreed to look at all of their operations at their new offices in Paddock Wood in Kent. I was still employing periodically my three programmers, and Clara Shaw as a systems analyst and consultant. Clara had remarried but was retaining her previous married name. I carried out my survey and proposed the new systems.

A couple of years after I had returned to Gypsy Hill, all lecturers were offered new Contracts of Employment. These offered an annual salary increase of one annual increment. The existing incremental system increased lecturers' salaries automatically each year. It was part of the 'Silver Book' Contract, which also guaranteed sixteen weeks of vacation time each year in order to enable lecturers to study, attend conferences, and indulge in other academic activities. However, these academic 'end of term' conditions were absent from the new contract. They were to be replaced by a conventional total of four weeks of annual vacation periods each year. To my surprise, the majority of lecturers agreed to the new contract. Less surprisingly, I declined. The 'Silver Book' was one of the most beneficial features of my employment as an academic. I could earn more money in any one week of a vacation than the value of any annual increment.

Shortly after I had received my master's degree, I was asked by Henley to give some computer management lectures to their outside clients and supporters. I duly presented lectures at Northampton, Brunel, and Amsterdam. The visit to Northampton was to a wholesale pharmacy company who were building a new national distribution warehouse there. The lecture went well, but I also observed the most frightening experience of my career. The new warehouse was in the early stages of construction and consisted only of forty-foot high vertical steel pillars. On the top of these were small platforms, which appeared to be less than two feet square. The horizontal joists were being carried and put into place by a sixty-foot high crane. On the top of one of the vertical pillars, a worker was standing. As soon as each horizontal joist was swung slowly in to place, the worker inserted bolts in order to secure the end of it. No safety harness or other security was visible. How this could have conformed to any known safety regulations was a mystery to me. Somewhat squeamishly, I was completely unable to continue watching the performance of the procedure.

The visit to Amsterdam to an ESSO headquarters was a less stressful experience. Unlike my previous visit by sea ferry many years earlier, I now had the experience of flying from the then new London City Airport. My talk was about Information Systems Processing to engineers of the company. As part of my lecture, I was extolling the virtues of designing and running their own custom-built computer applications. They could do this by using some of the flexible new software packages that were now available. This was instead of relying on programmers in Computer Departments to design and write programs for them. Computer programmers were unlikely to understand or even be interested in the technical engineering implications of the content. The reaction to my suggestion and comments was instantaneous. They responded that they agreed entirely, and in fact, they had been very dissatisfied with the company programs that they had previously been required to use. They had now started to write their own software. After the end of my visit, I received glowing reviews of my presentation.

Another feature of the end of the summer term was that lecturers commonly received promotional copies of textbooks that were about to be published or had been revised. The hope was that these would be adopted by the recipients for inclusion into their next year's syllabus. Usually, only the most enthusiastic and conscientious lecturers wished to change or make the effort to revise their next year's syllabus. I very rarely encountered anything that persuaded me to accept them. The only book that I ever encountered that persuaded me to include it in my teaching syllabus was a completely new concept of 'Soft Systems Methodology'. It was by two British authors, both of whom I met subsequently. I introduced the techniques to a class of computer science students who I was still teaching each week at Kingston. Unsurprisingly, it was completely new to them, and I gave them a number of extensive exercises with which to apply the techniques. I was astonished at their response. They were universally extremely enthusiastic and were very anxious that it should be included in the syllabus. Sadly, it was the last time that I was sent to teach the course, and it appeared to be of no interest to the School of Computing. Nevertheless, I used this new valuable technique frequently in my consultancy and later work.

After a few years of marketing lecturing, I received a letter during the summer vacation from the head of faculty. It was unprecedented to receive any communications during the summer vacation. The letter explained that since the Polytechnic had now become a university, it was important that it should be engaged in as many research projects and activities as possible. A director of the Midland Bank had been employed to discover what additional activities should be introduced to the university. He had concluded that Kingston had been involved in very little research and that there were few Doctoral staff. He asked that all lecturers should be encouraged and supported in any activities of research that they could propose. Rather than wait for the beginning of the next academic year, lecturers should submit immediately any proposals that they might have. I saw this as a golden opportunity for me to apply to engage in research in team structure and management. I had become fascinated and heavily involved in the subject at Henley, where the original research had begun; I was very anxious to pursue it, and I thought that it would be an ideal study for a doctoral degree.

Clara Shaw's new husband was an IT manager, and he and she had attended a conference on 'Business Schools and their relationship to the IT Profession'. The conference was run by academics and professionals from the computer industry. All of the delegates and speakers carried identification labels, and perhaps unsurprisingly, the Dean from Henley was one of the speakers. During a break in which the speakers mingled with the delegates to discuss their interests, Clara spoke to him and knowing my recent connections with the college asked whether he remembered me. She also commented that I was looking for an opportunity to register for doctorate. Apparently, the Dean's response was immediate. He said that of course he knew me and suggested that I should go and see him at Henley.

When Clara told me of her encounter with the Dean, I immediately contacted him at Henley. I asked whether I could be considered for a doctoral degree. I went to Henley for an interview with the Dean, and after he had commented that despite the fact that I didn't have much of a record in research, he agreed that I could be accepted. I immediately applied to Kingston University for permission, and somewhat to my considerable surprise, my application was approved. I could now become a real 'academic'. My proposal for research was to study 'Team Structure and Management'. Because of my continuing involvement and experience, I considered that the fire service would be an excellent field of study. I duly contacted the chief fire officer of Surrey Fire Brigade and received his permission to study throughout the whole brigade. I presented my proposals for my research to the Dean at Henley, and he approved. He cautiously warned me that the very latest and high-powered statistical methods would be involved in my research. At the beginning of the next academic year, I was given teaching relief throughout the year and allowed to submit expenses for travel once per term to Henley. Although this would not cover my actual costs, I would be continuing with my consultancy, which would also provide a very substantial supplementary income. My banishment to the School of Marketing was at last becoming less painful and humiliating to me.

Academia

At last, I could become a genuine fully qualified 'academic'. My doctoral studies began, perhaps unsurprisingly, with lectures at Henley of how to study for a doctorate. There were half a dozen other doctoral candidates, and we were all advised that the most important aspect of our research was the use of statistics. Our tutor explained to us that we would be required to use the most advanced and powerful statistical methods, many of which were now available only on computer. The essential package was 'SPSS/PC+', a convenient and perhaps fortunate abbreviation for 'Statistical Package for Social Sciences for Personal Computers'. Mercifully, its title was most commonly abbreviated to 'SPSS'. The package contained every conceivable statistical test and use of statistical theory. The documentation consisted of three manuals, supplemented by another explanatory book. They were A4 size and in total were four-inches thick. The other test and technique that would be essential for my studies was the '16PF'. This had been used in the original Henley Research into Management Group Behaviour. It was a non-computer proprietary test inspired by Raymond Cattel, an American psychologist and could only be used under licence. It was necessary for me to attend a one-week course and pass a test in order to purchase and administer it. I managed to do this and then devised my own computer programs with which to record and analyse my results. I would also be using the original Belbin Self-Perception Inventory, which had been developed originally at the college. Once again, although it was a manual test, I had written a computer program to process the results.

I soon began my field studies at Surrey Fire Brigade Headquarters. The chief fire officer was pleased to see me once again and welcomed research being carried out in the brigade. Roger Ticknor was once again appointed to help and look after me. Fire stations were all manned on a twenty-four hour day, seven-day week. The fire fighters were split into four 'Watches' of eight hours per Watch. In total, there were about thirty fire fighters in each nearly twenty stations. I planned to give my tests to all of the fire fighters at a dozen stations. My tests took roughly an hour to complete, and almost all fire fighters were happy to take the tests. I gave each fire fighter the results of their individual tests, and these were entirely confidential. I had specially agreed with their union that no individual information would be given to any senior officers or brigade headquarters. I wrote a computer program for a data base system that enabled me to produce personal reports automatically from the test data. It also allowed me to apply complex statistical analysis to individuals, Watches, and Stations.

My studies went well, and I learned a great deal about the fire service and came to admire them greatly. They were proud of being a disciplined service and were the only organisation I ever encountered in which the only route for entry was at the lowest possible level as a recruit. After one year of probationary training, fire fighters could only obtain promotion by serving successfully at every level and rank. There was absolutely no 'accelerated' promotion. I only ever encountered help and encouragement and never any hostility. My admiration for the fire service has never diminished.

Although it was not part of my research, I was asked by Roger Ticknor to give a couple of evening lectures on management courses that were being run at Reigate for outside organisations. The lectures were in the building that had been under construction during my master's degree study. My first lecture was in the evening to twenty managers from the Blue Circle Cement Group. They had been split into two teams and had just completed a hard day of 'Outward Bound' type physical activities. The first part of my lecture on Management Team Structure was to give them all the Belbin Test to complete. After twenty minutes, I examined their results. I concluded that one team was very unstable due to two of their members who were likely to have spent much of their time arguing with and 'scoring points' off one another. In contrast, the other team was well balanced. I revealed the results to the class as diplomatically as I could. The response was predictable. The arguing team absolutely denied my interpretation. The other team confirmed it. Apparently, earlier in the week, one of the arguing members had actually been asked to leave the team. I rested my case. It was typical of many similar situations that I encountered in the future.

Shortly afterwards, it was the end of the academic year and time for Shirley and my annual holiday. Previously, we had gone on many visits to Scotland. Our visits had ranged from Gretna to Wick and to the Hebrides. I had always said that we should never go abroad on holiday until we had seen the beauties of the whole of Great Britain. We had always supplemented our annual holidays with many long weekend visits during the year with our Birmingham Dental School friends. We had covered over forty parts of England and one or two locations in Wales. On this occasion, Shirley and I, for our annual holiday, went out to Australia to see our daughter Lynn, who had qualified as a medical doctor. After I returned from Henley, my daughter Lynn was working in a hospital in Sydney, and Shirley and I stayed in her flat, where we stayed for a couple of weeks. During that time, we went into Sydney and attended an opera in the unbelievably beautiful world famous Opera House. With my Hi-Fi knowledge from the long past, I was able to appreciate the superb quality of the acoustics. I also learned a lesson from forty years earlier in St Helens with Mark Griffiths when I had installed the new amplifier. The materials from which the Opera House seats were made provided almost the same sound absorption qualities as a human body. The effect of this was that it did not matter whether the seats were occupied or not, the sound absorption was exactly the same. I just wished that someone had told this to Mark and me forty years earlier. I fell desperately in love with Australia and all of its inhabitants. I decided that it was the only country in the world to which I would ever want to emigrate.

One evening, Shirley and I attended a symphony concert at the Opera House and returned later at night on the ferry back to the West Bank. The terminal was a couple of miles from Lynn's flat, and we had hoped to get a taxi. Due to our lateness, the whole site was deserted, and there were no other passengers from the ferry so we began to walk. We were overtaken by an empty corporation bus with its passenger lights out. To our astonishment, the driver stopped the bus, leaned out of his window, and asked us where we were going. After we had told him, he said he would take us home, as it was not far out of his way back to his depot. It was an extraordinarily kind action, unimaginable in the UK. Lynn also took us to the local zoo, which unsurprisingly contained a large range of Australian animals. At the entrance, we were offered and bought a bag of some sort of nuts for food for the emus. We were able to approach the animals closely, and just as I raised my bag to offer the nuts, the emu snatched the bag out of my hand. It then shook the bag violently, and emptied the nuts, and then ate the paper bag. I realised that I had much to learn about Australia and its residents.

A few days later, Lynn hired a car, and we drove up the West Coast to Brisbane and Cairns in Queensland. In Cairns, we went up to Kurunda Market, which is about thirty miles away in the rainforest above Cairns. I returned on the wonderful railway which provides spectacular views of the surrounding landscape and the sea. I had learned that the original Bungee Jumping Stadium was just outside Cairns, and I insisted that Lynn should drive me there. She did this reluctantly, only for us to find that the stadium had just closed half an hour earlier. Lynn rather curtly told me that I had 'enough treats for one day'. However, I discovered from the hotel in which we were staying that tickets for the jumping could be booked by the hotel. The next morning, I got on a special coach that was full of Japanese tourists, and I assumed that they were all anxious to see the stadium. We reached the stadium, and I was puzzled to find that I was the only passenger who got off the coach. The stadium was almost completely deserted when I entered, and I was asked to enter my personal details and sign a complete disclaimer for any possible injuries or ill effects from the experience. I finally entered my date of birth and was about to receive my ticket, but the attendant was somewhat surprised and amused. He explained that it was unusual for anyone of my age to apply, but as I was more than sixty years of age, there would be no charge for the event. He said that he would call my hotel and return my fee.

The stadium was surrounded by the beautiful rainforest and was completely deserted. A huge steel structure, the size of an electricity pylon was in the centre and a medium-sized lake was below it. I climbed up a very long staircase to a platform at the top of the pylon to find half a dozen short rows of seats leading up to its edge. The only other occupant was a young girl who was seated on the front row. She was wearing a set of harness and clearly was being prepared for a jump. After a short time, she announced that she would like to postpone her jump and come back later. The attendant then removed her harness and fitted it on to me. At the end of the platform was an overhanging kiosk containing the operators who announced my weight and added the somewhat puzzling comment, "No water?" After a few minutes, I was asked to step forward and put my arms out in the pose of a diver. I looked around the horizon and was absolutely enthralled with the view of the surrounding rainforest and the beautiful sight of the bright blue ocean beyond. It was the one of the most memorable visions and moments of my lifetime. The bell in the kiosk rang; I dived forwards and found it a wonderful experience. However, as I approached the water below, I reached the final extension of my jump and the elasticated rope came to a brief halt. It then began to spin slowly and retract. It continued behaving like a giant yoyo in a manner that no one had mentioned before, and I felt completely helpless. However, I decided that I was grateful for the option of 'no water', since the lake looked rather unclean. I thought that experience of being dunked up and down in the rather foetid water might have been somewhat unpleasant. Shortly afterwards, two men arrived in a small boat and released me. I think it would be fair to say that I found the whole experience unique, hugely satisfying, and memorable. I collected my certificate for the jump and returned to Cairns, where I re-joined the family.

When we returned to England, I submitted my doctoral thesis to the invigilators. I was interviewed by one of the ex-tutors from my days on the masters' course. He was extremely complementary about my thesis. He went so far as to say that my computer analysis methodology was almost good enough to be awarded a doctorate in its own right. He then followed this with what to me was a somewhat disappointing 'however'. He was very anxious to see my computer analysis methodology continued and extended. I should therefore continue my research for a further year. I really had hoped to have obtained my doctorate as a result of the work that I had already done, but it was very difficult not to be gratified by his judgement of my work. I continued to extend my work for another year. It had the consolation that I was able to have another year's 'Teaching Relief' back at Kingston. At the end of the year, I was examined again and awarded my doctorate. The award ceremony was in the summer in the grounds at Henley. It was in total contrast to my Master's Award Ceremony at Brunel. On this occasion, there were at least a hundred awards, of which only five were doctoral. There were now many affiliated overseas centres and students had come from many parts of the world for their awards. There were so many of them that the award ceremonies had to be held on two days rather than one.

I continued to teach marketing, but I was also asked to teach on courses in personnel management. These were adult classes, which included many middle-aged members of the nursing profession. These were mainly sisters and matrons of hospitals. My fellow lecturer Ian James, who had joined the Polytechnic in the same year as I, was a long-time friend. He also lectured to these classes but gave me a salutary warning. He said that the classes were always very attentive, but sisters and nurses tended to sit on the front row of lecture classes listening closely whilst knitting at the same time. He found this slightly off-putting. However, I never encountered this problem but repeated my Personality Testing exercise that I had used at Redhill Fire Service Headquarters. After the first two years, I used to predict confidently the probable personality make-up of the students.

There would always be a predominance of up to a third of the students who would have the same 'point scoring' personality profile that was likely to be disruptive if duplicated in small teams. The future performance of any such teams of which they were members would be better if there was only one of them in each team.

Doctorate

After my first year of teaching after receiving my doctorate, I decided to sample the annual Academic Conference circuit. Each summer, lecturers received a flurry of letters inviting them to attend academic conferences at many universities throughout the country. As well as attending the conferences, lecturers were invited to present papers. I had always ignored these events, since I always had more than enough to occupy my vacation, including consultancy activities and long overseas holidays. However, now in the light of my research and with my new academic status, I felt confident that I could present papers at such conferences. Therefore, I applied for three conferences at the universities of Stirling, Lancaster, and London. I submitted details of my lecture papers to each of them and was accepted by all of them.

I attended each of the events, and the experience was a revelation. Delegates were invited to attend all or any of the lectures that were presented. No records were kept of any of the attendees, other than the lecturers who were presenting the papers. It was therefore possible to attend a conference without ever sitting in on any session. However, I presented my papers at each of the conferences, and they were perfectly well received. I had presented slightly different versions of the same lecture, but with different titles at each of the conferences. My final presentation was at London University. The conference was held in Kensington and had been well attended. However, my presentation was on the final Saturday morning of the conference. By this time, most of the attendees had gone back home, and I had an audience of about five delegates. I got home in time for lunch, having had quite enough of the summer circus of academic conferences. However, I could see why these were so popular, although I never again attempted to attend one. I presented my expenses to David Smiles, who then managed to delay reimbursing me for nearly a year.

After receiving my doctoral degree, I had often pondered on the basis and method with which the general subject of management was taught. The vast majority of textbooks on the subject were American and many dated back to the very beginning of the twentieth century. I concluded that there was no 'General Theory' within which management was considered or taught. What was needed was a general theory of management. I decided to study the matter and try and produce such a theory. I went to Henley to see my Doctorate Supervisor Vick Dulewics. He was pleased to see me, and we had morning coffee on the beautiful lawn sweeping down to the river in front of the college. I introduced my thoughts on the lack of a general theory, and he was amused, and laughingly said that I was quite right but that no one could produce such a theory. After a moment's pause, he thought carefully and then looked at me very strangely. He said, "But probably you could." After leaving him, I thought that was as good an endorsement and encouragement as I could possibly receive. I finally became determined to write my first book.

I was also still in touch with the fire service. The Fire Service Staff College had moved from Wotton to Moreton-in-Marsh in the Cotswolds. This was the very large training establishment for all ranks of fire fighters throughout the country. I gave a number of lectures there, which were well received. I always had to stay overnight, and I was amused that the very comfortable bedrooms lacked en-suite toilet facilities. I had an interesting experience in dining at a very large long table with all of the senior fire fighters. For the first time in my life, I was always the last person to finish eating each course. I was told that fire fighters on Watch never knew when they would be called out to an incident. If the alarm sounded, they always had to leave immediately. It could be many hours before they would have the opportunity to finish their meals. I was also asked to allow extracts from my Doctoral Research Thesis to be published in the National Fire Service Journal. I was told that there had never before ever been a Doctoral research project in the fire service. As always, the deputy commandant was extremely supportive and invited Shirley and me to attend the centre's Annual Dinner Dance. It was a very grand and enjoyable event. I felt very privileged. I was also continuing to give occasional lectures to Surrey Fire Brigade, and they too showed me exceptional hospitality. They invited me to their annual dinner at a hotel at the top of Reigate Hill. All of the senior officers were dressed in their formal dress uniform, and I regarded it as a privilege to have been invited, since I was the only person who was not part of or related to the brigade.

At the end of the summer vacation, Shirley and I went to New England and Boston, where we hired a car for two weeks with our friends from Northampton.

It was just at the beginning of the Fall, and the trees were stunningly beautiful. Boston was also fascinating, with its historical heritage of the Tea Party and Battle of Bunkers Hill. We also went to the top of Mount Washington. We were able to drive the car to the summit, but although it was autumn, it was bitterly cold, and there was thick snow. Most astonishing of all was that in the continuously strong wind, all of the icicles on the flagpoles were horizontal. I had never seen this before, nor ever did again. We then drove down through New England, saw the site of the landing of the Pilgrim Fathers, and then went on to Cape Cod. It was the era following the Kennedy presidency and had a recent history of scandals. The North American residents were also of interest, and all of us were amazed at the sheer volume of food that Americans consumed. In contrast, I developed a liking to and weakness for clam chowder and managed to eat it every day. We returned home, determined to visit America again.

Shortly before I was due to retire, my old very close friend and long-time colleague Chris Palmer, who had retired a year earlier was killed in a car accident in Kingston. It was devastating news to me, and I had been looking forward to seeing him for many years to come after my own retirement. My external consultancy activities had progressed significantly. Brian Lee, with whom I had been at Brewing School, lived at nearby Cheam. Shirley and I were great friends with Brian and his wife and had been with them on a number of boating holidays on the Llangollen Canal and the Caledonian Canal from Inverness to Fort William and back. Brian had retired early from his position of head brewer at Courage Barclay and was now a manager with Higgins Robertson, a firm of hop merchants with a head office near London Bridge. He asked me to give a talk to the staff and demonstrate the possibility of the use of computers for their activities. They were about to relocate to Paddock Wood in the centre of the Kentish Hop Fields. My presentation was successful, and I was asked to visit Paddock Wood to conduct a survey. Therefore, I proposed, and Higgins Robertson agreed that I would write and provide a computer system specifically suitable for their use in the Hop Trade.

The Hop Trade was unique, and the transactions were exceptionally complex. All hops were 'picked' or harvested, seasonally at the end of summer. The hops were packed into special sacks known as 'pockets'. Each pocket had a unique identity, and was marked with the grower's name, the year, and the pocket number. Additional data had to be provided with each pocket. This was its variety name, individual weight, its grade, and it's Alpha Factor. Higgins

Robertson traded over twenty thousand individual pockets each season. If the pockets were not sold before a specified date variable rental fees had to be charged on a daily basis until the pockets were finally sold. The clerical effort involved in controlling all of this information required half a dozen clerical staff, many of whom were only required for two or three months at the end of each growing season. There was no existing computer system that could possibly be applied to these unique activities. I began by designing and agreeing the systems specifications, and then producing the record structures and the systems and file specifications that were necessary. I also designed a special transaction file that recorded the time and date of every processing activity that was carried out on every record. The time of every activity was not merely the time and date but was recorded to the nearest millisecond. This would be the most secure computer financial processing system that I ever created or encountered. In order to implement the system at Higgins Robertson, they had bought three powerful PCs, which I had networked together. After the successful completion of the system, only one female member of staff was required to process all of the twenty thousand complex records which had to be processed each year. For a few weeks during the peak of activity, she was assisted by a second part-time clerk.

Just before I finished my work at Higgins Robertson, I was asked by Michael Higgins to join him in his office. A second person was also present, who was introduced as the buying executive from the Whitbread Brewing Group. This was apparently a new appointment, and he was now responsible for purchasing all brewing materials including hops. This was a multi-million pound market, and the buying task had always been the responsibility of head brewers. The selection, evaluation, and pricing of hops were exceptionally difficult, complex, and highly skilled tasks. It was clear that the new buyer appeared to know absolutely nothing about hops. He was only interested in driving down the purchase price. Michael Higgins asked him politely which particular type or variety and quality of hops would he like to discuss first. His response was a breath-taking display of sheer ignorance and incompetence. He said, slightly patronisingly, that obviously there were only two types of hops – 'beer' hops and 'stout' hops, and he would consider purchasing both of these two 'types'. Because of the potential size of the order, he would, as a matter of policy, expect his company to receive a substantial discount. Michael Higgins managed politely to conceal his surprise, as did Brian Lee who was also present. Shortly afterwards, I asked to be excused, in order to attend to an 'important program' that was being tested. I left the meeting eternally grateful for not still being a brewer or having to tolerate such an ignorant idiot.

I was still employing the three programmers and Clara Shaw as an analyst. I also had a second analyst who had worked in Local Government. They continued to be superb, and we produced the new system very rapidly, and it worked extremely well. As a result, I was invited to visit the largest company in the Hop Trade. The company was English Hop Products, which had originally been a nationalised organisation. They produced a very wide selection of products, all of which were derived from hops. Their manufacturing plant and processing were unique and exceptionally complex. All sorts of materials and processes could be applied in a variety of ways to the hops that passed through their plant. Processing time duration was also a key factor. Fortunately, as an ex-brewer, I was able to understand easily the importance of almost all of the aspects involved. The production manager was David Gardiner, and he and I became great friends. I realised that what was required was a complex and extremely flexible Production Processing System. The system worked extremely well and required costing information to be incorporated to the processing. I got on very well with the financial director, who was always very helpful and supportive, and I discovered that the company was using a Sage Computer Accounting System. I discovered also that the input of the details of all transactions into to the system were stored in a single file. I realised that I could copy all of this data into my Production Processing System. With the help of the production manager, I created an extremely flexible Production Control System. This allowed every material quantity and cost associated with production could be calculated and displayed. Because of the very large number and wide range of processes and products, this had previously been impossible. The system revealed details and costs that were invaluable for effective management control. My ultimate success was revealed when at the end of one financial year, the financial director came to me and laughingly asked me for some of my systems cost figures. He had been unable to reconcile some of his own financial totals. He said that only the 'Raymond Bradforth' System could possibly produce the correct figures. I obliged immediately, happy that the value of my system was validated and so well received.

Shortly before the summer vacation, my head of school said that he wished me to become the admissions tutor for the school. This post, although it carried no extra pay, was always regarded by academics as a prestigious appointment.

However, it involved spending most of the summer vacation examining students' applications and interviewing those who were either selected or regarded as marginally eligible candidates. I had no ambition either for the post or the inferior vacation prospects. However, I could not avoid doing it for one year. With my proven work study skills, I analysed the task and how best it should be done. My first step was to process the application qualifications by simply ticking the potentially most likely candidates. I then made offers to these, but knowing that an unknown number would refuse, I made provisional offers to a number more. I did not waste time interviewing any of them. What I knew was that 'A Level' results and marks of student entrants to universities had almost no correlation with their final degree or other marks or performance during their following three years. The marks were almost useless for predicting the future success of students. The clerical staff who usually spent an enormous amount of time writing to applicants and arranging interviews was astonished at how little effort was now actually needed.

During the summer vacation in the following year, Shirley and I once again went to America with our Northampton friends. However, on this occasion, we had decided to travel right around that world. We flew first to San Francisco where we stayed for a couple of days. John and I were fascinated by the cable car system and managed to visit the central underground power house from where, to our amazement, all of the cables were driven. We felt obliged to drive over the Colden Gate Bridge, and we also visited Alcatraz. We then drove down the coast to Los Angeles, and on the way, we saw the astonishing home of Howard Hughes before flying to New Zealand. Shirley and I were due to stay in Auckland with Shirley's fellow Olympic Medallist, Evette, who had won the Gold Medal for the Long Jump in Helsinki. However, John and Sarah were flying on to Australia to see two of their Northampton neighbours who happened to be living there at the time.

Evette was something of a celebrity in New Zealand, and she and her husband Buddy insisted on taking us for a tour of North Island. Buddy had also been a national basketball coach and had travelled all over North Island as part of his career. Like all New Zealanders, Evette and Buddy were incredibly open, friendly, and hospitable. They took us first to stay in a bungalow on the nearby beautiful seashore. The bungalow belonged to the governor of New Zealand and apparently was his occasional summer residence. We were the only occupants, and after two days during which we were shown the local sights, we left to travel south. Buddy knew of my liking for Port Wine. In the middle of the morning, he stopped his car at a wayside café, where like almost everywhere else in North Island he was known. He had also stopped in order to register a bet on the nationally controlled horse-racing network. He came back with a bottle of 'Artillery Port', extracted glasses from the glove compartment, and then insisted that we should all toast our visit. I never before or after had the experience of drinking Port Wine during the middle of the morning.

We drove on to Rotorua, which was the centre of volcanic activity in New Zealand, and looked at the thermal springs. We stayed overnight with friends of Evette and Buddy. When we arrived at their bungalow, they welcomed us all but explained that they hadn't got sufficient bedrooms for all of us to sleep there. However, they told us that their next-door neighbours were away, and they had their house keys. Shirley and I could therefore sleep there. I appreciated that what would be regarded as unthinkable in British home society was simply regarded as normal neighbourly behaviour to New Zealanders. In Rotorua, we were taken to a local orchard, and I encountered for the first time kiwi fruit trees. I tasted the fruit and found it to be delicious. Buddy explained that it was a unique product of the country, and they had generously allowed cuttings to be sent to America. As a result, large quantities were then grown in California and provided heavy competition. On the way back to Auckland, we stopped at a tourist gift shop in Whitianga. I was unable to see anything that was of interest to me until we entered a small room in which there was a large low table. The eight-inch thick top was about five feet by three feet and stood two feet high on five very thick legs. The top and legs had an incredible, arguably grotesque, convoluted form, and the wood had a deeply coloured beautiful complex serpentine grain. I asked the owner what it was. He explained that the timber was Kauri Swamp Wood that had been buried for over sixty thousand years since a New Zealand natural disaster event. The table was not remotely similar to anything else in the shop and had been made by a local craftsman. I asked the price, which was a few hundred pounds but was assured that it could be sent to England safely. Nevertheless, I did not have the nerve to buy it but asked for his business card. When I told the story to my daughter Lynn a few weeks later, she insisted that I should buy it, regardless of the price, which she said I could afford easily. I duly agreed, phoned the owner, and he explained that the invoice would include, for tax reasons, a vastly expensive transport fee, but at a seriously reduced price, I happily gave him my bank details. A couple of months later, the table arrived home, suspended inside a specially manufactured crate, the timber of which was high quality planed pine. Shirley thought that the table ought to go in the back room out of sight. I insisted that it should be the centrepiece of our lounge. It has since been admired there by every visitor who sees it, and I admire it every day. Perhaps unsurprisingly, my relations with the non-academic clerical staff had never been close. The pinnacle of my success was when a student from another school had asked to seem me. The office assistant informed him that she thought that I was only rarely on site and was a part-time lecturer. My other encounters with the clerical staff had on a couple of occasions been somewhat trivial and irritating. All lecturing was done using blackboards and chalk, and overhead projectors and screens. The clerical staff ordered the chalk and issued it on request. All of the blackboards were made of black rubber, which could be rotated vertically within a frame. Unfortunately, the chalk that was being issued was hard and was actually scratching and destroying the surface of the blackboards. Every time lecturers had asked the clerical supervisor to order soft white chalk, she had refused, saying that only the present grade could be purchased from their main supplier. Lecturers had also asked for coloured chalk, which was also refused. In consequence, lecturers had to go to the nearest toyshop and buy soft and coloured chalk. Happily, during the next very few years, I gently wound down my activities, and we decided to go to Alaska and then come back over the Canadian Rocky Mountains for our next holiday.

The following year, I explained to my Head of School that my wife and I were due to go to Canada, and happily, I was relieved of the post of Admissions Tutor. Shortly afterwards, Shirley and I flew from Heathrow to Vancouver where we joined a Holland America twenty-thousand ton cruise liner. Unsurprisingly, the passengers were mainly Americans, and their company was a new experience for us. Shirley and I dined at a reserved table for two, and after a couple of nights at dinner, an American from on a nearby table came over and spoke to us. He politely and rather apologetically enquired whether we were on our honeymoon. He had noticed that we had a bottle of wine on our table at dinner on every night. We concluded that clearly, regular wine drinking was not normal American social behaviour. We also found it difficult to understand the enormous appetites of the American passengers. The food in the restaurants offered an amazingly wide choice, and American passengers seemed to require incredible generous portions. In addition to the restaurant facilities, food was brought around the ship's lounges two or three times a day. The American passengers seemed to display the eating behaviour of starving immigrants. However, they were universally sociable, and I had the privilege of sitting next to and talking to an ex-pilot from the Second World War. He had flown Liberator bombers over Europe and explained that they had been instructed, for safety reasons, to maintain a minimum height at which to fly. Unfortunately, the aircraft were incapable of flying at that height when fully laden. It was only after they had released their bombs that they were able to comply with the regulations. His wife also explained that his eyesight was now too poor to allow him to drive an automobile. However, they had managed to overcome this problem by letting him use her driving licence. I was very glad that I was unlikely to need to drive in their home area.

We continued sailing up the Inside Passage, and after a few days, we arrived at Alaska and were enthralled by the experience. We called in at Skagway and went on the White Pass and Yukon Railroad up to the top of the famous Chilkoot Trail. During the Yukon Gold Rush, prospectors had very laboriously carried all of their belongings up this very steep trail in deep snow. However, when we reached the top, there were a large number of bicycles available for hire. These were offered with the opportunity to cycle back to Skagway rather than return by train. It was actually downhill all of the way, so very little physical effort would be required. Shirley and I joined the group of people who were being led by the guide who was to cycle at the front. The guide suggested that the most elderly riders might find the cycling rather tiring and suggested that it may be better for them to keep to the back of the group. As I was only sixty-seven years old, I decided that I would like to keep to the front of the group and obtain the best view of the descent. The guide seemed to be somewhat surprised by my decision and on a number of occasions kept asking me whether I was all right. The ride was a delightful scenic experience, but halfway down, we encountered a barrier. It was a customs office. Apparently, we were leaving Canada and re-entering the USA. I was required to show my passport, which was then duly stamped by the officer. The stamp was an elaborate graphic image and record of my entry into the United States from the Klondike Trail. Some years later, this illuminated entry was admired with much amusement by customs officers in some Eastern European countries. Unfortunately for the rest of the riders, including Shirley, they were simply waved on, without having their passports inspected or stamped.

We returned to the ship, went further north, and had a seaplane trip to a glacier. We then went to a forest where we openly encountered and watched families of black bears who were fishing for salmon in a river waterfall a few yards away. Finally, we called at a small town with a salmon farm and cannery. The town was interesting, because it had a full-scale six-mile long motorway, which ran from north to south alongside the coast. It began and ended in the middle of nowhere. Apparently, because Alaska was part of the USA, it was entitled to a motorway. The fact that it was completely unnecessary and useless was regarded as irrelevant. However, we bought some smoked salmon from the nearby cannery. When we later attempted to eat it back in England, we found that it was quite inedible. Finally, we went to the northern limit of the voyage to the end of a glacier, where we saw huge volumes of ice collapsing into the sea. It was a most impressive sight, but in the context of later worldwide interest in climate change and global warming, it was somewhat salutary.

We returned to Vancouver and joined the Rocky Mountaineer train tour. It was a wonderful experience. As a life-long railway enthusiast, I was both fascinated and enthralled. As a result, I had studied the history of the construction of the railroad over the Rockies and realised that I knew more about it than the official guide. On one evening, we were allowed to dine in the local town, and in the restaurant, that Shirley and I chose, smoked rattlesnake was an item on the menu. I could not resist this unique culinary opportunity of a lifetime and duly ordered it. I tasted it cautiously, only to discover that it had the flavour and texture of soggy cardboard. It was something of a disappointment, and I was glad that Shirley had not joined me in my choice. We finally flew home overnight from Vancouver. Shortly after midnight, the plain called at Calgary, where two very large policemen in thick fur-lined clothing boarded the plane. They walked to the rear of the aisle and removed a passenger who was completely inebriated and blind drunk. The cabin crew passed the passenger's hand luggage to one of the policemen. It was a very interesting end to a fascinating and eventful winter holiday.

After a few more months, I finally reached my retirement. It was normally a routine university event at which there was usually a brief celebratory farewell meeting. Lecturers who had achieved twenty-five years of service or more were given a cash retirement gift. The Personnel Department explained that the cash value of this was one hundred pounds. However, since this was subject to the deduction of income tax, the recipient could ask to have it substituted by a one-hundred pound gift voucher, which was redeemable only in a department store in Kingston. In either case, the value of the gift was derisory and was less than half of my daily consultancy fees. It was to my great delight and relief that I had only completed twenty-four years of service. I was therefore not eligible for either of these generous financial rewards. The personnel director then attempted her final 'Coup-de-Gras'. I received a letter from her telling me that my final salary would be withheld, until such time as I received from the university librarian a signed form to say that I had no books or other papers on loan from the library. I was also required to obtain a signed slip from the Personnel Department to certify that I had handed in all keys that belonged to the university. I had never taken any books or other documents from the library for over ten years, and I had left all of my keys in my desk drawer, where they belonged. To my considerable delight and relief, I very deliberately avoided the insulting insincerity of a farewell meeting and simply left the world of academia at the end of my last lecture. I had hired a small conference room in a rather exclusive hotel on the other side of Kingston Hill. I had invited about twenty of my long-time colleagues and friends from my own and other departments to join me in the evening. It was a completely friendly low-key event in pleasant surroundings. It cost me somewhat less than the gift voucher that I might have received if I had served a year longer. The following morning, I sent a letter to the personnel director telling her that if she wished or attempted to withhold my final monthly salary, she could discuss the matter with my lawyer. My final salary arrived shortly afterwards.

Resurrection

I had finally left the world of academia and was looking forward to going on overseas holidays and sitting in the sun in the wonderful garden in Willow Grove for the rest of the summer. I would then spend the winter building and operating my extensive model railway in the roof. I would intersperse these essential activities with a modest amount of Computer Systems Consultancy. However, unforeseen events intruded into my plans. I was contacted by Clara Shaw. After she had finished working for me, she had been employed as an adviser by the European Bank of Recovery and Development, more popularly known as the EBRD. The bank had been established and was funded by all member countries of the European Union. Its role was to provide help and advice to medium-sized companies throughout Eastern Europe. None of the EU advisors were directly employed by the bank but were all independent individuals who received fees and all expenses for their consultancy and work as and when required. The EU advisors were all specialists who were sent out to the Eastern European countries for periods of a week at a time. They were required to provide advice and help in their own individual area of expertise. They were nearly all male, and their experience was mainly as senior managers or executives within a particular industry or business sphere. Clara had been one of the very few specialists with information technology experience or qualifications. She had successfully completed a number of assignments before leaving to take up a full-time job with Spillers, the flour manufacturers. They subsequently became part of the international Nestle organisation, whose head office was in Switzerland. She was strongly of the opinion that I should apply to become a part-time EU advisor, since the EBRD apparently were unable to find anyone with information technology or computer consultancy experience. I was grateful and somewhat flattered by her recommendation but reluctant to find work during my new retirement. However, I was rather intrigued by her account and after a few days of deliberation decided to contact the organisation.

I was invited to meet John McPhee who was the Head Advisor of the Turn Around Management Programme, more popularly known as the TAM Programme. The programme was run by the EBRD at their head office in London. The offices were an expensive rather luxurious tower block alongside Liverpool Street Station. John McPhee explained that the EU advisers were all from different countries in the European Union, and in each country, there was a Senior adviser. The role of the EU Country Adviser was to identify small to medium sized organisations that could benefit from the TAM Programme. He would then offer them a programme of the type of help and number of weeks of visits and support that were required. He would be responsible for organising the programme, selecting the appropriate EU advisers, and controlling the visits and budgets. All of the other EU advisors were Specialist Advisors, with experience in particular industries and businesses. They only visited organisations within their own specialism. However, I was to be the only systems and information technology specialist, and therefore, I would be required to visit clients of all types of industries and businesses. It was to prove to be a wonderful and most satisfying advantage to me.

Each EU adviser was required to make visits within the programme, provide reports and recommendations, and would be paid in Euros. John also commented that in reality, all of the EU advisers were highly qualified management consultants, but they had been asked not to use that title. The various city accountants who posed under the title of 'Management Consultants' had complained to the EBRD. They claimed that because the clients of the TAM Programme did not pay fees, this provided unfair competition. I refrained from responding to this pathetic claim. However, John offered to appoint me as a TAM EU adviser and suggested that my first assignment was to Riga in Latvia. I had no hesitation in accepting his offer.

I was totally ignorant of Eastern European geography, had no idea of where either Riga or even Latvia were. I arrived at Gatwick Airport on a cold winter afternoon to meet my first new TAM colleague, Brigitte Watson. She was a German who had an English husband, and she was an accountancy adviser. She had been on the TAM Programme for some time, and this was her third trip to Riga. The company that we were visiting was a very high-quality printer and map maker. During our flight, Brigitte gave me all of the background information on the company, its problems, and the progress that had been made. We arrived in Riga in the dark and were taken to a large concrete multi-storey hotel on the edge of a park on the outskirts of the city. Our bedrooms were on the seventh floor. I noticed that both the walls and floors of all of the corridors and rooms were bare concrete. However, the floors had long strips of quite good quality plain carpeting. The walls were covered fairly sparingly with soft curtain-type materials. It was my first exposure to a Russian-built building of the Cold War era.

I awoke the next morning to find that my room overlooked the park. The road, park, and landscape were covered in deep snow, and a worker was laboriously clearing the pavement below. Toilet facilities were further along the corridor, and they reminded me of Fire Service accommodation. I met Brigitte at breakfast, and she announced that we needed better accommodation. Shortly afterwards, we left by taxi with our luggage to visit our clients who were located in the main part of the city. The offices of the printers was a fairly modern large two-storey building, and we left our luggage in reception. We were welcomed by the manager who was an extremely well-dressed woman in her early forties. She spoke perfect English and after inviting us for coffee explained that they required a new computer system. She offered to arrange our hotel accommodation for us and said that she would be acting as our personal interpreter. She then left Brigitte to carry on with her previous work and took me around the offices to meet the other twenty staff. I soon identified the full nature and implications of the work and by the end of the day had a clear idea of what was required. At the end of the day, Brigitte and I were taken to a hotel just inside the ancient walled centre of the city. It was a two-storey building, in the reception area of which sat a female receptionist, and somewhat to my surprise, beside her sat a male armed guard. However, the hotel proved to be extremely comfortable, and the food and drink were excellent.

My work progressed well, and I went around all of the departments. The company also had a small factory at Cesis, which was about eighty kilometres from Riga. Brigitte and I were taken there by the manager in her car. On the way back, Brigitte in the course of a perfectly normal conversation asked the manager how she had become so fluent in speaking English. The manager explained that during the Russian occupation of Latvia, she had learned it as a girl from an English Language grammar book. The end of the 'Cold War' and Russian occupation had occurred only a very few years previously. The manager then continued to describe the circumstances. Apparently, her father was a farmer of a smallholding. When she was five years old, the family were sitting at home one evening when armed soldiers arrived at the house. They told her parents that the whole family had to leave immediately, since as farmers, they were 'Enemies of the People'. Unsurprisingly, her mother protested. In response, one of the soldiers went upstairs and came down with a bed sheet. He laid it down in the middle of the floor and lay a few pots and pans on it. He told her mother that she had better put the things that she might want in the future into the sheet, because she would not be returning. The family were then taken to a labour camp where they remained for the next fifteen years. She took the English book with her, and when they returned fifteen years later, she applied for a job as language teacher. Because she was the daughter of an 'Enemy of the People', she was not allowed to teach. However, the local school required a teacher of English, and she was allowed to become a temporary member of the Communist Party. After a year, she was allowed to become a full member. When the family finally returned home, they found their farm occupied by a Russian family, and they were not allowed to reoccupy it. Her story was one of the most disturbing, moving, and upsetting experiences of my sixty-five-year-old life. We returned to Riga, and I just about managed not to weep. As a very old man, I find it very difficult not to be sad to think of the manager's account and it still upsets me. It also makes me utterly ashamed of my countrymen and their unbelievably ignorant perception of the people and importance of the European Union.

I made three more visits to the company in Riga and fell completely in love with the city and its surrounding countryside. The old part of the walled city was medieval and contained a wonderful cathedral, opera house, and market square. The opera house was without exception the most beautiful and delightful of the many opera houses that I ever visited, and I attended half a dozen performances there. I also attended two or three splendid choral performances including a Haydn Mass in the cathedral. Riga had been occupied by the Russians, and now almost fifty percent of the population were ethnic Russians. One of the largest car factories in the Soviet-occupied areas was located on the outskirts of the city. However, the Russians had gone to extreme lengths to maintain and enhance cultural life, and absolutely no expense had been spared on the opera house. The decoration of the auditorium and seating was incredibly elegant and luxurious, and the scenery sets and costumes were exceptionally artistic. I was able to attend both classical operas and ballets there. The price for the best seats in the house were less than the equivalent of five pounds, and the local audience always, without exception were dressed in their very best 'Sunday' clothes. The operas were varied, and two were uniquely Latvian. The first was based on the story of the Hunchback in the Paris Notre Dame. It was by Kaspars Dimiters, a Latvian songwriter and poet. Both the music and singing were completely different from any opera that I ever saw before or since. After the end of the evening, I managed to buy a CD of the opera from a local store. The other extraordinary performance was a ballet based on Tchaikovsky's Sixth 'Pathetique' Symphony.

One Sunday in spring, I visited the small seaside resort of Jurmala, which was about thirty kilometres along the coast from Riga. I travelled there by train but had some difficulty in finding the right station at which to get off. The name of each station was displayed only on one large board at the end of the platform. Unfortunately, I was at the back of the train, and I was only able to see the board as the train was leaving. No one on the train spoke English, but with some sign language, and a great deal of luck, a very kind lady managed to enable me to get off at the right station. Fortunately, the train on the way back terminated in Riga. The seaside town was delightful, and the seashore had very long and wide sandy beaches, which stretched as far as one could see in both directions alongside the Baltic. The most notable feature to me was the colour of the sea, which although quite natural, closely resembled Brown Windsor Soup. However, the local Riga population had turned out in force. The scene was one that was reminiscent of the Edwardian era. Every single person and family were immaculately dressed in their most formal 'Sunday' outfits. They were just walking quietly up and down the beaches alongside the sea. No one was bathing. There was a market square in the centre of the old city. It had stalls at the weekend with all manner of traders and their goods. One man was very cheerfully selling his wares simply standing and holding out trinkets. The most memorable feature was that a cat was sitting contentedly on his head. As a cat lover, I was unable to imagine how any cat that I had ever known or seen would contentedly adopt such a pose. On another occasion, a man came up to me selling Russian Army black bearskin hats. He pulled the hat from under his jacket where he had been concealing it from a policeman standing nearby. He invited me to try the hat on. The price was the equivalent of a couple of pounds, but the hat was far too small. After revealing another hat, equally small, he made his final appeal to me. He halved the price. I still refused, and he promised to come next time with a larger hat. In fact, he did return later, and I became the proud owner of a genuine Russian Army real bearskin hat. I removed the brass star badge from the front of it and wore it when I went to the Arctic a few years later.

On one of my visits to Riga, my luggage and that of my fellow passengers' was left behind at Gatwick Airport. We were told it would be delivered the following day. However, I was due to give a presentation to the printing company, and I was not prepared to represent TAM wearing an open-neck sports shirt and jeans. I therefore went straight into Riga and clothed myself in a business suit and shoes. I sent the bill to British Airways, and they paid without hesitation. To my utter amazement, they also enclosed a free return flight for two on any of their services. I subsequently spent five days in New York with Shirley, which compensated for her preclusion from my visit many years previously.

There were also other TAM programs running in Riga during my visits, and I met a number of the EU Advisers, and Brigitte and I had dinner with them on a number of occasions. One dinner was in an old cellar restaurant. The food was self-service, and there was a wide excellent choice of food. However, the restaurant had a unique billing system that I have never encountered before or since. The food was presented to the cashier who then weighed it. The charge was based simply and entirely on the weight. In an age back in Britain of overeating, this would have been a very welcome innovation. On another occasion and restaurant when we dined, I ordered quails' eggs for a starter. The waiter spoke only Latvian, and I tried to ask for something with which to remove the shells from the eggs. The chef then appeared and explained that I was expected to eat the shells as well as the eggs. After four very profitable visits to Riga, I submitted my final report and decided that it was time for a holiday with Shirley at the expense of my generous TAM fees. I had already earned in Euros the equivalent of more than my pension.

After I returned home, I received my next TAM assignment, which was to Hungary. It was to a company called Ganz Rok, who were manufacturers of heavy engineering installations for the Electricity Generating Industry. In particular, they produced water-tube steam boilers. This was a subject that I had studied at Birmingham University and had a working technical knowledge of steam boilers. I flew to Budapest where I was met at Budapest Airport by my new colleague Jacques Girard. We were taken by car to the remote small-town Szolnok about fifty kilometres east of Budapest where the factory was located near what had once been a crossroads in the middle of the Great Hungarian Plain. The factory was large and relatively new and apparently had been built during the Russian occupation. We were taken to the head office where we were welcomed by the managing director. He had arranged for us to stay at a local hotel in the nearby town, and after outlining his requirements, we were taken there by car. The hotel was another Russian masterpiece of utility engineering, which could be used either as a factory, multi-storage carpark, or hotel. The building was completely concrete, as were the internal walls, floors, and ceilings. The floors and some of the walls were partially covered by cow skins, presumably from the local area. However, the beds were reasonably comfortable, and the food was good.

The next day, we were collected and returned to the factory. I was given a grand tour of the factory and introduced to its managers. I was fascinated to see 'in the flesh' equipment and components about which I had been taught at university but had never seen in real life. After carrying my survey over the next few days, I presented my findings to the managing director. The most significant of these concerned labour control and work recording. The plant was run on shifts during a six-day week. Before each shift, all workers had to clock in and register their names and times. As there were many hundreds of workers, there were very long queues at the factory gate. Clearly, this affected the time at which their arrival was recorded. I suggested that they should use a barcode system and a small computer to input the data and update the records. The managing director thought it was a brilliant suggestion and promised to implement it as soon as possible.

A few days later, Marc and I were invited to attend a board meeting and lunch with the directors and senior managers. It was a very interesting experience. There were about twenty members present, and all sat on either side of a very long table. I was asked to give a brief presentation and proposed a number of areas that I thought would benefit from the installation of a computer. The chairman asked me to present these and then opened the matter for general discussion. Almost all of the directors and managers were very positive and supportive of my proposals. However, one of the members gave a long speech completely opposing my suggestions. I suppose I should not have been surprised to discover that he was the chief accountant or finance director. He was listened to politely. After the end of the meeting, Marc and I were invited to join the directors for lunch. The director next to whom I had been sitting was extremely friendly and hospitable. He spoke good English, and we had been talking about my interest in Classical Opera. He insisted that we 'Opera Lovers' should sit together at lunch. The lunch was cold but superb. It had an unbelievable profusion and selection of Hungarian 'fish, flesh, and fowl' and instantly converted and committed my love of Hungarian food and wine. It also was my first experience of the wonderful Hungarian hospitality that I was to enjoy for the next few years to come. I visited Ganz Rok a second time a few weeks later and found that they were implementing my proposals. However, Marc and I were put in a rather superior hotel beside the river. It was a traditional, rather exclusive Hungarian Hotel, was very comfortable, and was not made out of concrete. The food was excellent.

Shortly after I returned home, we went to Jersey with my daughter Lynn and her French-Canadian husband Jean. We hired a cottage, and I hired a car. Whilst I was there, I looked up my old friend and ex-colleague from my days of running management courses for him. I told him about my recent TAM exploits and commented that the only problem was that my fees were being paid in Euros. He immediately offered to introduce me to his Barclays bank manager, who he said would be happy to open a Euro account on the island for me. I immediately took up his offer, and when I returned home informed the EBRD of my new bank details. From then on, my fees were always paid directly into my offshore Euro account. Since I was to spend a great deal of money in the European Union that was an extremely beneficial arrangement which saved me a small fortune in future unnecessary tax and currency exchange fees.

Czech Republic

My next TAM assignment was to the Czech Republic. I was to meet Marc at Prague railway station, from where we would travel to Ceska Trebova in Western Bohemia. The factory was a small specialist engineering company who manufactured high quality office copiers and photographic equipment. Ceska Trebova was about a hundred and fifty kilometres east from Prague, but there was an excellent comfortable trans-European rail service. The Managing Director, who was the principal owner, was extremely friendly, as were the rest of his staff. Marc and I discovered that the company ran an extraordinary method of sales forecasting and production. They consistently produced approximately five or ten of their very high-value expensive copiers and then simply waited for customers to buy them. They did not build or produce anything 'to order'. Marc became highly frustrated by being unable to obtain any reliable current or historical sales records. The owner simply excused this by saying that the production costs and sales figures simply were impossible to produce. I had been looking at their systems and computer records and had become very friendly with their Production Manager. Fortunately, he was also responsible for their computer system. After a morning's work with him, I was able to show and extract the necessary information from their computer database files. Marc was incredulous and delighted. He said that he had been unsuccessfully trying to obtain the information throughout his last two visits.

The largest nearby town was Bruntal, which was on the borders of Eastern Bohemia. It was the nearest place that had a technical college. Marc and I had offered to run a weekend course there for the benefit of their technical staff. Our course was for the use of computer spreadsheets, which would have been very useful to the company. The college staff was very helpful and offered their support. The course was to be paid for by the company and advertised as free to their staff. We also offered to include freely any of the local students or staff. However, the response to our offer was for about three delegates in total.

Apparently, none of the locals wished to sacrifice part of their weekend leisure, especially since they would not be paid for it. Marc and I were suitably chastened by our lack of local social sensitivity understanding.

Bruntal was near to the centre of the wine-growing area of Western Bohemia. The wine quality was excellent. I once asked the manager at Ceska Trebova why we had seen no wine growing in Eastern Bohemia. His reply was that Western Bohemia grows it, and Eastern Bohemia drinks it. We were also near the site of the Napoleonic War Battle of Austerlitz, which had proved to be a historic turning point. Marc and I had both wanted to visit the site but were unable to find any public transport. We considered that the private taxi cost would have been excessive. We also found a Chinese Restaurant in Ceska Trebova. We were the only customers in the restaurant, the food was excellent, but the Chinese staff could speak no English, and neither Marc nor I could speak either Czech or Chinese. It was a rather strange experience. I made three more visits with Marc, two in summer, and one in winter. On the occasion when we arrived in winter in Ceska Trebova, it was dark when we arrived. We emerged from the deserted railway station to find that the snow was about a foot deep everywhere, and there were no passengers, people, or taxis. We wearily dragged our travelling luggage for about half a mile through the deep snow to our hotel. It could easily have been a scene in a TV movie. The TAM program never proved to be boring or uninteresting. We spent the weekend in Prague where we met Clara Shaw. She was now working with Nestle at a town called Buk, which was just over the border with Austria. She had already worked with Marc when she was on the TAM Programme and, they were great friends. Prague was a very beautiful city, particularly the old town centre and market square. The food and drink in Prague were of course excellent, as were the exquisite Bohemian cut glass and other Czech products. I was to stay there a number of times in the future with other TAM colleagues.

During the summer, Shirley had been invited to Helsinki for an Anniversary Celebration of the Olympic Games at which she had won her Bronze Medal. We spent a splendid week there and also went on a short sea cruise to Tallinn in Estonia for a day and to St Petersburg for a few days. I was not terribly impressed with Tallinn, but I thought that St Petersburg was wonderful and magical. It had suffered unbelievably hardship during the Second World War, but there was no longer the faintest trace of those events. The hermitage was incredibly rich in artefacts, and I could happily have spent a week inside. We also went to the

Summer Palace, which had a heart-breaking history. The retreating Germans had completely stripped it of its treasures and attempted then to vandalise the palace. Immediately after it had been recaptured by the Russians, Stalin had insisted that it should be fully restored immediately. The quality of the restoration was almost unbelievable. It had been restored luxuriously to become one of the most beautiful and elegant historical buildings that I was ever lucky enough to see.

After my last visit to the Czech Republic, I was asked to go back to Prague to visit a manufacturer of women's undergarments. Apparently, there were problems with stock control. The industry was one in which Marc was not involved, and I only met the senior advisor briefly. However, the managing director explained to me that many of the materials that were used in the manufacture of their luxury garments were extremely expensive and valuable. Almost all of their factory workers were female, and both the materials and the garments they produced were both attractive to them and very valuable. I was introduced to the general manager who, like the majority of their staff, was female. On my second day, the manager took me to the main factory at Teplice, which was about sixty kilometres north of Prague and was very close to the German border. The manager took me in her company car, which was a rather superior and sporty saloon. It reminded me strongly of some of the versions of British Jaguar cars. To my utter astonishment, it was a Skoda. Contemporary opinion in England at that time was that Skoda cars were something of a joke, and no self-respecting motoring enthusiast would want to be seen in one. My TAM experience had taught me yet another lesson.

The factory at Teplice was large and populated almost entirely by women workers and supervisors. The workers were deployed in a very large open main workshop. On long tables, workers worked at cutting and sewing machines and passed their work along their table as the garments processed and took shape. At the far end of each table, the finished garments were inspected and packed. Each worker had small slips of paper on which were recorded the details of the work done by them. They passed on these slips of paper, along with the work, and after the final stage of the manufacturing process, these were collected by the supervisor. The workers' pay was determined entirely from these piecework records. The system was a classic mass-production manufacturing process. However, most of the materials that were being used were extremely valuable. In particular, there were large reels of very expensive and delicate elasticated fine lace. Apparently, it had proved to be almost impossible to measure accurately and cut off appropriate lengths of this material. The total length of the reels was stated at the time of purchase and delivery but was impossible to check. Furthermore, it also appeared that due to the expensive value of the attractive garments that were being produced they often tended to 'disappear' as rejects.

An unusual, if not unique, feature of the factory was that there were only half a dozen male workers, all of who carried out any heavy manual labour. In contrast, or as a result of this, the walls of the work areas were covered with large 'pin-up' pictures. These were, without exception, all of scantily clothed or naked males. At the conclusion of my visit, I drew on my years of Work Study experience. I reported that a new production and stock control system was necessary. Work in progress should be recorded electronically by workers and not by simply passing scraps of paper to one another in order to estimate work times. An electronic recording system would ensure that times were recorded accurately and allow standards to be set for work times. I also solved the conundrum of how to measure and issue delicate elasticated materials accurately. They should be weighed. Extremely accurate electronic weighing machine had become available at that time and would be completely suitable. On my return to head office, I reported to the managing director, and he appeared to be delighted.

I spent the weekend in Prague with Engel Hoefgeest and Marc Girard. Engel and we decided to visit the opera house for a performance of La Boehme. Marc decided not to join us. Engel and I sat through the first act, with which we were both familiar and were absolutely baffled. Neither of us recognised the story or the performance and found the language unfamiliar. When we visited the foyer in the interval, we found posters displaying the performance. Apparently, it was a Hungarian version by a Hungarian composer. We left the Opera House and headed for the nearest restaurant, where we met Marc. Engel had a Dutch and Hungarian dictionary, and he regaled us with a few choice phrases. One that we found amusing was one that Marc and I said could only be found in a Dutch dictionary. It was the Hungarian for 'Please pay for your own food bill'.

I returned to my hotel that evening to find a message from EBRD in London. It asked me to go to Hungary instead of returning to London. I was to visit a manufacturer of construction-site cranes. I booked a flight for the next morning and arrived in Budapest. I was met at the airport by a representative of the company and taken to Eger. Eger was about a hundred kilometres east of Budapest and was a very pleasant town in the middle of one of the best wine-growing areas in Hungary. I was met by the managing director who was extremely friendly and hospitable. The company's cranes were about ninety metres high, and the company was in the process of writing a computer system to record production costs. I met the author of the computer system who was a young engineer who was writing the programs in FORTRAN. FORTRAN was the standard scientific language used universally by academics in science departments. It was completely useless for any commercial purposes. I suggested to the director that a database system would be far more appropriate and offered to write a system specification for him. He accepted gratefully. The engineer programmer who had been somewhat unhappy with his past lack of progress seemed to be quite relieved.

I met the director again on the next morning. He had offered to take me around the site and see the cranes and plant in more detail. It was the middle of winter, and it was an extraordinary psychedelic experience. It was extremely cold but also extremely dry. We walked through the large yard of the site, and the air was completely filled with what appeared to be a weird form of snowstorm. There was no snow, but the air was cold and dry, and the sunshine was very bright. The air was completely filled with what appeared to be minute glittering ice crystals. They were not falling or rising; they were in suspension. As we walked through, it had no effect or feeling of extreme cold on my skin. I had never had such an experience before nor have I ever since. Before I left the director, he took me to the Works Canteen. One of the walls was completely covered with a huge tiled mural showing women repelling Moorish Invaders. From the top of the city walls, they were pouring all sorts of unpleasant substances and artefacts over the soldiers below. Apparently, it was a representation of a real historic mediaeval event during which the women of the town actually did repel the enemy troops.

I finally returned home after a very eventful TAM visit and submitted my reports. I also discovered that my General Theory of Management book had been printed, and I submitted it to a number of publishers. A few weeks later, I was bitterly disappointed by the rejection and feedback. Apparently, perhaps unsurprisingly, the publishers of technical books sent their books to academic lecturers for review. I realised that the last thing lecturers wanted was to completely change their existing conventional textbooks and lecture content. My book was certainly the only book with a general theory of management. Most importantly, I had made extensive use of 'Soft Systems' techniques and drawings as well as conventional tables and diagrams. My approach was obviously 'Beyond the Pale' and was probably not considered to be academic. I was glad that I did not need the money, and I really didn't need or want fame or recognition in the academic world. The book was meant for the benefit of managers and management.

After she had retired, Shirley had begun to play bowls at the nearby Bowls Club. She had never played bowls before, but as an ex-athlete and sportswoman, she had no difficulty in adapting to the game. The sporting and social life was excellent. Importantly, the members also had an annual two-week Bowls Holiday abroad. I was not and never had been interested in sport of any kind. I therefore never attempted to play the game but nevertheless joined as a social member. The overseas holidays were very enjoyable, and we were always joined by John Hunt, one of our closest friends from our days in Northampton. Unhappily, John's wife Sarah had died a few years earlier. Like me, John did not play bowls. Whilst Shirley used to accompany the other members and play against local teams John and I used to hire a car and tour the surrounding areas.

Hungary

My next TAM assignment was to Hungary. I was given the details of the senior adviser, who was Dutch, and had been a director of Philips Electrical in Holland. I was to meet him at the Keleti railway terminus in Budapest. We were to travel together to a large domestic appliance manufacturer in Debrecen, which was two hundred kilometres east of Budapest and close to the Ukrainian Border. Keleti Station was a magnificent terminus with a large booking hall. When I arrived at the hall, it was filled with at least a dozen very long queues. There were a number of booking windows, each of which were for specific destinations. I managed to find the correct one and after about twenty minutes of standing in the appropriate queue managed to buy a return ticket. I then fixed a piece of A4 paper around my neck with the letters TAM, which I had written with a felt-tip marker. I then waited for my new TAM colleague. After two hours of his non-appearance, I was beginning to feel somewhat alarmed. In desperation, I decided to use my new state of the art mobile phone. At that time, very few phones allowed overseas calls, but I managed, after some difficulty, to phone my new colleague's number back in Holland. Despite my triumph over the technology, when his wife answered the phone, she explained that he had left many hours ago. I attempted to assure her that I was sure he would arrive soon. My difficulty was that I didn't know the name of the company, and my airline ticket was dated for me to return on the following weekend. After another hour, a slightly short bespectacled gentleman introduced himself as Engel Hoefgeest. He apologised for his lateness but explained that his flight had been severely delayed. I little knew that he was to become one of my lifetime's best friends. After a very comfortable rail journey, we arrived in Debrecen in the dark and booked into the local hotel.

The next morning, we were taken to the manufacturing plant, where Engel had been visiting for the last three months. We were welcomed and taken to meet the managing director. I was then introduced to the senior managers and taken for a guided tour of the factory site. The factory had originally been a Russian ammunition factory and was in the middle of a forest. As a result, all of the buildings, other than the main offices, were single-storey, relatively small, and always well apart from one another. Presumably, this had been in order to limit collateral damage in the event of an accidental explosion. There was also Computer Department, but although I visited all of the departments and areas of the company, I only met the computer manager on a number of brief occasions. The computer manager, who was female, appeared to have a rather low status in the management hierarchy. Apart from the unusual physical separation of the buildings, the plant was very conventional and traditional. I pursued my usual work study practice of following all of the production processes and products through from beginning to end. The only stage which proved difficult to examine was the raw materials input. After numerous requests, I was finally taken to an area on the outskirts of the factory, in which the large rolls of sheet steel and other metals were stored. The store was in the open air, and to my considerable surprise, it was in the charge of a rather military-looking security guard. The guard was carrying a sub-machine gun, which was strapped over his shoulder, and an automatic pistol in his belt holster. It was politely explained to me that the materials were valuable, and they were being protected against theft by local criminals.

Among the many products that were being manufactured were domestic central heating boilers and water storage cylinders. These were processed on a continuous production conveyor line, which was very reminiscent of the classical car manufacturing factories of Henry Ford. A new computer recording system had been introduced recently, which produced production reports. The system was a commercial software package. The production details had to be entered by the foreman. He simply counted the items on the slowly moving conveyor belt and chalked 'five-bar gate' marks on an adjacent cast iron pillar. At the end of each day, he entered the totals by hand on to a written input document. The data was processed overnight, and the results of his day's production were printed the following morning. These historical results were of no practical value in production control. Instead, I recommended installing electronic counting detectors on to the production line. These could provide continuous real-time production control and could be used to improve output. This would be a very much simpler system compared with my bottling line system of many years ago. The managing director was always charming, but within a short time of meeting him, he reminded me of one of the main characters in James Bond movies. He was always absolutely immaculately dressed in exquisitely tailored suits. I never saw him wearing the same suit or necktie two days in succession. He always treated us both with extreme courtesy. He invited Engel and me to lunch with him every day in the director's small private dining room. The food and wine were always superb, and he made every effort to introduce us to the widest possible range of traditional Hungarian food and drink. The only time I failed fully to respond appreciatively to his choice of food was when we were presented with the Hungarian version of tripe. It was a dish that despite being a Northerner, I had never been able to eat. I tried not to be too embarrassed. However, despite our splendid lunches, Engel and I had nothing to do in the evenings, except go out to dine. We were staying in one of the main hotels in Debrecen, and there were less than half a dozen restaurants from which to choose. We found one, which was in a cellar and had a wonderful character and atmosphere. There were rarely many other clients there, but the food was superb. Engel and I always had caviar as a starter, followed by steaks and a whole range of delicacies. The bill was always less than twenty Euros. On one occasion, we mentioned to the factory Finance Director how much we were enjoying our dinners, and he politely asked us how much we were being charged. He was absolutely horrified. He found it difficult to believe how expensive they were and that we were paying so much money for them.

On my second visit to the company, I was asked to give a talk to the staff about production planning and stock control and how I was investigating it. The company had been considering buying a computer package, which was being promoted by the American consultants Arthur Anderson. Needless to say, the so-called 'consultants' were charging a premium, if not extortionate fee for what was a very simple and rather poor Excel Spreadsheet application. I explained this to the Managing Director and suggested that they would be far better served if they allowed their own Computer Department to use a database package. However, I duly gave my talk to about twenty of the company's staff. They listened very attentively but after my presentation asked absolutely no questions. I was extremely puzzled and somewhat concerned by what was to me a new experience. After my presentation, the computer manager thanked me and said that she found my advice very helpful and interesting. I asked her why the staff had been silent. She explained, rather apologetically, that under Russian Occupation all children at school and staff in organisations were taught 'never' to ask questions.

On my third visit to Debrecen with Engel, we discovered that the hotel was full and that it was the Annual Celebration in the town, and was a public holiday. The company therefore had arranged our accommodation at a small private hotel on the outskirts of the city. It was the height of a very hot summer, and there was no air-conditioning in the hotel. As a result, at the end of breakfast, my dark shirt was completely soaked, and I had to change before leaving the hotel. However, Engel and I were given complementary tickets to the day's events in a local park. It was highly entertaining, and a splendid holiday for Engel and me. We also went into the very large Lutheran Church, which was the equivalent of a cathedral and the largest in Hungary. The striking difference was that both the exterior and interior were completely devoid of any form of decoration or colour. After one more day of visiting the factory, Engel and I left Debrecen trying hard to decide how to present our TAM reports.

After our visits to Szolnok, Engel and I used to spend our weekends in Budapest with Clara Shaw who was working at Buk, which is to the West of Budapest. Budapest is a delightful city. Engel and I always stayed in Pest where there is a wonderful selection of civic buildings and markets, but we also visited the castle in Buda on the east side of the Danube on a number of occasions. One of the very many features of Pest is the Great Market Hall. Despite having had an excellent hotel breakfast, my great pleasure was to eat at eleven o'clock a fried goose leg at an open restaurant on the indoor balcony. Hungary is a great producer of geese, and inevitably, there was an abundance of the luxury pate-de-foie-gras in the market. However, I strongly disapprove of the method of production, and I never did or ever have tasted the delicacy. We also visited the beautiful opera house and attended a performance of Wagner's Flying Dutchman. Although I was very familiar with the music and the opera, to my embarrassment I sat through the First Act without realising that the cast were singing in Hungarian.

My next assignment was to Poland to a bus company in Grodzisk Mazowieki, which was about thirty kilometres South West of Warsaw. The town was usually referred to more simply as Grodzisk. The company leased but did not own about fifty local single-deck buses. They also leased a similar number of buses, which operated in Warsaw. The company was originally state-owned and operated both during and after the Communist regime. It had been privatised two years earlier and was now wholly owned by the three hundred employees, all of who were members of one or other of four trades union. One of these was the one that had led the ship-workers' historic overthrow of Communist Control in Gdansk. Although the company was profitable, no dividends had been paid to shareholders since privatisation, nor had the shares been revalued. Shares were not allowed to be sold. The President of the company owned twenty percent of the shares and the Finance Director owned ten percent. I was welcomed by both of these officials, and within a very short time, they became very great friends. At the time, there was no senior TAM adviser, although apparently one was on his way from running a bus company in Ceylon. One of the problems that that the company feared most was loss of revenue. All buses had an elaborate recording device for fare collection. At the end of each shift, drivers had to hand in a recording cassette on which records of all ticket issues and takings were stored. The cassette was then analysed, and the number of tickets and takings were reconciled. The problem was that drivers allowed passengers to board and pay without issuing a ticket. They would then keep the difference between the takings and the ticket records. By the time I examined this problem, the EU advisor from Ceylon had arrived, and he claimed that in his experience, revenue losses could easily be fifteen percent. I considered that this was nonsense and proposed a computer-based statistical control system. This would quite simply test statistically the expected taking of any particular route or driver. This was a technique that I knew was used by Birmingham Corporation some fifty years earlier. With the help of the computer manager, I produced a prototype system. This immediately detected a driver whose takings differed significantly from all other drivers on that turn. This was confirmed when a ticket inspector boarded his bus unexpectedly and checked the takings and tickets. My system produced a provisional estimate for total losses of revenue for the whole company to be of the order of two or three percent. This was in total contrast to the fifteen percent predicted by the senior EU advisor.

Warsaw was a wonderful city, and I was staying in an apartment just beside the Old Town and Market Square. Like many other parts of Poland, it had been completely destroyed by the Nazis. However, it had been perfectly and wonderfully restored by the Polish authorities after the war. I also went to a splendid concert in the cathedral. At Whitsuntide, I witnessed a very large procession of people walking along the main street to celebrate the Christian Event. They were led by clergymen, and every few hundred metres, the whole procession stopped, knelt down and listened to, and responded to incantations from the priests. I also visited the top of the huge Soviet-built 'Wedding Cake' building in the centre of the city. It gave a marvellous view of the city. The other memorable occasion was in attending an open-air Chopin Concert during a beautiful summer day in the large local park. There was only a solo pianist and an absolutely superb public sound reproduction system.

One of the most memorable events of my visits was the Annual General Meeting. Since all of the workers were shareholders, all of them and their families attended the event. The meeting was held in a very large hangar-like bus garage. The directors sat behind a long table at one end of the floor, and everyone else stood on the floor in front. Along one side was another long table on which was a large selection of refreshments. I and my interpreter sat at one end of the top table. The president addressed the audience whilst sitting at the table and using a hand-held mobile microphone. After some time of announcements and discussions with the members, he passed the microphone to me and asked me to say a few words to explain my activities. It was completely unexpected, and I was taken entirely by surprise. I decided that it was the lecturing opportunity of a lifetime. I rose to my feet and immediately left the table to stand right in the middle of the audience who parted to make room for me. This gave me a short time in which to decide what to say. I told them that the first thing to understand was that they were all wearing three hats. One was as workers, the second was as union members, and the third was as shareholders and owners of the company. It was therefore to everyone's benefit to make the company as efficient and profitable as possible. That was what I had come to help them to do. My comments appeared to be very well received. I am rather ashamed to admit that it was something of an ego trip, and I felt rather like a Communist orator during a revolution. I also considered it to have been my biggest challenge since ten years earlier when I was asked unexpectedly by a student how to sell British fighter planes to Germany.

On one weekend in winter, I visited the delightful mediaeval city of Krakow with Clara Shaw who was living and working in Warsaw at the time. I found that the city had a delightful market square and a clock tower in which was displayed an animated trumpeter. Before finishing sounding the number of hours, the trumpeter stopped abruptly. Apparently, a trumpeter had once sounded the alarm from outside attack but had been killed by an enemy arrow before completing his task. There was also a splendid symphony hall in which the excellent local symphony orchestra played a concert of Tchaikovsky's Manfred Symphony. The only notable site that I very deliberately refused to visit was nearby Auschwitz.

I had no wish to pay tribute or examine the appalling atrocities that had been committed there.

My investigation of the company was very successful, and I was asked by the president to run a training course for twenty of the managers. I used my Management Profile test and also an IBM Intelligence Test that I had used for many years. I first had to satisfy the four Trades Union Shop stewards that all results would be completely confidential to the candidates and not available to the management. They were somewhat suspiciously hostile at my meeting alone with them, but I happily explained to them my previous experience with working for Trades Union and the TUC. The course that I ran was six full one-day sessions at a local small hotel. Sixteen managers were selected, and both the president and finance director attended throughout. Unfortunately, I had been nine times to Poland on the TAM Programme, and my contract ended before the end of the course. However, uniquely in TAM Programme history, the finance director agreed to pay fees directly to me by the company. The only minor problem was that under Polish law, they were only allowed to pay me for work on site and not for any preparation work off-site. My fees were therefore adjusted accordingly. My TAM colleagues were astonished by what apparently had no precedent. However, I also had to acquire a new interpreter. Clara Shaw was working and living in Warsaw at the time, and she recommended one to me. The interpreter was a charming young female. For the only time in my life, I was greeted on the first occasion that I met her, by her curtseying to me.

Before leaving Poland, for the last time I went to Masuria with Clara Shaw. It was autumn, and I found the Masuria Lakes to be utterly delightful. That part of Poland had originally been part of East Prussia, and very few of the population could speak English but unsurprisingly were fluent in German. A hand-paddle boat was provided by the hotel and was ideal for exploring the local sylvan scenery. On one occasion in the local town, I was standing beside the lake whilst feeding a swan. Apparently, the practice of feeding swans from the palm of one's hand was unknown to the locals. To my astonishment, a small crowd of onlookers surrounded me to observe this strange and dangerous behaviour of a 'foreigner'.

In contrast to my Eastern European travels, Shirley and I went to South America. We flew first to Lima in Peru but unfortunately had to change planes at Miami. Instead of providing a painless simple transfer, the Americans in Miami appeared to make it as unpleasant and difficult as possible. After being forced to go out through US customs and waiting in a holding area, we then all had to queue for half an hour in order to go back through US customs in a different part of the airport. We nearly missed but just managed to catch our onward flight to Lima. We stayed in Lima for a couple of days and found it to be an interesting city. We then flew up to Cuzco and were warned that since the altitude was 3,400 metres, we were likely to suffer from altitude sickness. We were advised to rest for twenty-four hours and drink plenty of water. When we arrived at the hotel, Shirley took the advice, but I ignored it and went to explore the city. I found it very interesting but quite unlike anything I had seen before. Parts of the town were ancient stonewalls that had been constructed by the Incas. The design was unique and the blocks were huge lumps of stone which had been trimmed but were all different shapes and sizes.

After a few days, we took the train to Machu Pichu, which was at a more modest altitude of 2,500 metres. We were taken up to the site by bus and enjoyed the wonderful Inca structures of the Temple of the Sun, and all of the surrounding buildings. On one of the beautifully manicured green lawns, a local man was lonelily trimming the grass with what were no larger than a pair of kitchen scissors. He spoke English, and I talked to him and discovered that he lived down in the village beside the Urubamba River, which was over three hundred metres below. In 'Old Money', a thousand feet was regarded as the height at which hills were called mountains. This man was walking up and down the 'mountain' every day with his pair of clippers to trim the grass for the benefit of visitors. I apologised to him and hoped he would not think I was patronising him for giving him the equivalent of ten pounds for the dedicated work that he was doing.

Shirley and I descended to a restaurant overlooking the Urubamba River. The river was actually the upper reaches of the Amazon, and the restaurant overlooked a rocky beach where a large tributary joined it. I decided that I would like to go down to the rocky beach and left Shirley in the restaurant. When I reached the beach, I had an extraordinary unnatural experience. I began weeping uncontrollably and was quite unable to stop. I had absolutely no idea what was causing my genuine distress, but I eventually composed myself and returned to Shirley in the restaurant. I did not mention the incident to her, but after we had finished our lunch, the waiter had a brief conversation with us. He mentioned that the site below on the river was where some hundreds of residents of a small village further up the tributary had been swept down by a 'flash flood' and had drowned in the river below. As a result of his revelation, I was not sure whether I was more or less embarrassed.

We went on from Machu Pichu to Lake Titicaca, which was just on the border with Bolivia. We visited a late nineteenth century iron gunboat, which had been made in Glasgow. It had been carried up in pieces from Lima by black African slaves; I was not sure whether I should admire the British craftsmanship of the boat or apologise for its transport. Just before we returned to Lima, I was accosted by a friendly young boy who was anxious to clean and polish my brown leather shoes. He had been demonstrating his skill on one or two other visitors. After repeatedly refusing to use his services, I finally decided that it was time to teach him a lesson. I sat down on his small stool and demonstrated my long nearly forgotten army skill of boot polishing. I sat on his small stool and laughingly showed him how to really spit and polish leather shoes. He was not only amused and somewhat surprised but so was the small audience that had gathered. I perhaps rather foolishly paid him anyway. On our way back to Cuzco, we stopped at a hotel for lunch. On the lawns beside the river was a selection of beautiful Peruvian hand-woven hammocks slung between the trees. I was unable to resist buying one but was told that they could only be woven to order. However, I was told that if I ordered and paid for one, it could be delivered the next day to our hotel. Needless to say, I did order one, and it was delivered to our hotel in Cuzco, which was thirty kilometres away, at eight o'clock on the following morning. Finally, Shirley and I flew back to Lima and then on to the Galapagos Islands. The islands were wonderful. At that time, very few Europeans or others had visited them, and there was only a relatively modest tourist trade. We saw George the two-hundred-year-old tortoise that had been sat on by Lord Nelson, and the famous Galapagos Booby birds and dolphins. We visited a number of the smaller islands in the group and had a thoroughly enjoyable and educational time. We returned home, where my next TAM Assignment was waiting for me to go to Slovakia.

Slovakia

I joined my new TAM senior adviser at Bratislava Airport. We were taken from there by car over the border to Ruzomberok, which was in the Tatra Mountains in the far North of the country. The road journey was terrifying. It was a well-maintained highway, which was used by large numbers of very large commercial lorries. The driver attempted frequently to overtake these, only to be confronted head on by a vehicle coming the other way. Fortunately, the oncoming vehicles usually seemed to give way, but I was unable to work out what the rules were, if any. Unfortunately, this experience occurred on every occasion that we were taken by road in Slovakia.

The factory was a very large modern papermaking, packing, and storage plant. Like the company in Poland, it had been privatised after the end of the Russian Occupation and was wholly owned by the employees. Unlike the Polish example, they were also allowed to sell and buy their shares. As a result, the most senior directors and managers owned a very large proportion of the shares. They had borrowed money from financiers in order to do this. They were now in the process of selling the whole company at a huge profit to themselves, to a company in Israel. The consequence of this to our TAM Contract was that the directors were not faintly interested in our mission. They politely allowed us to see all over the highly automated plant and warehouse and arranged for us to stay at a nearby hotel. The plant had been built by the Russians and was very impressive. The hotel was near the top, a nearby mountain, which was apparently a winter ski resort. However, it was now summer. The hotel proved to be excellent, but the Senior Adviser and I were the only guests. The only visitors were a mother brown bear with her two cubs, who we used to see through the dining room window each morning. After a week of splendid isolation, we were taken back to Bratislava where we spent a couple of pleasant days seeing the sights. My opinion was that as a city it didn't compare with any of the other capital cities that I had visited.

When I returned home, I discovered that Shirley and I, and our great friend John Hunt from our Northampton days, were due to go with Shirley's Bowls Club to the Algarve in Spain. Since neither John nor I ever played bowls, we took the opportunity to visit other resorts on the coast. As always, the hotel, food, and drink were excellent. John and I toured the Algarve, and we all had a thoroughly enjoyable fortnight. When we got home, I had decided that the days of the Peugeot Cabriolet were finally over. I decided to buy Shirley a newly introduced BMW Convertible. Unfortunately, there was a nine-month wait for potential customers in England. However, after searching the internet, I discovered that they were more readily available in Europe. I found a dealer in Belgium, from whom I was able to order one. It would be newly built to my specifications in less than three months. With the help of my French-Canadian son-in-law, I ordered one. I was also able to use Euros from my Jersey Bank and buy the car more cheaply than I could in England. It also had a surprising number of 'standard' features, all of which were expensive 'extras' if bought in England. The most bizarre of these was a 'ski tunnel', which ran alongside the engine transmission tunnel and could be accessed from the boot. Unfortunately, neither Shirley nor I were ever able to take advantage of this obviously invaluable European 'standard' feature. However, an even more beneficial feature was a free, for the first owner, lifetime AA rescue service. I duly collected the car from Lille in Belgium with Shirley's new personalised English number plates under my arm. Despite his earlier fears, the dealer had no difficulty in identifying me at the railway station.

After my trip to Belgium, I received another TAM Assignment to Hungary with Marc Girard. It was to an agricultural plant and machinery manufacturer at Szolnok, which was about a hundred kilometres east of Budapest. The company was large and was in the process of introducing a new American computer system. The managing director was young, very dynamic, and enthusiastic about the new system. He had worked in America for a couple of years with General Motors, where the computer system was used. Apparently, his computer manager was equally enthusiastic about the new system and had been working on it with three programmers for the previous three months. The environment and its problems were subjects with which I was totally familiar and completely at home. It looked to be a 'dream' assignment.

My first step was to visit the factory with the factory manager. It was a classical engineering manufacturing works with more than a hundred engineers and workers. The manager and foremen were extremely friendly and sociable, and I was very impressed by the scale and extent of the works which were spread over a number of buildings on a very large site. The company manufactured a wide range of products ranging from farm tractors and vehicles to hand-held implements. There were many hundreds of processes and many thousands of components and assemblies. The most important issues, as always, were production planning and stock control. The computer manager was an exceptionally well dressed and poised thirty-year-old female, who looked as if she had just walked out of a fashion parade. She also spoke perfectly good English. I asked her to explain the system to me, and the work that had been done. Apparently, she and her programmers had been familiarising themselves with and testing the computer package. I asked to see some examples of the input and output documents of the new system. It was intended that data would be entered from half a dozen terminals installed throughout the plant, but output would be printed in a separate administrative building. I asked the manager to take me around the plant to see the data entry terminals. Although she agreed, she seemed very reluctant to do so. As we approached the main factory building, I asked her how often she visited the plant, and what had been the response of the managers and foremen to the proposed new system. I discovered to my horror that neither she nor any of her programmers had ever visited any part of the factory. None of them knew any of the factory staff, nor had any idea of the manufacturing processes or working procedures. It was one of the most surprising revelations I ever encountered in my career. We discovered that none of the data entry terminals had been installed, and they were not expected for another two months. The output documents were to be sent back to the foremen of the works. I was shown samples of the output documents and discovered that the foremen would each receive nearly a thousand of these on each shift. We returned to the offices, and apparently much to the computer manager's relief, I left her there. I continued my tour with my interpreter and the foreman and was shown the materials and parts store. This was run by one man in a separate building, which was like an Aladdin's Cave. There must have been more than a thousand parts of all shapes and sizes, none of which, or their locations were labelled. The storekeeper simply knew all of the part numbers and their locations by heart. I explained to him that he must never ever fall sick or go on holiday; otherwise, the whole factory would have to close. My next discovery was an open air store in which were stored raw materials and many hundreds of rusting and partly assembled obsolete parts and components. These had clearly been there for many years and were obviously only fit for scrap. Finally, when I returned to the offices, I estimated that there must be at least twenty thousand stock and production items, none of which had been entered into the new system. The new data entry terminals had not been installed and were not expected for some months. None of the production staff or workers were familiar with the new system, and none of the computer staff had any knowledge of the production processes. It was a nightmare scenario, and I was trying desperately to think how I could break the news to the managing director.

The company also had a smaller plant at Eger about eighty kilometres away. I had been to Eger before to visit the Tower Crane Company there, and I remembered it well. However, I now met the manager who had been running the tractor plant there during and since the days of the Russian Occupation. He was very friendly and amiable, and he regaled me with a comparison of life under the Russians, and the present time, and how best to cope with both situations. After I had been taken around the small factory, I was determined to test the computer system. I had arranged with the computer manager back at the head office to carry out a test of their new system on the production of a small item manufactured at Eger. A computer terminal had been installed at Eger but had never been tested or used. After about two hours of intensive trial and error, the manager, his staff, and myself were eventually able to produce a single invoice. It was not a promising start. I had become increasingly aware that the computer system may well have been suitable for General Motors in America but appeared to be completely inappropriate for the needs of the company. There was absolutely no possibility of the very expensive system being implemented by Christmas, which was the planned starting date. It was difficult to see how a new system could be introduced by means of the TAM Programme. I had absolutely no idea of how Marc could break the news to the Managing Director. However, I managed to preserve my good relations with the managing director by offering him a suggestion about sales. Apparently, the manufacture of farm equipment was very, very seasonal. Farmers bought their new equipment in the spring and rarely bought anything in the winter. I suggested that the company should try exporting to Australia and New Zealand where the seasons were reversed. As a guilty gesture of goodwill, I gave him my copy of an antipodean map that showed the Antarctic at the top of the world and the arctic at the bottom. Happily, Marc and I left on good terms. However, we heard later that the system was scrapped, and the Managing Director resigned.

Shirley and I made our final trip to Australia. We flew to Perth, first to stay with the daughter of our great friends and neighbours John and Beryl Kemp. We found Perth to be a delightful city but almost completely detached by a thousand miles from all of the other cities in Australia. It might just as well have been in another country. We flew from Perth to Broome in a small aircraft, which had single seats either side of the central aisle. The interior of the plane was very warm. The airhostess was sitting on a folding seat opposite to two young men who were the front passengers. They asked her whether they could have the air conditioning on. She removed a flight magazine from the rack beside her and wafted in front of the faces of the two young me. It was a classic example of Australian humour. From Broome, we went by Land Rovers to the Bungle Bungles in one of the remotest parts of outback Australia. The temperature was in the eighties, but we flew over the sacred site in a small helicopter, which because of the temperature had no side-doors. The flight was a stimulating experience. We returned by coach to Perth before flying to Singapore where we bought a set of Chinese crockery and chopsticks. I visited a fortune-teller who told me that I would live to be very, very old. I was not sure by Chinese standards, how old that might be.

My next assignment was to Budapest to the largest software company in Hungary. I had another senior EU adviser, Ed O'Sullivan. He lived in Western Ireland with an Irish passport but had lived in East London most of his life and had an 'Estuary' accent. The company was in offices in Buda, about a kilometre away from the river. The company was split into independent departments and profit centres, each of which specialised in different aspects of computer packages. The teams were an ideal subject for the use of my Belbin Team Analysis Test and programs. I had these translated, and after completion by the team members produced the results to the managing director. One group in particular was composed of an almost ideal group of members, and I predicted that they would be the most effective and profitable. The managing director was impressed and admitted that the group was indeed the most profitable in the company. We were asked by the managing director to run a management course at Lake Balaton, which was about seventy kilometres South West of Budapest. Ed O'Sullivan was supposed to be a personnel specialist, and he took charge of the proceedings. He proceeded to try and relate every aspect of management to the personnel function. He appeared to know nothing about statistics, and confidently added up rankings, and then averaged them. It was meaningless, but his presentation skills dominated all events. I found the whole weekend embarrassing and was glad to return to Budapest. The managing director took us out to dinner beside the Danube at the foot of the Castle in Buda. It was excellent, but I discovered a new dish of Hungarian Fish Soup. It was full of pieces of fish that had simply been cut up, and the soup contained all of the fish bones. Finally, I visited an open-air display of statues and memorials from the days of the Russian Occupation. The number and sizes of statues was astonishing and very impressive. However, apparently there had been some difficulty in preventing citizens from destroying them all when the Russians had left.

Shortly after I returned home, Shirley and I went on a cruise to the Antarctic. We flew directly to Rio de Janeiro and then to Ushuaia at the southern tip of Argentina. Ushuaia was an interesting small town with a market. We joined our cruise liner there and then sailed later on the same day that we arrived. The trip to the Antarctic was magical, and we landed a number of times to see the various varieties of penguins and other wild life. We were taken ashore in powered Zodiac rubber dinghies, each of which was in the charge of a middle-aged man. Apparently, these were regular passengers who were ships' captains enjoying a free vacation. The penguins seemed remarkably unconcerned by our presence and seemed to find us even more curious than we found them. It was a delightful experience. The ship had a ballroom for entertainment. During the ballroom dances, two of the dancers were middle-aged men immaculately dressed. They were the equivalent of the long-since past 'Lounge Lizards', whose role was to politely invite elderly single unaccompanied ladies to dance with them. There were educational lectures by various speakers about Arctic and South American life. One of these was an ex-diplomat and was incredibly well informed about historical events in Brazil. In particular, he described the inside diplomatic events in Montevideo during the first Second World War naval Battle of the River Plate. The cruise then went on to sail up the west coast of Chile. Initially, I was rather disappointed that we didn't sail past Cape Horn but instead went through the Straits of Magellan. However, it was a fascinating experience. Despite its imposing title, the straits were little wider than parts of the River Thames where the Boat Race takes place. At one apparently famous location, the straits go through a hundred and eighty degree turn that is similar to the Thames near Richmond. I found it incredible that a fifteen-thousand-ton liner could be manoeuvred around such a bend. Instead of emerging into the Pacific Ocean, we then sailed up the Chilean Fjords. These were considered to be remarkably similar to the Norwegian Fjords, but in the opinion of the captain were superior. We went ashore once to see the Napa Valley, which was a remarkable wine growing area. The valley had originally been settled in the nineteenth century by German political immigrants. In fact, we found that the residents still appeared to be Germanic and certainly spoke German rather than any other language. It was our first experience of Chilean Merlot, a wine that was unknown in England at that time. We subsequently managed to buy for a ridiculous knockdown price a dozen bottles from the Co-Op back home. At that time, no one had heard of, nor wanted to buy Chilean Merlot.

We arrived at Valparaiso at the end of our voyage and were taken up to Santiago. It was a fine city, which we toured, and in the hotel, we were offered the opportunity to take a tour to the top of the Andes at the Argentinian border. The only snag was that the tour company were only prepared to be paid in cash. Since we had no Chilean cash, they suggested that we could obtain it from the local bank. This was extremely inconvenient and was clearly a tax evasion fiddle on the part of our tour company. I flatly refused to contemplate this and declined the invitation. However, the hotel manager approached me shortly later and offered to arrange a private taxi tour for a lower price, and he would happily accept credit card payment. The next day, we were taken up to the top or watershed of the Andes. It was a fascinating journey, up a very quiet normal main road, on which there was very little traffic. At the summit near the border, the scenery was completely unexpected. It was just like a grassy Scottish Glen, with green hills on either side of a modest, fairly flat mountain road, which began to fall on the other side of the summit. There was no border post. On the way back to Santiago, we were held up briefly by a party of horsemen, including a young boy, who were driving their cattle up from the valley. The riders were all dressed in completely authentic gaucho blankets and 'Mexican' straw hats. They could all have been in costume for a Hollywood movie, or a Mexican cowboy film. Our driver gave way to them, and we delightedly watched them pass around the car. On the following day, we returned home to England.

Serbia

When we arrived home, I discovered that my next assignment was to Serbia, with a Danish Senior EU Adviser who was an expert in the furniture industry. We were met at Bratislava Airport by the female managing director of the company and were taken to Novi Sad. Nov Sad was a quite large modern city, which was just over a hundred kilometres up the Danube from Bratislava. The company manufactured office furniture and was located at Temerin, a small town about fifteen kilometres outside the city. The president and rest of the staff were all very friendly, and we conducted our study without any difficulty. The small factory had a fairly large timber store near the centre of the plant. Particularly in the light of my years of experience with the English Fire Service, I was appalled by the fire risk. Unsurprisingly, there were vast quantities of wood shavings and sawdust everywhere throughout the adjacent works. An accidental small fire near or in the store would be very likely to destroy the whole plant. I reported this to the president who appeared to find it highly amusing. He explained that next door to the plant was the Town Fire Station. I was even more appalled that the fire prevention officer next door was either unaware of it, or didn't think it was important.

One of the problems of the company was an exceptionally high labour turnover of clerical office staff, particularly women. The turnover was about forty percent per annum. The main office activities were in accounting. I suggested that a business and accounting computer system should be introduced, and the women should be trained to use it. The suggestion was welcomed by the president, who shortly afterwards arranged for the purchase of a system and the training of the staff. The president came from a small village near the Croatian border. His village had been wiped out during the recent conflict, but he had some photographs, which he had been unable to view because they were recorded on a floppy disc. I found a suitable micro-computer and was able to display them for him. He was utterly delighted. Subsequently, he and the

Managing Director took me out to dinner in a completely traditional Serbian restaurant. The food and drink were excellent, including the tradition of drinking Serbian alcoholic spirit along with spoons full of strawberry jam.

The Senior Advisor had apparently disagreed with the president, and my later visits, apart from the final one, were alone. I was booked into a modern hotel set in parkland on the outskirts of the city. It had been a favourite hotel of the deposed President Tito. Once again, the menu was superb, and I extravagantly began each dinner with caviar. Apparently, President Tito had been particularly fond of the delicacy, and the hotel had large stocks of it in tins. Since none other of the guests seemed to be ordering it, my portions were enormous. The catering staff apparently decided to empty the tins on my plate rather than throw the caviar away. The Managing Director also took me out to dinner to another exclusive traditional Serbian restaurant on the banks of the Danube. My leisure life in Novi Sad was even more luxurious than it had been in Debrecen with Engel Hoefgeest. The Managing Director also took me over a brand-new bridge over the Danube. The original bridge had been destroyed by the Allies during the recent war. This was the first time that the ancient castle on the other side of the bridge could be reached without a twenty-kilometre detour since the war. On my final visit to the company, I joined the Senior Adviser for our conclusion meeting with the president and managing director. We were kept waiting for nearly two hours before seeing him. Apparently, this was one of the reasons that the Senior Adviser had avoided visiting the Company with me on the previous occasions. However, I gained some important knowledge from the meeting. Apparently, it was general practice for Serbian companies to have three sets of financial accounts. One was the official version for tax purposes. The second one was for the shareholders. The third one was the real one. Only this one revealed the real profit. Despite the coolness between the president and my Senior Advisor, my services had been recommended to a company in Bratislava who manufactured domestic furniture. The company not only sold their furniture as wholesale items but also had large retail sales from their premises in Bratislava. All of these sales were subject to VAT. Once again, the financial arrangements were interesting. All tills carried cash record rolls. These could only be removed for inspection by the tax authorities. If customers required an invoice, they paid VAT. If they paid in cash and did not receive a till receipt, they did not have to pay tax. However, I carried out my survey, the work was interesting, and the Managing Director was well satisfied with my work. He and his secretary took me to dinner at an extremely pleasant restaurant overlooking the City Zoo, with the Danube in the background. Once again, they occasionally revealed to me some of the horrors of the recent war. My first visits to Serbia had been extremely pleasant, educational, and satisfying.

At the end of summer, Shirley and I went on a tour to China. We began at Shanghai, before joining a river cruise up the Yangtze River. I regretted not having travelled from the airport via the wonderful 'Maglev' Train connection. However, we went to the top of the highest building and visited a genuine delightful tea garden to drink tea in the correct traditional manner. We were also taken to an old part of the city to see inside homes there, and the residents' way of life. We travelled by train to Nanking where we were to join our boat. We visited an open-air market, and later, the presidential palace and found it difficult not to forget the Japanese atrocities there before the Second World War. At the market, I was tempted to buy a translated copy of the 'Little Red Book' of Chairman Mao Tse-Tung. However, I decided it was too expensive, and the lady behind the stall would not accept my preferred price. After returning from the palace, we passed beside the market again, and the bookselling lady saw me again and recognised me. She called me over and said she would sell the book at my suggested price. I really did not have the heart to refuse but insisted on paying her the price that she had previously stated. She was equally determined only to accept my original offer. We parted on very good terms. My love of the Chinese, which had begun in my Hong Kong days, grew even stronger. I found it difficult to imagine any similar behaviour in many other places in the world.

We travelled up the very crowded Yangtze River to the Seven Gorges Dam and were taken in a small boat on a short trip up one of the tributaries to a newly built modern town. There we met families whose villages had been flooded by the dam, and they had been rehoused in the brand-new small town. The villages that had been flooded had never had any road communications, whilst the new town gave them excellent access to the nearby city. The electricity power station at the Seven Gorges Dam was vast and was not only supplying large parts of China but also exporting power to Hong Kong. The whole enterprise was a wonderful replacement of the original Seven Gorges, up which all river traffic had to be hauled manually by hundreds of local labourers. We returned to our boat and continued up to Chongqing, which had been the capital of Nationalist China during the Second World War. It was now a very modern city of over a million inhabitants and was surrounded by motorways. From there, we flew to

Xian to see the Terra Cotta Soldiers, where there was also a zoo in the town in which there were many panda bears. Whilst visiting the zoo Shirley and I were amused to be asked to be photographed holding a small child of a visiting family. The family had never ever seen previously a European. The Terra Cotta Soldier Museum was fascinating, and as part of the facilities, a very old man was autographing copies of the Guide Book. I duly asked him to sign ours and discovered that he was the local farmer who had first discovered the soldiers. I had absolutely no reason to disbelieve him, and I was very privileged when he allowed me to shake his hand.

Shirley and I flew on to Peking, where the city was amazingly modern. However, the most noticeable feature was a huge pall of yellow pollution permanently hanging over the city. Bicycles were everywhere in the city. On the main highways, intersections when traffic lights were red completely blocked the road with waiting cyclists. One of the local Peking jokes was that if someone shouted 'there is my stolen bike', at least a half a dozen cyclists would jump off their cycles and run away. Shirley and I also visited a local restaurant and were introduced to Szechwan food for the first time. We found it to be very hot and spicy. It was explained to us by the restaurateur that Szechwan food like females from that province was all 'Hot and Spicy'. In contrast, Cantonese food with which I was familiar was made by 'people who will use anything that swims or flies, except Boeing 747 Jets'. Nevertheless, we felt that we were obliged to eat Peking duck, with which we were both very familiar. We decided that it was no better than the cuisine of our local Chinese restaurant at home. Finally, we were taken to see the Great Wall of China. It was a fascinating experience, and I was amazed at the gradients on the top of the wall. I thought, somewhat wryly, that troops who had been required to patrol it could easily have become Olympic Athletes. We finally returned home, and I became fully aware of the amazing ongoing economic development in China. They were constructing more new motorways in one year than had been built in ten years in the United Kingdom.

My next TAM assignment once again was to Serbia. It was to a timber merchant about a hundred kilometres south of Belgrade at Uzice on the border of Croatia. Once again, the managing director was very hospitable, and after the first day, my senior adviser left me to carry on alone. The Managing Director discovered that I had been a college lecturer and asked me if I would give a talk in the local Technical College. I was surprised, as this was my first visit. However, I agreed and was encouraged by the very warm welcome that I received when I delivered my presentation, since I had no visual aids. An even more surprising experience was my overnight accommodation. I was driven about twenty kilometres out of the town deep into a remote forest near to the Croatian border. There were a number of timber-built holiday cabins there, but all were unoccupied. I was taken into one of them and found inside that it was well furnished, beautifully warm, and there was a plentiful supply of food and drink in the cupboards and refrigerator. There was also a television set. To my utter astonishment, the driver gave me the keys to the cabin and left me, after saying that he would collect me on the following morning. As the cabin was at least five kilometres away from the nearest village, I felt, and was, completely isolated. However, there was every requirement for my comfort, and I was collected on the following morning, after I had received a very brief visit from a cleaning lady. It was one of the most extraordinary experiences of my TAM assignments.

Engel Hoefgeest was also in Serbia at the time, and we had decided to spend the weekend in Zurich, where we met Clara Shaw who was working in Switzerland at the time. Zurich was a beautiful city, and although expensive, the hotel and restaurants were excellent. I returned home to find yet another TAM assignment to Serbia, which I was determined would be my very last assignment. However, this time it was with my very dear friend and colleague Engel Hoefgeest. We were to go to an electrical component Manufacturer in Pristina, which was nearly three hundred kilometres southeast of Belgrade, near to the Croatian border. We met at Belgrade at the height of summer and were taken by car to the factory at Pristina. On our arrival, the most noticeable feature was a huge pile of compost beside the main door to the directors' offices. The other noticeable feature that there were fly swatters on every desk. During our introductory discussion with the president, we realised that there appeared to be an infestation of small flies, against which the fly swatters were being plied expertly by the staff. We were also introduced to the managing director who was in his mid-thirties and appeared to be very keen and business-like. The company manufactured an astonishingly wide range of electrical products, and there were permanent storage areas scattered all over the premises. I soon discovered that the company had a huge problem of stock control. I had only rarely seen their method before, which was to manufacture products in order to fill all vacant spaces in storage areas. Many of their stocks were sufficient for at least a year's sales. Clearly, there was no Sales Forecasting and the value of the stock was costing the company a fortune. I discussed this with the Managing Director and suggested that the computer should be used for Sales Forecasting and Production Control. He immediately responded defensively, saying that the computer was out-of-date, and he had been unable to get any sales information from the computer manager. I immediately went to see the Computer Manager. He was in his early thirties, and we both understood one another well. Astonishingly, the computer installation was an ICL machine, with which I was completely familiar from nearly thirty years earlier. I asked him to print Monthly Sales Records for twenty products for the past year. He was able to do this for me within ten minutes. I returned to the Managing Director and Prresident and presented them with the figures. The President was delighted, and perhaps unsurprisingly, the Managing Director was extremely displeased. He insisted that the Bulgarian System that he intended to introduce was far superior. However, it would not be available for some time. The President asked me to give a talk to the staff about Sales Forecasting and Stock Control. I did this, and I presented them with monthly forecasts for the next year for about a dozen main products. My presentation was well received by all of the sales and production staff. They were all very anxious to get similar information about all of their products.

Engel and I were staying in a most extraordinary hotel in the town. It had been built during the Tito Communist Era and unsurprisingly was clearly of Russian influence. It was a seven-storey building with a large central space, which stretched from the ground floor to the roof. The bedrooms were accessed from galleries on each floor. Engel and I were on the seventh floor and were the only guests or residents in the whole of the hotel. The food and wine were excellent, the beds were comfortable, and unsurprisingly the room service was good. However, the eating arrangements at the factory were somewhat different. Management meetings tended to last from mid-morning to mid-afternoon. Lunchtime consisted of consuming local alcoholic spirit, which was served with very light snacks of crisps or biscuits. We discovered that the spirit was distilled from wine, which was made from grapevines in the yard. The heap of compost and the profusion of fly swatters were the results and necessary requirements of the activity. Even more surprising was that in the large modern department store in the town, Engel and I had seen small domestic spirit-distilling plants displayed in the window, on sale for domestic use. In contrast, I was equally surprised to see in a local stationer's shop normal A4 white paper being sold by the sheet. Obviously, we were in a very different world from any that we had visited before.

After our visit, Engel and I spent the weekend in Belgrade. We went to the opera, visited the splendid markets, and had a wonderful dinner alongside the River Danube below the city. I returned home very contentedly. In the winter, Shirley and I went to Canada to see Lynn, Jean, and our two grandsons. We visited Niagara Falls, which had frozen solid for the first time in decades. It really seemed to me like the end of an era.

Afterlife

After sixty years of working life, I was now seventy-five years old. It seemed to me to be absurd that a geriatric Briton should be advising thirty-year younger Eastern European managers and businessmen on how best to run their organisations. It really was time for me to have far fewer shakes of my kaleidoscope. I was continuing to go on overseas holidays each year with Shirley and spending a fortnight in Mid-Wales with Mark Griffiths. For the last ten years, I had been earning almost as much income in Europe, with considerably less effort and far more enjoyably than I had done at Kingston. However, I considered that paid employment for my most wonderful last ten years, whilst welcome, had not even been necessary and should no longer be part of my life. I was also slightly thankful for the fact that my experiences had not occurred whilst I was still teaching. I would probably have bored my students to death even more successfully than normal, with endless reminiscences and anecdotes of Eastern Europe. I looked forward to the final pleasure of sitting in summer in our wonderful tree-surrounded garden in Willow Grove, and looking at, rather than 'working' on, my model railway in the roof in winter. My 'unwise' purchase of the house for eleven thousand pounds, despite 'professional' advice fifty years earlier has left me slightly concerned about its future. How will it be disposed of now that it is valued at well over a million pounds?

Shortly after I 'retired', I submitted the third edition of my Management Text Book to the Chartered Management Institute, more popularly the CMI. It became a runner up in the category of 'The New Manager' in the competition for the 'CMI Management Book of the Year'. I received rave reviews from the three judges. They were worthy of repetition. 'One of the best books on management theory that I have ever read.' 'I wish this book had been available when I was studying management.' 'This will be a handy reference book for years to come for new and old managers alike.' Despite this gratifying praise, I did not even get short-listed on the final assessment. I was very disappointed. I left London to join Shirley in Tokyo, where she had started our cruise to Japan, Taiwan, and the Philippines the day before. My consolation was that I saw the Northern Lights when I flew over the Polar Route from Heathrow. I boarded the ship, and we visited Hiroshima and Nagasaki. I have never been unable to develop any empathy with the Japanese, and a female guide on a bus tour demonstrated how to behead victims with a Samurai Sword. She explained jocularly that it was important to hold the sword correctly, otherwise it could injure the executioner. I am as disgusted today as I was at the time, with a cultural attitude that belongs in another universe. We also visited Taiwan and Manilla, where I was equally appalled by being shown a cave where two thousand Japanese Soldiers had committed suicide rather than be captured. Similarly, there was a museum celebrating and commemorating the Kamikaze Pilots of the Japanese Air Force. However, the Japanese had their revenge on me for my views, since I returned home with a very severe fever condition and spent the next ten days in bed.

Despite my 'retirement', Shirley and I continued to take our annual holidays abroad, and joined with John Hunt in the Annual Bowls Tour to the Mediterranean. Shirley and I went to Australia twice more and to Tasmania. Our visit to Darwin allowed us to see the 'Top End' and Alice Springs. We also visited Ayres Rock, where to our utter amazement, in the hotel we were offered freshly caught fish that had been flown in from the South. Our trips to Adelaide, Melbourne, and Brisbane completed our visits to all of the main cities of Australia, except Canberra, which we were assured by many people would be uninteresting. However, we also spent ten days in Tasmania. We visited the Penal Establishment at Port Arthur, where we went into the rooms originally occupied by the Tolpuddle Martyrs. It was a very sad reminder of penalties of the days of the very beginning and foundation of Trades Unionism in Britain. We also travelled across the country to the other Penal Establishment at Macquarie Harbour. This was completely isolated from the rest of the Island by impenetrable forests and originally could only be reached by entry from the sea through a very dangerous narrow entrance known as Hells Gate. The establishment carried even sadder stories of civil inhumanity and religious hypocrisy. Apparently, three prisoners had been hanged for murdering a warder. Because of the appalling conditions, they had wished to commit suicide. However, their Christian religious belief was that, unlike murder, suicide precluded the individuals from going to heaven. From then onward, I continued my policy of never entering religious establishments, unless it was unavoidable.

My policy on visiting religious establishments was confirmed when Shirley and I visited the Caribbean. In Jamaica, we were taken to see a beautiful small church on top of a hill. As usual, I did not join the other visitors in entering the establishment. However, whilst I was waiting outside I examined a commemorative plaque to the original founders. All of the benefactors had contributed their wealth in the form of tons of sugar, the most generous of which was fifty tons. I found the hypocrisy and evil of the ownership of the slaves who had produced that sugar to be nauseating. A couple of years later when Shirley and I visited the Duero River in Portugal, I was equally appalled to discover that the Portuguese Catholic Church, unlike that of Rome, had continued the practice of inquisition until the end of the Nineteenth Century. I was very contented that I had absolutely no political or religious allegiance to any party or cult.

I needed to review and revise my car-owning policy. I had bought my last Jaguar by mistake. I had never been knowledgeable about cars, but I had been driving a four-litre Jaguar Sovereign for a few years, and it now needed to be replaced. I contacted the firm in Kent from which I had been buying my Jaguars for some years. I thought I should 'downsize' to a Jaguar X Type. After a few weeks, the salesman telephoned me to say that he had been unable to find an X Type for me but could supply an FX. I had no idea what this was but nevertheless agreed. He delivered the car to my home, and I was surprised to see that it seemed larger than I expected an X Type to be. The car was absolutely stunningly beautiful, painted in a colour that I later discovered was called 'Emerald Fire'. It had a 4.2 Supercharged V8 Engine, and the car was immaculate. I took it for a test drive and fell utterly in love with the best Jaguar that I was ever to own. In the following five years, I never saw another one on the road. A few years later, I took an Advanced Driving Test, which lasted three hours. During the journey, the instructor kept looking at the rev. counter. Apparently, he couldn't get over the reading at seventy miles per hour. That was far too technical for me to appreciate. Happily, I passed the test and was gratified to be told that I was the best driver of my age that he had ever seen. I was not sure that was necessarily a compliment, but I gave him a bottle of malt whisky when he finally left.

Finally, I decided that it was ridiculous for me to be driving a luxury five-seater saloon car. What I needed was an open-top convertible; I had been very impressed by Shirley's 3-Series BMW that I had bought new. However, I now bought a 3-Litre slightly later version. It arrived from Yorkshire and was immaculate. After the first few days, I became utterly appalled by it. It was the most badly designed car I had ever seen. First of all, the wing mirrors had to be retracted manually. In order to get into and out of my garage, I had to get out of the car and walk around both sides. I had last seen that on the Triumph Heralds, designed fifty years previously. Secondly, the backseat headrests were so high that it was impossible to see out of the rear window. However, these were said in the manual to be retractable. In practice, this would only have been possible with the use of a hacksaw. It had the worst all-round vision of any car I had ever driven. It was a disaster. I sold the car ten days later. In its place, I bought a Mercedes CLK350 3.5-Litre Sport Convertible. In contrast, it was the most superior and sophisticated convertible I had ever encountered. It also has more features than any other car I have driven. Unfortunately, Mercedes were unable to provide me with a proper manual. However, at least I know how to retract the wing-mirrors.

I am very happy to know that our daughter and our two sons have all been able to shake their own kaleidoscopes successfully and happily. When they reach their age of retirement, they may lack the golden opportunities of the TAM programme, but equally, they should not need them. There have only been three occasions when I have sought or accepted advice on major changes to the direction of my life. They were the decision to enter the Brewing Industry, my decision to marry Shirley, and the decision to join the EU TAM programme. All of these decisions changed my life dramatically and were and have been completely successful and beneficial. In contrast, I had hopefully anticipated only gentle shaking of my kaleidoscope in the future. However, like everyone else, I could not possibly have expected or predicted that I and the rest of the world would experience the worst pandemic since the Black Death. Surprisingly, the outcome may well create more economic, social, and political change than any previous event during my lifetime. I shall not be sorry to miss the party. Perhaps the saddest shake of my kaleidoscope has been the revelation of national political delusion and inadequacy. The claim that a referendum majority result of fifty-one percent of the adult population represents the 'Will of the People' is an interpretation worthy of the belligerent prejudice of the Queen of Hearts, or the madness of the Mad Hatter, in Alice in Wonderland. If the referendum had been on the reintroduction of 'Hang, Drawing and Quartering', would any sane person consider that a difference of one percent in the votes of adults in the nation would justify its enactment? Perhaps fortunately, I plan only to be shaking my kaleidoscope very occasionally in the future.

The Chessboard

Alice said at last, "It's a great huge game of chess that's being played – all over the world. Oh, what fun it is! If only I might join."